Women's Rights and Religious Practice

York Studies on Women and Men

General Editors: Haleh Afshar and Mary Maynard

Alison L. Boden
WOMEN'S RIGHTS AND RELIGIOUS PRACTICE
Claims in Conflict

Nikki Craske
GENDER AND THE POLITICS OF RIGHTS AND DEMOCRACY IN LATIN AMERICA

Celia Davies
GENDER, DEMOCRACY AND INCLUSION IN NORTHERN IRELAND

Myfanwy Franks
WOMEN AND REVIVALISM IN THE WEST
Choosing Fundamentalism in a Liberal Democracy

Shirin M. Rai (*editor*)
INTERNATIONAL PERSPECTIVES ON GENDER AND DEMOCRATIZATION

Carmel Roulston and Celia Davies (*editors*)
GENDER, DEMOCRACY AND INCLUSION IN NORTHERN IRELAND

Yvette Taylor
WORKING CLASS LESBIAN LIFE
Classed Outsiders

York Studies on Women and Men
Series Standing Order ISBN 0–333–71512–8
(*outside North America only*)

You can receive future titles in this series as they are published by placing a standing order. Please contact your bookseller or, in case of difficulty, write to us at the address below with your name and address, the title of the series and the ISBN quoted above.

Customer Services Department, Macmillan Distribution Ltd, Houndmills, Basingstoke, Hampshire RG21 6XS, England

---

Women's Rights and Religious Practice

Claims in Conflict

Alison L. Boden

Princeton University

palgrave
macmillan

First published 2007 by
PALGRAVE MACMILLAN
Houndmills, Basingstoke, Hampshire RG21 6XS and
175 Fifth Avenue, New York, N.Y. 10010
Companies and representatives throughout the world

PALGRAVE MACMILLAN is the global academic imprint of the Palgrave Macmillan division of St. Martin's Press, LLC and of Palgrave Macmillan Ltd. Macmillan® is a registered trademark in the United States, United Kingdom and other countries. Palgrave is a registered trademark in the European Union and other countries.

ISBN-13: 978–0–230–55144–2 hardback
ISBN-10: 0–230–55144–0 hardback

This book is printed on paper suitable for recycling and made from fully managed and sustained forest sources. Logging, pulping and manufacturing processes are expected to conform to the environmental regulations of the country of origin.

A catalogue record for this book is available from the British Library.

A catalog record for this book is available from the Library of Congress.

10 9 8 7 6 5 4 3 2 1
16 15 14 13 12 11 10 09 08 07

Printed and bound in Great Britain by
Antony Rowe Ltd, Chippenham and Eastbourne

For Jarrett, Timothy and Martha

Contents

Introduction

What is freedom? Is it the capacity to do exactly what one wishes? Is it the knowledge, joy, and comfort of feeling that one's life flows through and towards eternal and ultimate streams of meaning and goodness? Is it the absence of any practical restrictions on one's life? Is it an inner state? Should it – or can it – be all of the above? What is freedom of religion? Is it the ability to practice one's religion without the interference of persons from other religious or secular communities? Is it the ability to interpret for oneself how to live faithfully? Should – or can – religious freedom permit both inter-religious and intra-religious independence?

What does one do with the fact that some people seem to choose against what appears to be their own self-interest, and on the grounds of religious freedom? Who should judge both the veracity of the relevant religious teachings and their value in the lives of the people in question? Should – or can – the evaluators be both the agents themselves and those outsiders who believe they are being supportive of them?

This book hopes to complicate two sets of criteria. The first is religious arguments against human rights norms; the second is the criteria of arguments made in the name of human rights against religious practices and beliefs. By exploring the inability of the human rights construct to secure concrete rights for some religious women the intention is to reinforce respect for the role of religion in individuals' lives, to confirm the validity of the human rights idea as a tool for securing social justice, to challenge human rights advocates to consider the broader social, legal, and spiritual dimensions involved in implementing human rights, to challenge advocates of religious freedom to consider issues of power, justice and spiritual autonomy, and to provide a framework for considering when the rights construct will not be the most effective way of securing justice and equality for religious women.

A multiplicity of voices has weighed in on the topic of rights abuses (particularly for women) substantiated by religious ideology. Numerous writers have sought to prove that particular religions are quite compatible with human rights (and they are correct), but have not acknowledged the extent of rights abuses legitimated by the religion in question. A second group of writers has suggested that the conflict be resolved by subordinating religious issues to women's rights norms. A third group of writers insist that freedom of religion is so inviolable a human right that no challenges can be made to religious teachings or practices, no matter how much they compromise what are popularly considered to be human rights. Some within this last group also insist that all legitimate human rights are actually guaranteed by the practice of their religion.

This book will not try to harmonize or reconcile these three perspectives. It will challenge their shortcomings while affirming their helpful contributions, all in an attempt to clarify how religious women's rights might best be secured. Its perspective will fully acknowledge the culpability of the religions in perpetuating some rights abuses, without viewing religion as some external, complicating factor or the disposable "problem," and also without portraying traditional religion as the sought-after answer, the panacea. It is from a hermeneutical starting point between these two perspectives that the inability of the rights construct to promote some religious women's human rights becomes most clear.

Some writers in the third camp, defenders of religious freedom, insist that gender subordination, if lamentable, is divinely ordained. Religious adherents may not pick and choose from holy teachings with which they do or do not agree. Any changes to religious practice open the door to the destruction of both theological integrity and the protection of religious freedom. The religious fabric of communities will unravel. Those human rights categories that are truly necessary are already enshrined in religious law.[1] The eternal results of not following divine law far outweigh the temporal (and, ultimately, temporary) inconveniences experienced in the present. Denying claims for equality made by women in his community, a religious scholar once said, "Some people do not know what is good for them."[2] This approach, in total, is troubling and impractical. It permanently subordinates questions of justice and equality for women to religious and family leaders whose interpretations of their traditions may support many rights infringements.

There are, in the second camp, those whose idea it is to subordinate religious rights to other rights norms for women in cases of conflict between them. This resolution, also, is troubling and impractical. Some writers very intentionally view the conflict through the lens of another discipline, including law, philosophy, sociology, gender studies, and political science. But there is an unfortunate and irresponsible tendency among some commentators in every discipline to suggest that religious arguments be summarily dismissed – religion is the problem so it must be eliminated from the context in question. This suggestion is rarely put so straightforwardly. Often, it informs comments such as the following: "Although a balancing of concerns must be achieved by States Parties in the cases where different human rights potentially compete, it is inappropriate to require that the balancing of women's rights and religious rights be undertaken by the women's Convention [*sic*], or to suggest that guarantees of women's rights must accommodate religious rights instead of the other way around."[3] (In fact, the Women's Convention, as drafted, has no real potential for balancing women's rights and religious rights, a key reason why the rights construct is unable to promote religious women's rights in some situations.) A footnote to the above comment reads, "As a practical matter, this world does not appear to be in great danger that any country will develop political climates that will foster radical legislative innovations in furtherance of women's rights in such a way as to trample upon other human rights."[4] No, women's rights are hardly in danger of being misused to trump other rights categories, but the answer to this (or any) conflict of rights claims must not be simply to reverse the scale of dominance, to fold one set of rights claims into another as a subsidiary, or to make one set of rights norms so inclusive of others that they are rendered toothless. The minimization of other legitimate rights claims is not an acceptable resolution to conflicts between them.

The "subordinate religious rights" perspective is impractical on two levels. First, it ignores the fact that international rights covenants, even with their vague language about when religious practices are to be curbed, do make illegal the blanket trumping of religious rights with other rights categories. And second, it excludes from the conversation the religious women who are the very topic, women who may not wish to abandon the controversy between their human rights and their religious practices but who want to find a way forward that respects both the integrity of their religious beliefs and their integrity as women. There are women in every society who do not view the two as contradictory or mutually exclusive, and neither does this study. In every region of the world there are women who enjoy both human rights and committed religious observance. They are not necessarily elite, educated, or in liberal democratic, industrial societies. Modernity and higher education are not the crucial ingredients in religious women's rights enjoyment but rather the characteristics of patriarchal religious ideology endorsed by those who are closest to them. This book assumes that its subjects do not wish to be rid of religion but to be rid of patriarchy, and that the two are separable.[5]

The "trump religion" argument is manifested in many ways in the current literature on rights and justice. One theorist, for instance, while writing against androcentrism in human rights discourse, laments the fact that various theoretical and practical problems will endure "as long as we continue the mystified search for ultimate truth or reality."[6] Whether the truth sought for is theoretical, rights-related, or religious, the work of many a rights activist and theorist is summarily dismissed (Gandhi and King leap to mind). Also dismissed are, again, the very women that the conversation is supposed to empower – religious women who do not wish to be freed of their religion but of the discrimination, patriarchy, or subordination that it currently supports. In the end, the refusal to take religion seriously is extremely counterproductive in the dialogue on conflicts between rights claims. Such a stance essentializes both religion and women of faith, excludes these women from the conversation about themselves, and may patronizingly assume that any resolution to the conflict can have no input from the religious traditions themselves.

The constraints of space and the desire to avoid pedestrian wordiness mean that terms such as "religious women" will be used in the chapters to follow. The phrase is not intended to suggest that all women who endure gender subordination through religious ideology – or all women who participate in religious practice, whether subordinating or not – meet some criteria for being "religious." They are not assumed to have particular beliefs or to adhere to certain customs. They may be atheists. The term refers to women whose lives are strongly influenced by religious ideology. That religious influence may be discriminatory; it also may be extremely empowering. Certainly, women have independent levels of belief (and sometimes none) in spite of sometimes having to conform to "religious" practices. References to "religious women" do not assume that all women under consideration have an equal (or deep) level of personal faith or compliance. It applies to women in secular democracies as much as it applies to women in an "Islamic republic" whose personal observance is considered orthodox. Arguably, it applies to women anywhere who may not choose to participate in religious community (if they do have the choice) but whose perspectives, nonetheless, quietly have been shaped by the values of their community's religion.

Similarly, references will be made to whole traditions, such as "Islam," "Christianity," and "Hinduism." A central point of this book is that religions encompass an extraordinary amount of diversity within their communities – they are diverse *within* themselves. Again, to write succinctly will sometimes require making reference to a religious tradition as large and varied as the ones named above, but the implication is never that these traditions are monolithic. In fact, the discrimination towards or the subordination of women within the same religion, *if it exists*, will be very different. Also, while gender subordination in different religions has many points of commonality, sometimes the differences *within* traditions will vary significantly.

A pitfall awaiting those who write on women's rights and religion is the construction of false norms for religious women out of a few eyebrow-raising texts or practices, as are conversations about what comprises "authentic" religion. Both are a losing battle for women, continually returning the upper hand in the argument to those religious authorities that may wish to perpetuate subordination. What makes any practice a religious one is the sacred value that is accorded to it by individuals and by communities, be it snake-handling, hymn singing, polygamy, giving generous amounts of money to justice-related causes, relationship to a particular land, resting from work, working one's fingers to the bone, never leaving the home, clitoridectomy, or dying to secure another's human rights. The only way to make progress with a subordinating practice that is held as an item of faith is to treat it as such.[7]

These pages are written by a "partisan of religion,"[8] one who thinks that patriarchy and religion do not have to be partners, and that what is patriarchal about the religions are elements of their theologies and the social structures that they consequently reinforce – religious legitimization for male dominance in society, patrilineal families, social and religious organizations controlled by men, and overwhelmingly male images of creative power.[9] Patriarchy is just as prevalent in secularism, if perhaps more cloaked. The religions do not enforce patriarchal structures alone but in an infinite variety of recipes with factors such as race, class, and caste, depending on the society. The author believes deeply in the radical equality of human value between men and women, and knows that schools within each of the religions do as well, even though some of their practitioners evince a very different ethic. The best apologist for any discipline is one who also acknowledges its flaws, and this study will attempt to walk the line of cherishing religious faith while pointing out those ways in which it is abused or manipulated, those sites of religious legitimization for male dominance, the disempowerment of women, and violence towards women. A kind of universalist view of human rights is assumed, one that does not hold any particular religious or ethical system in higher esteem than others but one that claims emphatically that gender subordination is unacceptable in any moral system that would employ it. It is possible to honor individual women's dignity (and agency) at the same time that one honors the integrity and authority of religious teaching. One can support both social justice, broadly understood, for women, and also support the claims of religious organizations and communities to represent the transcendent and eternal, their claim to truth of a *religious* nature, their claim to truth on a higher plane, one that perhaps trumps all other truth claims because of its religious origins. Women's rights and religious practice do not have to be pitted against one another. The human rights idea can bridge the gap between women's rights and religious practices, and bring social justice to women whose rights are compromised by such religious practices, *but the crucial factor in all of this requires making changes to patriarchal religious ideology*.

Examples throughout the book are drawn particularly from India; this is for several reasons. First, India is a secular democracy whose Constitution draws heavily on the rights notion for its vision of securing social justice for every citizen. Second, the three religious traditions that are the focus of the study – Islam, Hinduism, and Christianity – are substantially present in the country, making it possible to study the religious traditions in the same national context. While the Indian subcontinent also encompasses a number of sub-cultures and languages, it has a comprehensive set of national laws and a coherent sense of national identity that affect each of the religious communities. And third, the presence and impact of personal status laws for all religious groups in India is significant, providing a particularly substantive setting for studying the ramifications of such laws on religious women's rights.

Profoundest thanks are rendered to those who have made the present work possible. Such gratitude is due to colleagues and students at the University of Chicago, where this book was written, especially those affiliated with Rockefeller Memorial Chapel, the Human Rights Program, and the Divinity School. The friendship of numerous people provided invaluable support, especially Dirk Ficca, Sharon Berlin and Jim Ketelaar. This book's first incarnation was as a doctoral thesis for the Department of Peace Studies at the University of Bradford, and could not have been completed without the guidance of Sarah Perrigo and Donna Pankhurst, plus the insights of examiners Oliver Ramsbotham and Haleh Afshar. Haleh and Mary Maynard at the University of York, and Jill Lake and Melanie Blair at Palgrave, saw it through to publication. Lastly, and most of all, deepest thanks go to my husband, Jarrett Kerbel, and to our children Timothy and Martha, who came to us as these pages were first being written. They each made many compromises so that this project might go forward. To them this book is dedicated with love and gratitude.

1
A Conflict of Rights Claims

> *In a small village in rural Bangladesh, a handful of women organize to train themselves as weavers and to collectively market their products. Each of them has several children; each has been widowed, deserted, or is caring for an invalid husband. The religious custom of* purdah, *or seclusion, circumscribes the private and public life of all of the women. It stipulates that they may not work outside their homes. Those who have land to cultivate do so only at night, in the moonlight, for fear of censure or beatings by neighbors and relatives. Their inhibited attempts at farming are not adequate to feed their families. Along with those women who have no land, they now find themselves facing starvation. They say, "*Purdah *does not feed us." As they begin to organize, they encounter strong resistance from the local religious authorities. They explain, "Then the* mullah *does not allow us to talk in the road or to go out of the house. A social barricade is created. 'You will not be allowed to take water from the tubewell. If you go into the field, your legs will be broken.' " One woman explains, "The* mullahs *say: 'When they will die we shall not bury them.' Villagers say, 'Wherever they want, they go. They do not cover their heads. They talk with men. They will be sinners.' I said: 'If Allah does not see us when we stay hungry then Allah has sinned.' "*[1]

In innumerable instances every day and in every corner of the globe, religious practices and human wellbeing are in conflict. The opportunity to follow the principles and to observe the rituals of one's religious tradition is accorded tremendous importance in the international community. States' constitutions and international covenants codify and protect the possession and expression of religious sentiment. Freedom of religion is widely considered to be a human right.

The same is also true, of course, for human wellbeing. Bills of rights, constitutions, declarations, and covenants enumerate the categories of harmful or unjust behavior that may not be visited upon any person. International courts of human rights and other bodies are charged with overseeing the implementation of these rights principles. Strenuous disagreement proliferates between individuals and states as to which rights are "basic," to whom they should be accorded, what duties might adhere to the person possessing a particular right or to the government in question, and so on. There remains, however, a panoply of agreed-upon human rights that are definitively outlined in a variety of texts, documents to which states have voluntarily become signatories. In so doing, their governments have promised to safeguard these rights.

The subject of this book is those instances of conflict between the right to the free expression of religion and the human rights of women. Certainly, such conflicts exist regarding the rights of children and of men (and, some would add, also animals and the environment). However, the situation of women's rights in general and the role of women in the world's religious traditions add extra dimensions to the question of this particular rights conflict. As illustrated above in the Bangladeshi community, women's very lives are in the balance.

The situation of the village sheds light on several issues undergirding the rights conflict in question. First, religion and culture are commingled. A firm boundary between where one ends and the other begins is often impossible to construct. Arguments may be made for the immutability of the practice of *purdah* within Islam, but counter-arguments might also point out that the custom is not universal to the religion but rather is determined more by region and economic status. Culture suffuses all religion, and religion suffuses many (if not all) cultures. Is one of those categories inviolable and the other not? Should the perpetuation of practices with roots in either be considered protected, even if these practices discriminate against some members of society?

Second, the public and private spheres are thoroughly blended, the boundary between them completely obscured. Religion is often said to be one of the most private of matters in human experience, but as the Bangladeshi situation makes clear, religious sentiment is often a matter of public policy, officially or unofficially. Religion becomes a public tool to legislate much of what happens in private. Public authority ensures private conformity, with particularly potent ramifications for the world's women.

Third, some observers might argue that the case of the Bangladeshi women does not involve a question of basic human rights. The women simply wish to earn wages; the opportunity to do so, they would say, is not a fundamental human right, such as freedom from torture. Desire for personal comfort or advancement must always be subordinated to the very real need to protect the religious integrity (and social order) evinced in the long-held custom of *purdah*. Others would argue that the right to work outside the home is only marginally an issue in the case in question. The situation is actually one of the right to life, which is almost everywhere agreed to be a fundamental human right; the resisting women chose to act as they did because they wished not to starve – or to watch their children do so. Significant disagreement as to the importance of women's claims occurs frequently in such rights-related discourse.

Fourth, there is an economic dimension to the scenario. Those observers who say that the women's fieldwork would improve their financial situation are not incorrect. At present the women suffer from extreme economic disempowerment. Their proposed labor would likely make them economically self-sufficient for the first time in their lives. Such self-sufficiency points to a fifth element common to many conflicts between women's rights and religious practices, the power-related dimension. The demand by the women to be able to work in their own fields or market their own products carries an implicit challenge to male authority and to women's subordinated status in their society. They challenge the gendered division of labor in their village. If successful, these women will survive independently as the head of a household without adult males. At the most local of levels their autonomy will significantly increase. Their antagonists counter all of these possibilities with the weight of religious argument.

The human rights idea was devised to promote basic criteria for social justice and a basic quality of life for every person in every society. Certainly the women of this Bangladeshi village are perfect candidates for the implementation of human rights norms. Ironically, however, the human rights idea may not be a helpful method for securing their human rights, given the face-off between religion and gender and the competing rights claims that can arise (one to religious freedom, the other to gender equality). In fact, a host of factors may render the human rights idea ineffective in the procuring of social justice for the women involved, as this study will show.

An argument for the inability of the rights construct to address some conflicts between women's rights and religious freedoms

The development and codification of the human rights idea, especially since the end of the World War II, have provided the international community with an extraordinary tool with which to advocate for and implement basic levels of social justice and human wellbeing – that is, to enable human rights. It stands to reason that human rights law, along with organizations and activism grounded in the human rights notion, are the optimal tools for securing human rights. Rights law and theory have been constructed for just that purpose. This book will argue that, when the persons for whom rights are being sought are religious women, the human rights construct is not always the appropriate tool because in certain circumstances it cannot be successful. The question is not whether religious women should enjoy human rights, or if the rights idea is valid, but whether the discourse of human rights can be effective in securing actual rights given the women's particular situation.

When women's rights categories are pitted against religious freedoms, a handful of internal inconsistencies and incompatibilities – theoretical, legal, and theological – rise to the surface. Simultaneously, there can be complicating factors with both internal and external manifestations, factors which on a practical level significantly compromise the efficacy of the rights idea in relation to religious women. Some inconsistencies lie between the rights construct and gender issues, some between rights and religion, and some engage all three categories. A primary inconsistency is simply internal to the rights notion itself: the very language of human rights creates an impasse. Two legitimate rights norms are pitted against one another with no legal or philosophical resolution to the standoff, stalling real progress and extending the tenure of patriarchal religious ideology. A theoretical locking of horns produces a discursive battle of competing valid claims, one to gender equality and the other to spiritual authenticity and autonomy.

Because there is as yet no real consensus on the "ground" of human rights – the essential source of the rights construct – a focus on elemental rights theory is only of limited help in solving this conflict of rights claims. Is individual wellbeing – the end of harm to a person – the ground of all rights? Religious communities teach a variety of perspectives on what comprises harm, and some have different criteria of harmful behavior for women and men. Is community welfare the ground of human rights? If so, what is proclaimed as good by a religious community may differ substantially from codified rights norms, and require vastly inferior rights enjoyment for certain individuals in the society. Are human needs the ground of human rights?[2] As the Bangladeshi example shows, the content of basic human needs also has no consensus within communities and in the international community, generally. Without a ranking of human needs contestations arise, as do demands that rights discourse be removed from anything related to distributive justice. If the ground of human rights is in God (as John Locke wrote), issues develop regarding the variety of manifestations of the divine in human societies and claims (on behalf of the divine) against certain rights norms. Similarly, while some theorists identify the ground of human rights as human dignity[3], there is no consensus (particularly when religion is involved) on what comprises a life of dignity. Consequently, without consensus on the source and goal of the human rights project, the corpus of human rights law that flows from human rights theory is equally undecided on the ranking of religious freedom and discrete gender-related rights. No template exists for the resolution of such rights conflicts nor is one likely to be articulated, as Chapter 2 will discuss.

A variety of factors internal to the rights concept frustrates the securing of women's rights and gender equality, generally, and are at play in the obstruction of religious women's rights. First, the state is most often the entity referenced by and held accountable to human rights standards, in both the law and theory of human rights. The state is assumed to be both the initial abuser and/or the ultimate guarantor of rights. In cases of women's rights abuses, however, the culprit may be a relative or a member of one's religious community and not an individual or institution representing the state. Human rights laws are significantly less effective in their applicability to the private sphere, and national and local governments frequently show themselves unwilling to prosecute rights violations that happen to women within their families or communities.

Similarly, women are disserved by the strong emphasis in rights discourse and law on the so-called "first generation" of human rights, which comprise civil/political liberties.[4] Priority is given to the public sphere, and to activities there such as political organization, free association, and free speech. These are activities in which many women are not free to participate. In addition, negative rights prevail in the first generation. Civil liberties are said to be best secured when citizens are left alone to pursue their own welfare, unimpeded by intrusive legislation or domination by the state or other actors. Anyone in a secondary or inferior situation is harmed by a strong emphasis on negative liberties, which leave imbalances of power unaddressed and permit the stronger actor to continue in his or her ways.

While women are certainly affected by first generation rights, the terms of and emphases upon first generation rights abuses often neglect the most pressing rights issues for women. For example, the right to life is commonly understood to require due process before the imposition of capital punishment, or the elimination of extra-judicial executions. It is not interpreted as requiring states to prevent the deaths of 500,000 women around the world each year from complications during pregnancy.[5] Similarly, definitions of torture in international documents often are confined to abuse that happens at the hands of a police officer or other agent of the state.[6] Women, many of whom are prevented by law or religion from participating in the public realm, may not experience torture while in police custody. They will, however, be tortured at home by a spouse or other family member who punishes them with increasing severity, sometimes to the point of death. Both in the international covenants and in national reports of human rights initiatives, rape is seldom regarded as a form of torture, as a tool of warfare, or as cruel, inhuman, or degrading treatment.[7] The Universal Declaration of Human Rights does not include rape in its inventory of rights abuses. Most governments do not recognize the crime of rape within marriage. The 1995 United Nations Beijing conference on women saw the first international-level agreement on a right to say "no," even to a husband.[8] While the major rights documents decry violence and bodily injury, they do not speak directly to the most dangerous place in women's lives, which is the home. Domestic violence results in some 25 percent of all emergency room admissions of women in the United States. While it is against the law in every American municipality to beat someone randomly on the street, and while states are held responsible for prosecuting the offender, the same aggressor may inflict even more injury at home upon his wife or girlfriend and not be charged with any crime. While murder between siblings is an offense for which police will certainly intervene, the murder of a woman by her husband and sometimes of a female infant or child by a parent may not be deemed worthy of prosecution in some societies.[9]

Citing these concerns and numerous others, some feminist rights theorists have concluded that the construct of "human rights," as an idea and a body of law, is an inherently gendered construct. The whole of the discourse is understood as androcentric and the concept of "human" as reflecting men's experiences, bodies, agendas, and ascribed attributes.[10] The preponderance of men's experiences, reflected in human rights discourse, creates an implied universality and objectivity to existing human rights law, while tacitly presenting men as human and women as "other."[11] Radical feminists conclude that the human rights idea, international covenants, and domestic law serve to reinforce heterosexism, mandatory childbearing, and the patriarchal family.[12] Some feminist theorists question whether the human rights construct can ever be of real help to women at all.[13] The working perspective of this book is that gendered and patriarchal elements exist in the human rights construct (as they do in religions), and that they contribute to the internal inconsistencies in the rights notion that compromise its effectiveness for religious women, but that they are neither inherent in the human rights idea nor manifesting themselves in every instance. They are most potent when combined with discriminatory structures external to the rights idea, such as local culture, legal institutions, and familial ideology.

Like gender, the category of religion also has internal inconsistencies in relation to the notion of human rights. Most importantly, there is a clash between the normative imperatives in human rights discourse and some schools of religious thought. One norm central to the rights idea is that of human equality regardless of any social or physical category, including gender, religion, and race. Claims for the validity of a *human* right are eviscerated by theologies that insist that women have different "natures" than men and that therefore justify different (inferior) rights standards for women and girls. If there is no such thing as a single value and essence to every human being there is no such thing as a human right, only rights by category: women's rights, men's rights, Christian rights, heterosexual rights, and so on.

There are inconsistencies between religion and the rights construct even in those religious communities that understand all humans as being of equal worth and the same essence. The modern rights notion has been shaped by such philosophical factors as Kant's "categorical imperative," his idea that human beings are ends in themselves and never to be viewed solely as means. The essence of all human rights becomes a relationless freedom embodied by individuals with an inherent, unqualified value and importance. Religion, however, puts human beings first into a category as humans (before any subdivisions, if applicable), then puts the whole of that category in relationship to a divine source, project, or entity. Human beings are not always ends in themselves but reflections, representatives, vassals, or members of the divine. As a group or as individuals they serve as the means for a different holy purpose; they may understand themselves as members of a total community before or in addition to understanding themselves as lone, rights-bearing individuals. The human position and condition are relativized, and set in the context of what are believed to be far greater and more ultimate ends than the individual human being itself.

A similar inconsistency exists between the understanding of duty in the modern rights notion versus that in some religious traditions. Many contemporary theorists would assert that human rights are actually claims that entail duties from others. In the words of one, rights are "merely the shadows cast by [other people's] duties."[14] This logical correlativity of rights and duties is defined by Joel Feinberg as "the doctrine that...all duties entail other people's rights and...all rights entail other people's duties."[15] Some religious traditions understand rights and duties in a very different light, not as unearned and inuring to the human being in every condition but as being earned in proportion to the fulfillment of initial duty. While secular human rights theory questions whether or not an individual's rights inherently require compliance duties from *others*, some religious sources, in a reversed version of moral correlativity, affirm that individuals' rights issue first from the duties that they *themselves* perform. R.C. Pandeya, a Hindu philosopher, writes that communities must not accord "the same set of rights to people who work for it and those who do not,"[16] an idea that is anathema to mainstream human rights theory. Carl Henry, an evangelical Protestant, has written, "The Bible does not teach that human beings simply on the basis of existence have inherent or a priori rights, or that they have absolute rights accruing from sociological or political considerations. The Bible has a doctrine of divinely imposed duties; what moderns call human rights are the contingent flipside of those duties."[17] Religious communities may have very specific criteria – required duties – for the enjoyment of human rights, quite the opposite indeed of the modern liberal rights notion.

Some conservative religious communities, therefore, resist the idea of rights as a valid discourse or view them as a tool of ethical imperialism and recolonization. Relativism presents a critical internal inconsistency within the rights notion, generally, regarding questions of difference and universality. The challenge does not belong to human rights alone, certainly, and is a vital question in feminism, law, ethics, and other disciplines. Absolute values, and concepts such as "objectivity," "truth," and "justice" are contested. At every level, human rights theory is laden with universal moral absolutes. On the most overarching of levels, the human rights idea regards all persons as having equal value; arguably, the human rights construct views human life as having infinite value, and the saving of human lives as the highest good in any society. On the micro level, the human rights concept now includes access to medical care, equality within the family, and the right to live in an unpolluted environment as universal moral absolutes. Similar moral absolutes also guide the world's religions. As Chapter 4 will describe, moral relativism presents a particularly potent inconsistency in regard to religion, and a great challenge in using the rights rubric for acquiring religious women's human rights. The challenges have both internal and external manifestations, some rooted in the theory of human rights and others in communities' application of the relativist critique of rights to enhance their own agendas or to preserve aspects of their power.

The very validity of the rights notion is challenged by those critics who say that its roots in liberalism, and its corresponding emphases on individualism, personal rights as claims, and legalism, fundamentally contradict the ethical structure of particular societies. Rather than having the individual as the fundamental unit of society, they say, families or whole clans appropriately play that role. Rather than having personal rights at the center of claims for justice, practiced duties are the foundation of personal entitlement. Rather than legal methods of redress and the formal codification of criteria for social justice, it is reconciliation, repentance, and education that should be used to address grievances and process petitions.[18] Consequently, rights language will not only be unhelpful but may actually limit women's protest within religious communities, as defensiveness against perceived moral relativism delegitimizes the concept in some locations.

There are other practical issues that complicate the applicability of the rights notion to both gender and religion simultaneously, issues that in part also have internal inconsistencies with the rights notion. The first is the embeddedness of the public/private dichotomy, both in the liberal discourse out of which the rights notion philosophically was born and consequently in the rights idea itself. "In liberal philosophy privacy is central to individualism as an area of life not subjected to the power of society," writes Kate O'Donovan.[19] As mentioned above, international human rights law refers continually to the state; where individual actors are referenced, only vague permission is given to states to call persons to accountability. The religious discrimination or persecution that a person may receive from someone of a different faith can find redress in international and domestic law, but much less so a person who, thanks to familial and/or religious ideology, is beaten by her mother-in-law or whose husband will not allow her freedom of movement. In spirit, the human rights notion properly considers each of these justice issues a question of real rights but in practice they are, legally, very difficult to redress. Rights norms as currently articulated only reinforce the notion of separable public and private spheres. "The emphasis on the state and public sphere is problematic for women," write V. Spike Peterson and Laura Parisi, "because it does not recognize the masculinist state's complicity in naturalizing – depoliticizing – the public–private dichotomy, masculinist citizenship, patriarchal families and heterosexism."[20] The public/private dichotomy is deeply, deeply rooted in the rights notion as it is now employed, as well as in some religious ideologies, and this tremendously disserves the rights of religious women and the ability of the rights construct to help them.

The rights notion's roots in liberalism also result in a strong emphasis on the individual in rights theory. Consequently, the rights construct is challenged in its ability to address the family, a primary site of gender and religious rights issues. Seyla Benhabib has pointed out that liberalism, with its roots in the Enlightenment, emphasizes justice as "the core of collective moral life" in such a way as to leave out the family.[21] Critical legal scholars have unpacked the Enlightenment emphasis on individualism that pervades the rights notion, and questioned whether a rights framework could therefore substantively address the systemic and structural oppression of some groups.[22] As one commentator has noted, neo-liberalism has an ally in the Judeo-Christian notion of personal sin: human rights violations are always the fault of an individual and never a structure (such as the family, but also religious institutions and theologies).[23] As a corrective measure, in the last few decades the liberal rights notion has been restructured to formally include the family (as with clauses in the Women's Convention), yet the primary emphases on the public sphere and on the individual seem to be unsalvageably intrinsic to the rights idea. Some feminists have concluded that liberalism lacks the potential ever truly to serve women, which begs again the question of whether the liberal rights notion may as well.[24] Because religion is further considered literally to be sacred – that is, off-limits to outsiders – the rights notion is even less able to secure the rights of women in religious communities.

Fiona Robinson has written of the inseparability of the rights notion from liberal and libertarian ideas of "individual consent as the legitimate basis of rights."[25] An added quality of the rights construct that impedes its applicability to some religious women is the assumption that what is of primary importance is that individuals are free to *choose*. An extreme articulation of this perspective perceives the making of choices as the great single indicator of rights enjoyment. Equating choices and liberties, Devaki Jain and Nirmala Banerjee ask, "Where there are no choices what freedoms are we taking away?"[26] Radhika Coomaraswamy has written that the whole question of the universality of rights can be resolved if people are allowed to choose whether they wish to have certain rights norms applied to them (as in, "what really matters is what individual women want for themselves").[27] Similarly, Martha Nussbaum, arguing for a "capabilities approach" to human rights theory and policy, has written that the maintenance of "choice as a good" can eliminate paternalism in devising and advocating for certain rights categories for all women.[28] The job of rights advocates is to make all human rights available to all women. If, in the end, the women in question are able to choose whether or not to accept particular rights for themselves, no religious or cultural interference has occurred.

The ability to make choices for oneself is unquestionably a good thing. Chapter 6, concerning agency, endeavors to illustrate, however, that the categories of religion and gender terribly complicate the question of choice-making and rights enjoyment. Particular religious communities and societies do not accept the idea that women (in this case) are entitled to choose to enjoy various rights norms, and consequently some women are instructed not to want them in the first place, believing that choice in such matters is religiously unacceptable. They genuinely do not choose certain rights for themselves. The great emphasis on personal agency in the liberal rights construct is significantly foreign to the religious contexts and practices that affect some women. If rights enjoyment is dependent on making choices, many religious women will never have them. To the extent that the rights notion (and the criteria for rights enjoyment) are founded and dependent upon personal agency, they cannot be applicable to many religious women. Fiona Robinson has suggested that other central ideals of the liberal rights construct are ones that make it potentially viable for women, to the extent that they truly can be realized – the end of hierarchy, arbitrary rule, and the creation of a broad space around each person so she can discover and implement her own idea of the good.[29] However, patriarchal religious ideology and its compromise of women's agency present an ongoing challenge to women's ability to develop their *own* ideas of what is good. The subject of agency thus offers a double inconsistency, one with the rights construct and the other with religious ideologies.

For some religious women, rights language is problematic in its very nature because it makes claims upon others – another reason why rights law and theory cannot enable rights in some situations. Research by Carol Gilligan, for instance, has shown that some of her subjects found the rights concept a dilemma in their own moral decision-making because they had been socialized to be so other-oriented that they understood any claims they make as examples of selfishness.[30] Certainly the socialization of Gilligan's respondents must be unlearned, and the ways in which it enhances others' agendas unpacked, but in the short run the idea of working for one's own rights, as such, with the claims and duties they involve regarding others, will be difficult for the women concerned, especially when their perspectives on the matter are taught to be religiously appropriate. Similarly, some research in Africa has also shown that the idea of making a claim against another person or institution is inimical to some women's ideas of what is appropriate. Much more accessible there are notions of corporate justice rather than individual right.[31] Other researchers have found that rights language is not considered by some women to address – yet – their real concerns.[32] This study will argue that patriarchal religious ideology is one category that remains beyond the reach of rights law and discourse as they currently are formulated.

The human rights construct has been devised to promote justice and wellbeing for every person. While it is far from the only tool for enabling justice, in practice the rights idea has become the most universal and accessible discourse for justice. It is a powerful tool, having achieved legitimacy in sectors of every society. Consequently, the rights construct has been given the task of righting wrongs of every kind, and of addressing seemingly limitless situations of oppression, discrimination, and injustice. It has been transformed by its supporters into the bearer of a phenomenal task – the creation of a universal code of moral and legal responsibility among states, between states and individuals, and between individual persons themselves. It has been set up with the task of dismantling many sites and methods of domination, not only in the state but also now in the home. We ask of the human rights construct nothing less than the reorienting of gender relations and of religion-state relations, among others.

But the rights construct is not always up to the task. Gender and religion (and particularly the combination of the two) present profound challenges to the ability of the rights notion to fulfill this mandate. In part, this is because of the aforementioned theoretical, legal, theological, and practical complications to do with gender and religion. Equally important inhibitors are the fact that questions of morality and justice in relation to gender are influenced by the persistence of patriarchy, and that questions of morality and justice in relation to religion face competing ideas of morality and justice, and particularly what makes for justice and a moral life for women. Understandings of morality and justice are relative to particular religious communities. They are also strongly inherent – and yet inconclusive – within the idea of rights (see the discussion below). As globalized as the idea of human rights has become, its inchoate assumptions regarding justice and morality may render it ineffective in addressing competing, discriminatory claims to gender and religious rights.

The focus of the following chapters will necessarily concern those religious communities and situations in which the human rights construct does not promote human rights effectively or practically. There are, however, numerous instances in which the human rights idea can promote rights for religious women. The difference lies in a handful of factors explored below, including the particular theological disposition of communities, the structure and accountability of their courts of law, states' willingness to implement human rights law, the existence of secular courts and the quality of their rulings on gender- and family-related matters, communities' resistance to what they perceive as moral imperialism, and the entrenchment of the idea of an untouchable private sphere. The rights notion can overcome the internal inconsistencies and practical challenges involved in gender and religion if most or all of these criteria are positively met – if there is theological support for gender equality, acceptance and appropriation of the idea of rights, a willingness to implement rights law, a willingness to address gender violence or discrimination in the home, and so on.

The most important criterion is theological, and for two reasons. The first reason is that there are theoretical and practical limits to the human rights idea. While the human rights concept continues to evolve, and certainly could be improved in its relevance to women and to religious communities, the serious structural impediments discussed above may always remain. Additionally, the actual enforcement of rights norms in participating states seems too daunting to the international legal and political community at present. Requiring compliance would mean significant intervention in states' affairs, intervention that offending states do not want to encourage and that other states are reluctant to enforce. Also, because of broad opposition to infringements on the right to freedom of religion, human rights law will not likely be redrafted to give states sweeping authority to address rights abuses within religious communities and families.

The second reason why a community's theological perspective is the most important criterion in the usefulness of the rights idea is that without religious validation of gender equality, such equality never will be truly available to women. The human rights construct and any other method of ending gender subordination will fail in communities and families until patriarchal religious ideology is undone. As long as the international community continues to uphold a right to freedom of religion (and one sincerely hopes that they do), discriminatory or violent religious practices and teachings will trump gender rights. As described in Chapter 7, religions are always in the process of change. When gender equality becomes a part of every community's theological make-up, the conflict between gender rights and religious freedoms will no longer exist. Religiously endorsed infringements of women's rights cannot be ended through more effective codification and enforcement of human rights law but through changes within religious communities to the theologies and practices that support gender discrimination and human rights abuses.

Women's rights

Amnesty International has concluded that women suffer more rights abuses than any other group, whether in times of war or times of peace.[33] This situation prevails largely because abuses of women's rights are perceived, as Susan Moller Okin has described it, as somehow benign.[34] Appalling instances of discrimination (some mandated by government policy) based on race, ethnicity, class, or religion, occasionally meet with international protest. Flagrant abuses of women's rights infrequently receive such attention, and when attention does come it may be politically motivated (such as the sudden concern for Afghan women's rights by the American government in the fall of 2001). The number of "missing" women in the world (through female abortion, infanticide, and neglect),[35] the trafficking of women,[36] and the selling of women on open markets[37] or into prostitution[38] remain critically under-attended rights abuses endured by women. Apartheid based on race is an offence to humanity; apartheid based on gender is culture, is religious sentiment, is private opinion beyond the reach of international commentary.[39] In the words of one 1973 working paper from the United Nations, discrimination based on sex is viewed simply as "idealized heritage."[40] Serious rights abuses that proceed from religious belief and are based on race, ethnicity, class, or religious differences may meet with strong international disapproval (racial apartheid in South Africa, for instance, received the strongest biblical and theological endorsement in many white churches). Religion-based infringements of women's rights receive less of a response.

Certain religious practices are occasionally challenged as forms of slavery. *Purdah*, the veiling and/or seclusion of women, results in their virtual immobility and withdrawal from the public realm. They are often confined to their homes. Child marriage, a religiously sanctioned (if not encouraged) practice in traditions such as Hinduism, is also considered by some commentators to be slavery. The same is true for brideprice, the custom (in some places supported by religious ideology) in which a man pays a considerable sum of money to a family in order to marry a daughter or sister. In reality, he has bought her, and his subsequent treatment of her often indicates that indeed he views her as his property.[41] The "women's rights are human rights" campaign of the last decade sought to insert into rights legislation and enforcement the understanding that the categories of injustice experienced by many women are indeed the very categories of rights infringements covered by international law, such as slavery and murder, and must be redressed as *bona fide* human rights abuses. The deep cultural and religious acceptance of many practices, and the "benign" or "natural" veneer of gender subordination, have made the campaign an uphill battle.

The world's religions contribute directly to the limiting of women's rights in every category. States and communities practice a wide variety of theological interpretation; consequently, women from the same religious tradition will experience very different levels of rights enjoyment depending upon which country, region, or local community is their home. Because of religious teaching, women cannot vote or stand for election in Bahrain, Oman, Qatar, Saudi Arabia, and the United Arab Emirates.[42] They may do so, however, in many of the other 35 states with a majority Muslim population. In Pakistan, the law permits women to hold a maximum of ten percent of the seats in the national legislature. The same condition prevails in Bangladesh, yet there the female candidates are not voted for by the plebiscite but by the existing male legislators.[43] In Nigeria, religious law prohibits a woman journalist from any background to interview a politician who is a Muslim (and presumably male).[44] In some Muslim countries, doctors refuse to perform pap smears or other tests to detect cervical cancer, saying that "the Muslim proscription of premarital and extramarital sex protects women from the disease." Some physicians in Malaysia refuse to perform such procedures for women of any age who are unmarried.[45] The women's cancers go undetected until the late stages, when the chance of survival is drastically reduced.

India is a multi-religious country whose national legislation defers to religious teaching on matters of personal status. The majority of the country's women, who are Hindu, may have a significantly compromised level of rights enjoyment in comparison with men if conservative interpretations of personal status laws prevail in their community. Dowry death, custodial rape, the marriage of little girls to older men, limited inheritance of land and wealth, and other customs have their roots in religious precepts and traditions. In traditional Hindu teaching, women are considered to be lesser beings than men in the great chain of rebirth in Hindu cosmology.

National legislation in majority Christian countries, such as those in Latin America, bears the strong influence of church teachings. Argentina, Costa Rica, and Bolivia, for example, have constitutions in which Catholicism alone is said to be supported by the state. In such countries the Roman Catholic Church exerts great pressure on lawmakers to prevent the legalization of abortion. Illicit abortion attempts are the leading cause of death and of all health problems for women of child-bearing age in Latin America.[46] Public debate continues in many countries as to whether or not abortion is a woman's right, yet all would agree that, in principle, women have a right to remain alive. That religious ethics should influence a society's lawmaking is not problematic, and is a fact in every region of the world. The problem occurs when such ethics are interpreted to support gender (or other) subordination.

Religious freedoms

While women's human rights are occasionally abrogated by practiced religion, that practice is also protected as a human right, and importantly so. Recent decades are replete with examples of discrimination – even genocide – based on religion. The same rights violations visited upon women are also endured by persons on account of their religious identification. Denial of the right to vote or run for office, to receive an education (particularly in a religious school), to receive medical care, to own land or enjoy freedom of movement and assembly, even the right to go on living – each of these is experienced by persons simply because of their religious beliefs.

State-sponsored discrimination on the grounds of religion exists in every region of the world and in every style of government, from democracies to "theocracies" to one-party systems. According to Human Rights Watch, minority religious groups (and in some countries, every religious group) are persecuted in East Timor, Pakistan,

Bulgaria, Vietnam, India, China, Israel, Saudi Arabia, Turkmenistan, Romania, Georgia, Greece, Hungary, Kazakhstan, Uzbekistan, Kyrgyzstan, Turkey, Algeria, and Egypt. Physical attacks, blasphemy charges, economic restrictions and discrimination, interference in the selection of leaders, jail sentences, and the prohibition on gatherings for worship are a few of the curbs on religious freedom.[47] Unfortunately, gross violations to religious rights have not been left behind with the twentieth century but endure in many countries.

Interference in the worship and other practices of a religious group is considered a serious offence for a government or members of a different religious tradition. Outsiders to a religion are not permitted to determine what is acceptable in that belief system and what is not. At the same time, some religious practices are deemed so reprehensible by a majority of the population that limits are placed upon religious freedom in the name of the public interest. The 1948 Indian Constitution includes a ban on the ancient (and inherently Hindu) custom of untouchability. The document includes a stipulation that no person may be barred entrance to a Hindu temple – a reference to common practice concerning untouchables and in complete defiance of religious teaching. The provision is a clear instance of the intrusion of secular government into the personal religious and social sensibilities of citizens. So is the sentencing in the United States in August 2001 of five years in prison for a Mormon man convicted of polygamy. His defense was religious freedom, but the court (and popular opinion) decided that he had broken a valid law. In any society, members of minority religions (such as Mormons) may be excluded from participating in the formulation and expression of that society's corporate moral norms. Simultaneously, a certain religious group may deny such activity to particular members within its own body. Discrimination against whole religious groups is almost universally condemned, while discrimination *within* religious groups is viewed as a delicate matter. This latter instance is most applicable to women's rights vis-à-vis religious practice, and is the point at which rights law on religion fails women.

In the chapters to follow, the point will be made that the very notion of human rights is a construct – not an organic or natural fact but an idea created by human beings as a tool to promote social justice. Human rights are a mutually agreed-upon, lowest-common-denominator standard for how humans should treat one another, and for what constitutes a life of "dignity." Much the same is true concerning the category of religion. Religion, also, is a construct. Like the human rights idea, what *is* organic or natural about it is humanity's desire to create a better and more intentional ordering to the lived world, and even to metaphysical life. What are natural and organic are the human impulses that lead to its construction, but not the exact terms of its codification.

Religion, rights, and the language of justice

The concept of a human right has been devised intentionally to circumvent appeals to religion, culture, legal tradition, or other factors in order to name those categories of justice from which no person should be excluded. Users of rights discourse base their appeals for justice not on relative or subjective grounds, such as what is "good" or "right" or "compassionate" or even "just." Instead, they anchor their justice claims within the very entity for which they advocate: the human being itself. Beneath all cultures, beyond all religions, above every positive law, comprising every tribe and nation, is elemental humanity, born into innumerable contexts but of the very same essence. Human rights are items of justice to which all human beings are entitled, in the words of many a contemporary rights theorist, "simply because they are human." However, beneath many conflicts of rights claims are conflicts of metaphysical truth claims, including the relative worth of humans generally, of women in particular, the goal of human living, and so on. This is certainly the case in conflicts between religious rights and women's rights.

Human rights and religions have compelling similarities and fundamental differences. The most important similarity is their shared source of moral power: an emphasis on the transcendent and a grounding in what is ultimate. The very concept of human rights has spiritual overtones. One Muslim writer points to the "declaratory character" of rights claims as they are enshrined in authoritative texts and commanded to be honored as promises by those choosing to adhere to the rights concept. These methods and attitudes – the very model of "practicing" human rights – mirror the practicing of religions; they add to the power of the rights idea by buttressing it with claims to normativity and ethical authority, providing what he calls its "mystic sustenance."[48] Furthermore, "The message conveyed by human rights as we conceive them," he writes, "pertains originally to the religious dimension of the individual, that in which he has revealed himself in the most mysterious, deepest, darkest and most promising ways."[49] The content of human rights discourse, then, includes many of the ultimate concerns of human existence, topics shared by religious teaching. Human rights language is but one way of speaking of these moral and ethical issues, as is religious language. A North American Protestant describes the similarities as follows:

> On the basis of ultimate meanings and concrete relationships, all religions set forth a social ethic – a more or less coherent set of moral guides about what is right and what is wrong, good and evil, fitting and unfitting – to prevent chaos, alienation, and tyranny. All this is rooted in a fundamental sense of what is holy, in a metaphysical-moral vision of what is "really real."
>
> Claims about human rights are religious in this sense: each view of human rights entails an ultimate metaphysical-moral vision about what is meaningful, about what relationships or memberships are sacrosanct, and what social ethic should be followed in order to prevent chaos, social alienation, and tyranny from destroying essential humanity.[50]

Concrete moral norms are actually foundational to both human rights and religion. The liberal humanism that undergirds the human rights idea is a philosophy with as many moral assumptions as have the religions. This fact is not a problem, but the source of the power of both rights and religion. Any attempt to enforce value-neutrality would rob either construct – rights or religion – of any substance and ought not even to be desired, yet numerous theorists (particularly in the legal community) assert that value-neutrality is both desirable and achievable. For example, one scholar of law has written, "Gender distinctions in religious law rest on the nature of the gender roles that have been shaped by the religious tradition itself; those roles cannot therefore be asserted as 'objective' or 'reasonable' bases for the distinctions made in the law."[51] Religious commentators on rights (the present writer included) might respond that what is "objective" and "reasonable" to this lawyer, conditioned by the liberal humanism that informs her practice of international human rights law, is just another point on the continuum of relative ideologies, and as incapable of objectivity as self-consciously theological perspectives. Even international rights law is not at all value-neutral. The religions are perhaps more transparent in their defenses of patriarchy and of gender discrimination, which secular ideologies have also managed to perpetuate since the "metaphysical rationalism" (in the words of one historian) of the Renaissance and Enlightenment. A particular point of tension between secular and religious rights theories may be the fact that the mere existence of each underscores the relativity of the metaphysical starting point of the other, and the fact that neither has categories or teachings that are universally accessible or applicable.

The objectivity thought to be so crucial by some secular theorists is both impossible and ill advised.[52] Objectivity is understood as foundational to scientific inquiry, and in an attempt to earn credibility for their schools of justice claims some rights theorists (such as Donna Sullivan)[53] have claimed objectivity as a hallmark of their discipline. They posit that the very legitimacy of their discipline rests in the fact that it avoids the pitfalls of particular identity-based positions in order to speak to irreducible commonalities of human wellbeing. However, human rights theories gain their very substance, their relevance, their influence, and their basic appeal thanks to the metaphysical claims that they make. These uncompromising claims, rooted in an essential, ineffable nature inherent in the human being, give the human rights idea its power. The human rights notion is therefore in the difficult position of drawing its authority, power, and universal validity on the basis of its metaphysical truth claims, all the while asserting (at the hands of some theorists) that contradictory rights theories are groundless because they are rooted in metaphysical perspectives which, by their nature, can never be universal. Contrary to the implicit assumptions of much contemporary rights theorizing, these secular theories appear to be, inherently, claims for the superiority of one metaphysical perspective over others. In fact, those secular rights theories that are most influential are the ones that do not camouflage their metaphysical claims but rather proclaim them boldly.

Mahatma Gandhi has been said to have founded his vision of a free and equal society not on the prevailing (secular) understanding of "rational man" but on the notion of "ethical man."[54] This dichotomy could also describe the intentional (fundamentally different) hermeneutical starting points of many humanistic rights theories and religious rights frameworks. One manifestation of the difference is evident in the objections of some religious theorists to the anthropocentric, rather than theocentric, nature of liberal rights theories.[55] "Human rights are inherent in one's humanity," writes one social scientist;[56] human rights, in other words, are possessed by a human being independent of any relationship she may have with persons, states or deities. If any relationship is implied, it is with governing authorities. "[H]uman rights are grounded in a rejection of the state's claim to ultimate authority," writes another researcher.[57]

Some religious rights theories would agree that no state is to have ultimate authority, but would argue that the moral authority behind human rights does not inhere to the human being but to the divine.[58] Liberal humanistic rights theories give autonomy to the individual; religious rights theories understand the human being to be in intimate relationship to a divine element, and perhaps also to a community of believers. Different theories may advocate similar moral visions and virtues, yet religious commentators may still take issue with the fact of "the idea of rights itself: the notion that individuals possess, on their own, rights that do not come from the community or from God."[59] It is a problem of independence, a fear that rights must come to the individual at the expense either of the community's integrity or of the belief that all moral authority originates in a deity and not human beings. As one scholar of Hinduism has noted,

> No matter how similar religious values and human rights might seem, the ideological basis for traditional religious values is not ultimately the same as the humanistic secular version. From a traditional communitarian point of view, the stark individualism and laissez faire attitude toward personal expression run fundamentally counter to the spirit of collective loyalty and disciplined demeanor that is typically found in religious life."[60]

Both secular and religious human rights theories root their truth claims in metaphysical perspectives; however, issues of autonomy, relationality, and ultimate moral authority create vastly different interpretations of the rights concept. Not only are the metaphysical starting points in different locations, but the trajectories taken off of those points are equally dissimilar.

And yet, secular and religious rights theories share much in common. Both have as a central concern the moral dimension of individual and corporate life. The so-called "first generation" of human rights boldly claims that human life has value. In some articulations of an irreducible "right to life," human life takes on ultimate value. So-called "second generation" rights extend this infinity of value to the human being who suffers from structural harm, such as from economic injustice, racism, or sexism. Michael J. Perry, a North American legal scholar, writes that the underlying assumption of international human rights law "is that the good of every human being is an end worth pursuing in its own right because every human being is sacred."[61] Another writes, "Most of the laborers in the field of human rights believe that there is a moral inevitability to human rights. I believe that."[62] Contrary to stereotypes of morality and sacrality, human rights law may hold persons in higher metaphysical regard than religious traditions.

In general, natural law theory (in which few rights theorists now intentionally ground their work) would seem to have left a significant imprint on liberal human rights theory.[63] Natural law assumes a higher authority and a pseudo-divine, intentional, inescapable, righteous ordering to nature and the universe. The language of the opening statement of the Universal Declaration of Human Rights is a case in point, with declarations regarding "the inherent dignity and...the equal and inalienable rights of the members of the human family." Article 1 proclaims, "All human beings are born free and equal in dignity. They are endowed with reason and conscience and should act toward one another in a spirit of brotherhood."[64] A Spanish/Indian philosopher of religion has outlined the assumptions contained in the liberal human rights idea in terms that illuminate its strong influences from natural law. In his opinion, the human rights concept assumes a universal human nature that is knowable (presumably through reason) and that sets humanity above other living things. The individual is assumed to have an irreducible dignity, to be a separate entity, to have autonomy, possibly to be *imago dei*, and to exist as an absolute – an end in itself.[65]

Michael Perry describes the natural law perspective underlying the liberal human rights concept as assuming the following:

> [T]he fundamental subject matter of morality is human well-being...[A]ll (or virtually all) human beings share some significant characteristics. In that sense they share a "nature," in virtue of which some things are good for every human being – some things are valuable for (and so, should be valued by) every human being – and some things are bad for every human being – some things are harmful to (and so, should be disvalued by) every human being.[66]

The religions, of course, have deep concern for morality, for what is good and bad for all (or some) human beings. Underlying many conflicts between human rights precepts and religious teaching, then, is a defensive battle of ideas of morality.

Both rights and religions ground their authority on the absoluteness of their moral truth claims. Liberal human rights theories hold different truths as self-evident, but each school of thought has its absolutes ("the inviolable dignity of the human being," "the human being as an end in itself," "the human being as having, everywhere, the same essence and value," etc.). The religions certainly have their absolutes, truth claims codified in sacred texts and practices. From these cosmological and doctrinal foundations emerge understandings of morally appropriate behavior for individuals. As the discussion in the chapters to follow will attest, some schools of Christianity teach the moral appropriateness of women's self-denial or self-sacrifice; some schools of Hinduism teach the moral appropriateness of wives' viewing (and serving) their husbands as gods; some schools of Islam teach the moral appropriateness of *purdah* for women. Unlike rights theory, each religion teaches morals that are universally appropriate to humanity in addition to morals that are appropriate to certain types of persons (women, believers, non-believers, etc.). Each, however, is understood as an absolute. The point of a human right is that it is applicable to every single person on earth. A fact of religious interpretation is that absolute truth sometimes indicates different treatment for different categories of persons, and *what is fair in the religions is not always what is equal.* While the human rights idea makes absolute moral claims about what is good for all humanity, the religions make such claims about human wellbeing on a variety of levels. The two sets of paradigms frequently conflict on what it means to be good, moral, lawful, self-controlled, self- and other-respecting.

There are points of convergence. The meaning and the end of religion do share common elements with those of the humanistic human rights construct. Human wellbeing, a just society, justice for individuals, and the common good are just a few. But the criteria of meaning and end are vastly different. The religions create, and are themselves reinforced by, powerful symbolism. The religions concern themselves with ultimate issues of human existence in a universe ordered by some quality of divinity or supreme purpose[67] – concerns such as the origin of the planet and of individual human societies, soteriology, sin, and failing. All of reality is structured by religious understandings of a deity, or a supreme or divine element, that is caring, punishing, aloof, intervening, internal, impregnable, doting, attainable, or an infinite combination of these qualities and many more. The perception of all of reality is structured by the perspectives that result from the understood character of divinity or supreme purpose. The world is known to be temporary, fallen, eternally recycling itself, inconsequential, infinite, or reflective of divine glory; humanity is understood to be blessed or punished with the fact of being alive. In some religious communities, women are particularly understood to be cursed by being alive.

The religions teach their adherents what it means to be human, the costs (eternal and temporal) of disobedience, their particular terms of obedience, how to find harmony and peace both spiritually and socially, the meaning of truth, equality, wisdom, and the criteria for all that is to be valued. The religions teach their followers the proper way to make meaning of life's joy and suffering. Cosmic order and divine intention may be applied to the best and worst of life's experiences. Believers and practitioners learn how to understand every element of their living, from a sunset to a terminal disease. Women and men are instructed continually, whether overtly or subtly, in what is the "true" nature of men and women, on how they should relate to one another, on how the divine element views, uses, evaluates, and ranks them. The religions give to people much (in many cases all) of their fundamental identity. They teach people what it means to *be* a Baha'i, a Sikh, a Jew, and in the process teach them what it means to be a human being. Basic ways of understanding humanity and "ways of seeing and feeling the world" (in the words of one historian of religion) are based in and continually reinforced by scripture, tradition, history and experience, law, and revelation.

Liberal human rights theory claims the human being as its universal reference point and the grounds for the validity of rights claims. As the following chapters will show, the religions, however, teach different understandings of the human being. The religions eliminate any universal perspective on the human being, on its value, origins and destiny; some religious teachings fly in the face of liberal humanist moral claims that individuals are of equal worth, deserve equal respect, and should have equal expectations of ability and opportunity. As Wilfred Cantwell Smith has noted, religious practice is not an addendum to a human being but a *way* of being a human.[68] Some rights theorists betray, in their work, the belief that the essential human condition is a "secular" one, with religion as an added, optional "extra."[69] In fact, the great majority of the world's people whose spiritual sensibilities are integral to their being may be proof of just the opposite: humanity is essentially religious, while a distinct minority have chosen a political, cultural, economic, philosophical, or social ideology as their central ethic.

It may be said, perhaps, that the human rights idea is primarily concerned with the quality of a person's physical life, while religions are primarily concerned with a person's metaphysical life, yet an influence on one sphere can only have practical implications for the other. The difference in focus[70] will create tremendously different answers to questions such as the following: What makes life valuable? What makes life good? What circumstances are acceptable or ideal? What is real quality of life, and how is it improved? What is human dignity – is it decided by the material conditions of a person's existence or is it something interior, a feeling about oneself or an intrinsic quality endowed by a deity? Do certain categories of people deserve certain (different) treatment? Is a good life one in which personal desires are fulfilled? Is it a life in which one is happy? Is it a life in which one can fulfill one's personal potential? Perhaps the most difficult question would be whether rights standards should be tailored (i.e., effectively reduced) to accommodate what particular individuals want for themselves, independent of what an external group (religious, legal, activist) decides is just.[71]

If religious perspective permeates many individuals' worldviews and lives, it is still and always, in its details, a learned perspective. Teachings and interpretations are inculcated from one generation to the next. Critics of religiously based injustices are correct to suggest that individuals may choose to teach different perspectives within the particular religious tradition, ones more consistent with human rights norms.[72] The issue remains, however, of women (and men) who deeply believe things about themselves that others might consider negative or harmful – that they are, for instance, of lesser human value than others, that they deserve harsh circumstances as a punishment for sin, that their bodies are a source of evil. Women who truly believe derogatory things about themselves do so with a positive outcome in mind, one instructed by their religious tradition. They believe that their conformity with the teaching will result in positive judgment by God, the return of a deity to earth, enlightenment, the sending of a messiah, the continuing balance of all the elements of creation, rebirth to a higher order of creation, the redemption by God of the chosen community, and so on. For these women, the human rights abuses they endure are theologically justified and offset by future gain.[73] They are also legitimate religious perspectives that are protected by human rights instruments. In practice, they sometimes legitimate systemic gender oppression, physical and sexual violence, abandonment, even murder.

2
Hierarchies of Rights Claims

> What they call human rights is nothing but a collection of corrupt rules worked out by Zionists to destroy all true religions.
>
> Ayatollah Khomeini

Makers and interpreters of international law have, at various times, sought to adjudicate among competing valid human rights claims by trying to establish a definitive hierarchy among those rights values. The hope is that an agreement upon a static ranking of human rights in order of importance will provide an objective tool for solving future conflicts. Despite growing bodies of legislation, no such hierarchy has been created. This chapter will show that principles internal to human rights law effectively prevent any such ranking. While this may be to the good, preventing an inflexible ladder of value and importance between actual rights norms, it is also the case that some contests between the right to free expression of religion and to discreet rights issues will remain unresolvable. Furthermore, the vagueness, imprecision, and indecisiveness of the language of human rights legislation leaves so many loopholes of interpretation that discriminatory religious practices are able to remain unaddressed. In its legal manifestations, then, the human rights construct is frequently unhelpful in ensuring the human rights of religious women because of its compromised effectiveness. As a result, attempts to resolve some conflicts with heavy reliance on greater implementation of existing human rights law are ill-advised.

The two international instruments most at issue in the conflict between women's rights and religious practice are the Convention on the Elimination of Discrimination Against Women (the Women's Convention) and the Declaration on the Elimination of All Forms of

Discrimination Based on Religion or Belief (the Declaration). Provisions within the Women's Convention that are most in conflict with the freedom to observe religious precepts are equality in protection before the law [Article 2(c)], the abolition of all laws and practices that discriminate against women [Article 2(f)], equal rights regarding nationality (Article 9), equality in all areas of economic and social life (Article 13), equality in all manner before the law (Article 15), and equal rights in family life (Article 16). Some legal scholars and states' representatives have suggested that these provisions render the Women's Convention itself a discriminatory text, restricting associational and religious rights.[1] These assertions have further encouraged the international legal community to attempt to codify a hierarchy of rights claims. The effort has not been fruitful.

The Women's Convention does not seek to eliminate all discrimination based on sex, but rather any discriminatory behavior that adversely affects women.[2] Differentiation in the treatment of males and females is not the Convention's subject. Equality of value between women and men is proclaimed in the Convention's Preamble, yet the document does not call for absolute, unqualified equality of treatment between women and men. The Convention's stated purpose is the elimination of any impediments to women's enjoyment of the rights codified within its own articles, as well as any of the other rights-concerned documents of the United Nations.[3]

A central problem in the language of the Declaration in regard to religious women's rights is the emphasis on the protection of the rights of religious minorities as groups. The Declaration also may be seen to cover the rights of religious individuals vis-à-vis the state, and both of these issues are important, certainly. In the way that it privileges religious groups, however, the Declaration could be used to support the power of religious leaders over individuals in their communities – for instance, reformers who advocate gender equality. The Declaration (which is absolutely non-binding and holds no force of law) clearly gives protection to religious freedom between groups, but not so clearly does it address religious freedom within them. At worst, it may reinforce the power of whole religious communities, including (or especially) those that seek to repress internal, reformist dissent.

Two additional characteristics of the Declaration particularly impact its potential to facilitate the resolution of the type of rights conflicts in question. First, the Declaration is focused primarily on government action. It assumes that the "plaintiff" will be a group, particularly a minority religion, seeking redress from discrimination endured as a result of state policy. The document does not provide obvious assistance, for instance, to a Hindu woman, a member of the religious majority in Nepal, who wishes to challenge the pervasive religious culture that may contribute to her discrimination or challenge a male relative who insists that she underfeed her daughter in order to ensure more than adequate nutrition for her son. Secondly, the Declaration speaks mostly to western-style religious expression, authority, and institutions, which are separable (and separate) from political and social institutions.[4] Conceivably, a Muslim woman in Libya, whose national laws are based on religious ones, would hardly be able to point to the Declaration as support for a change in national law to eliminate the discrimination that she might endure because of prevailing theological sentiment. The Declaration is intended to assist those who have been discriminated against because of their religious affiliation. It has little or no bearing on the discrimination endured by an individual or group whose gender, race, class, or other status earns them discriminatory treatment due to religious practices *within* their own tradition. They do not endure discrimination because of their religious affiliation, but because they are women within a religious tradition. The Declaration, in short, is not specific enough to address the problems of patriarchal ideology that are internal to individual religious traditions.

Which rights are fundamental?

The question of what is a "fundamental" human right, as opposed to a valid but less crucial human right, is not answered but actually obscured by the international treaties themselves. The Charter of the United Nations, the Universal Declaration of Human Rights, the Political Covenant, the Race Convention, and the Women's Convention use interchangeably the terms "human rights," "freedoms," "fundamental human rights," "fundamental freedoms," "rights and freedoms," and "human rights and fundamental freedoms." As they are used in these instruments, there would seem to be little or no legal difference between the terms – "human rights" are not less crucial than "fundamental" rights and freedoms but in fact are very much the same.[5] Scholars of law and philosophy have suggested a variety of definitions and criteria for distinguishing between fundamental (or "basic") rights and more generic rights.[6] In the words of one social philosopher, "Basic rights are the morality of depth. They specify the line beneath which no one is allowed to sink." He adds that "[p]reventing or alleviating helplessness" is "a central purpose" of basic rights. "Basic rights, then, are everyone's minimum reasonable demands upon the rest of humanity." They are basic rights because without them all other rights cannot be enjoyed at all. Other rights may be sacrificed to maintain a fundamental right, he writes, but if such a basic right is forfeited, no other rights enjoyment is possible.[7] The lack of definition or consensus as to what is the bottom line of suffering or depravity for human beings, or as to what is "helplessness" or a "reasonable demand" upon other persons renders the sentiments above too vague to be of practical assistance in the formulation of a corpus of fundamental rights.

Some lawyers have, at times, equated fundamental (or "absolute") rights with those outlined in national constitutions.[8] This approach adds little to cross-cultural (and inter-religious) attempts to outline fundamental norms relevant to conflicts in international treaties. Individual states retain the ability to create hierarchies of rights claims, further entrenching their own perspectives, and perhaps causing increased division rather than consensus. Even constitutionally guaranteed rights are rarely absolute. Free speech, for example, is circumscribed by laws against fraud and defamation.[9] According to another theorist, those rights that are fundamental will be "universal, paramount, categorical." He understands only the civil and political liberties of life, freedom, and property to suffice.[10] Another writer on the topic has claimed that a basic right is one that "is essential to all other rights," and that can be narrowed down to those guaranteeing security, subsistence, and liberty. Any distinction between civil and political liberties and economic, social and cultural rights, he maintains, is artificial.[11] Indeed, human rights are seldom grantable as single entities but entail other specific rights as well. The right to life is about freedom from extrajudicial killing as well as access to sufficient food. A single "fundamental" right brings many others in its wake.

Others write that social and economic rights can never be absolute, since they are not justiciable rights claims but merely goals or aspirations. One such philosopher understands possible absolute rights to be those practical, deliverable claims to goods that can never be in short supply, such as a fair trial and equal protection of the law (for positive rights) and freedom from torture or cruel treatment (for negative rights).[12] Another school of thought advises that basic human needs are the source of basic human rights. "Needs establish human rights," writes one theorist,[13] and "It is legitimate and fruitful to regard instinctoid basic needs... as *rights* as well as needs," declares another.[14] Again, consensus on basic needs as the ground for basic rights is lacking because of the vague nature of the criteria. There appears as yet to be no common, mutually acceptable standard of measure by which to gauge what items or conditions are absolutely and irrevocably necessary to meet human needs.

While the international legal community continues to work towards the creation of a short list of legal principles that may guide adjudicators of rights conflicts, there seems to be growing consensus that the effort to arrange individual rights into a hierarchy of fundamentality may be more damaging than helpful to the cause. Scholars of law have noted that efforts to stratify rights into categories of different value may actually work against "the credibility of human rights as a legal discipline."[15] Another reason for caution is that a list of "basic" rights risks devaluing all rights that are not on that list, encouraging states and individuals not to observe them. By the same token, the very idea of human rights is a construct – it is aspirational rather than factual. The idea of "basic" aspirations as opposed to "common" aspirations seems somewhat ludicrous. A better tactic might be to accord every human right equal weight as a fundamental or basic aspiration, and demand compliance with them all.[16] Other scholars argue that labels such as "fundamental" or "basic" will always be inaccurate since even the most widely accepted legal right becomes provisional when met with a competing claim or legally protected circumstance.[17] The inconsistent use of terms such as "fundamental" with "human rights and freedoms" in the various instruments may lead to excuses for denying people a wide variety of rights because they cannot be proven to be the fundamental rights referred to in the texts. Because of each of these issues, plus differences in political and cultural emphases between different states, the international community has yet to make real efforts to formalize a hierarchy of rights claims. It would indeed seem better that they do not.

The international instruments also incorporate lists of rights that are declared to be non-derogable, suggesting that the resolution of conflicting rights claims might be possible through reliance on treaties. Between the Political Covenant and the European and American Conventions only four rights are commonly held as non-derogable. They are the rights to life, to freedom from slavery, freedom from torture, and freedom from retroactive criminal laws and punishments.[18] The Political Covenant's full list includes as non-derogable rights freedom from imprisonment for non-payment of debts, recognition before the law, and most importantly for this study, freedom of thought and religion. Yet each of the documents contains savings clauses, guidelines on the few acceptable instances in which the rights delineated in the instrument may be restricted. These savings and limitations clauses have provided lawmakers with a second avenue for constructing a hierarchy among codified international rights obligations.

Savings and limitations clauses

Article 103 of the United Nations Charter contains the only explicitly stated rule by which to prioritize international obligations. It declares that, in the case of a conflict between the Charter and any other international obligation, the Charter is to take precedence. This injunction is intended to cover all international law, whereas the other treaties' savings clauses make reference only to instruments concerning particular topics or regions.[19] Women's equality rights and religious freedoms are both upheld within the Charter (the same is true for the Universal Declaration of Human Rights). The Charter thus assures that no other international law can invalidate either, yet it offers no practical assistance in conflicts between the two.

Stipulations in international law concerning freedom of religious expression converge on four general points. First, individuals have an actual right to have a religion or belief, and to manifest that religion or belief in a variety of ways. Second, the separation of religious institutions from the political institutions of the state is not mandated. Third, religious laws that may be a component of national legislation may not be invoked to exempt a state from complying with international law. Fourth, the various instruments concerned with religious liberty permit states to restrict that liberty for the sake of protecting other human rights.[20] (The only international agreement that names no restriction on religious rights is the African Charter of Human and People's Rights.)[21]

As noted above, the Declaration on the Elimination of All Forms of Discrimination Based on Religion or Belief lacks the force of law that is enjoyed by actual treaties. Nonetheless, the framers of the Declaration clearly intended the document to have normative status, as evinced by the form of, and terms within, the Declaration. Both the Secretary General[22] and the General Assembly[23] of the United Nations have made clear that they consider the document to be normative, and encourage the international community to do the same.[24] The Declaration, therefore, lacks force but still is to be considered normative. (It is possible, however, that its savings clauses may be secondary in weight to those of the international treaties since the Declaration continues to be without the force of law.)

The Declaration generally places greater restrictions upon states' abilities to constrict religious practice than do similar injunctions in the other documents. Its first article makes clear that such interference is to take place only in the protection of the "fundamental rights and freedoms of others," begging the question (which it does not answer) as to exactly which rights are fundamental and separate from those other rights categories that may validly be overridden by religious freedom. Similarly, the language of the Declaration permits a very broad array of practices to be protected as religious expression. Its first article states that the freedom of thought, conscience, and religion "shall include" the several practices it names, leaving wide open the field of other practices that may also be included for protection. The freedom to administer religious law in almost every conceivable way, including through religious tribunals, would seem to come under the scope of the Declaration.[25]

The savings clause of the Women's Convention (Article 23) declares that the scope of that treaty will be altered only by provisions in other international agreements or states' legislation that are "more conducive to the achievement of equality between men and women." It implicitly claims priority over those beliefs, practices or teachings that are not conducive to equality between the sexes and the elimination of all forms of discrimination against women. Additionally, because the Convention's savings clause is relevant only to other international treaties, the Declaration is not included. Only the Universal Declaration of Human Rights and the International Covenants are so implicated. Essentially, the savings clauses of both the Declaration and the Women's Convention do not resolve normative conflicts between the two instruments.[26]

The savings clause of the Women's Convention is both broad and simple. Without referring to the murky area of "fundamental" rights it defers instead to the actual aim of the Convention – the elimination of discrimination against women. While this approach might seem to decrease the possibility of conflict between positively stipulated rights, some reservations to the Convention (such as that registered by Egypt) point out a distinct weakness. Egypt declares that the marital relationship prescribed by Islam is the actual guarantor of women's equality in the family, rather than the very different conditions described in the Convention. The savings clause of the Women's Convention avoids the issue of the prioritizing of rights (such as those to equality and others to religious expression) at the cost of opening up the issue of cultural and religious challenges to the very concept of equality. As the texts of the reservations make clear, Egypt and other states have found in the savings clause the needed loophole with which to attempt to subordinate women's equality to religious practice.

While the freedom to have a religion or belief is declared in the Political Covenant to be a non-derogable right, the savings clause of that same instrument would seem to contradict the supposedly inviolable character of the right. From notes taken during the crafting of the Political Covenant it is apparent that those who drafted the document wished to provide a balance between the ability to fully support or restrict religious freedom.[27] Article 4 of the Political Covenant permits states to derogate from their obligations in times of "public emergency," yet only to the extent absolutely necessary under the particular circumstances, and never in a way that discriminates solely on the basis of race, color, sex, language, religion, or social origin.[28] Article 5(2) of the Political Convention is similar to the "most-favorable-to-individual" stipulation of the savings clause of the Women's Convention; it prevents states from using the Political Covenant to limit rights that are more favorably outlined elsewhere.[29] One commentator has concluded that "few if any" human rights delineated in the Political Covenant are actually non-derogable since, for the sake of "public interest," they can be abrogated at any time.[30] Two relatively recent documents, the Vienna Declaration and Programme of Action[31], and the Declaration on the Elimination of Violence Against Women[32] (both 1993) acknowledge the existence of conflicts between women's rights norms and religious practices. While keeping religious "considerations in mind," the Preamble to Article 4 of the Declaration on the Elimination of Violence Against Women declares that states "should condemn" violence legitimated by religion, but in Article 4(j) does not include religion in its appeal to states to modify educational systems to negate discrimination or violence against women. Neither document mandates a clear trumping of religious rights by other categories; indeed, the international community would seem to be unwilling to require just that.

Both the Political Covenant [Article 18(3)] and the Declaration on the Elimination of All Forms of Discrimination Based on Religion or Belief [Article 1(3)] include in their savings or limitation clauses identical language that would circumscribe religious rights in order to protect "public safety, order, health, or morals."[33] Because no definitions are offered for these conditions, the ability of the clauses to provide effective guidance in rights conflicts is again compromised. In fact, these clauses may obfuscate the issues behind human rights claims or play into states' desires to reserve power for certain religious groups.

"Public morals" has proven to be a particularly challenging concept, taking on quite different meaning in different contexts and religious cultures. The issue came to the fore in the case *Handyside v. U.K.*,[34] in which the European Court of Human Rights found that domestic law in the European states revealed no uniform understanding of "morals." The court wrote that the requirements of morals "var[y] from time to time and from place to place, especially in our era which is characterised by rapid and far-reaching evolution of opinion on the subject."[35] Appeals to religious morality have more recently been used by representatives to the United Nations whose intention would seem to be the safeguarding of privilege for majority religious groups. The Constitution of Colombia guarantees freedom of religion only to those other traditions that it considers consistent with Christian morality; the Colombian government defends this position on the grounds that Christian morality is the practice of the majority of Colombians.[36] Panama[37] has stood firm in holding Christian morality as a legitimate basis for limiting the freedom to practice all other religions since Catholicism is the majority religion.[38] Appeals to public morals have been the basis of many instances of discrimination against women, as with the Pakistani Olympic committee's circumscription of female athletes' participation in the Olympic games.[39] Permission in the various treaties to limit human rights on the basis of public morality offers states the option to declare that it does so for the sake of the best interests of women or religious minorities. Paternalistic states are made the arbiters of morality, and given the power to enforce adherence with the norms they choose to proclaim.

Jus cogens

A third, and related, legal strategy for solving conflicts of rights claims centers on the doctrine of *jus cogens*. *Jus cogens* are the peremptory norms of international law. The concept acquired particular international acceptance after its inclusion in the Vienna Convention on the Law of Treaties 1969, Article 53 of which states that, "a treaty is void if, at the time of its conclusion, it conflicts with a peremptory norm of international law." The Vienna Convention defines a peremptory norm as "a norm accepted and recognised by the international community of States as a whole as a norm from which no derogation is permitted and which can be modified only by a subsequent norm of general international law having the same character."[40] *Jus cogens* requires, in the necessary prioritizing of international laws, that certain norms assume the status of fundamental significance, based on their overarching acceptance by the international community and their consequent evolution into customary law. Laws and instruments that conflict with these peremptory norms are to be considered void.[41] While there is as yet no catalogue of fundamental human rights, these peremptory norms are sometimes regarded as the best resource for creating a hierarchy of criteria – and in some cases positive laws – that will serve to settle rights conflicts.

As with the nature of a "fundamental" human right, however, no firm consensus exists concerning which norms constitute *jus cogens*. A small number of norms appear repeatedly in states' legislation, suggesting that they are closest to achieving peremptory status. They are, generally, injunctions against extralegal killing, genocide, slavery, torture, and systematic racial discrimination. On the basis not of positive law but of court decisions (mostly from the United States), one legal scholar has compiled a list of 11 customary international human rights norms. "The list includes

(a) the right not to be murdered;
(b) freedom from torture;
(c) standards for the treatment of prisoners embodied in the UN Standard Minimum Rules for the Treatment of Prisoners;
(d) freedom from arbitrary detention;
(e) the right not to be subjected to cruel, inhuman, or degrading treatment or punishment;
(f) the right not to be a slave;
(g) freedom from disappearance defined as (1) abduction by state officials or their agents, followed by (2) official refusals to acknowledge the abduction or to disclose the detainee's fate;
(h) freedom from loss of consortium;
(i) freedom from racial discrimination;
(j) freedom from genocide; and
(k) freedom from a consistent pattern of gross violations of internationally recognized human rights."[42]

Arcot Krishnaswami, Special Rapporteur to the United Nations on religious discrimination, has written that *jus cogens* in reference to religious freedom ought to include the prohibition of "the sacrifice of human beings, self-immolation, mutilation of the self or others, and reduction into slavery or prostitution, if carried out in the service of, or under the pretext of promoting, a religion or belief."[43] Krishnaswami has also written that freedom of religion should itself be considered a peremptory norm, as it is codified in so many states' constitutions and laws.[44] While many might agree that freedom from religious discrimination *should* be a peremptory norm, few would say that it has actually achieved that status,[45] or that clitoridecomy and infibulation are included in the proposed norm of "mutilation of self or others."

Similarly, there are some who believe that non-discrimination on the grounds of sex has become a customary norm.[46] While the principle is stated forcefully in a number of international treaties, the general absence of state-level compliance would suggest that the concept is not at all a justiciable part of customary law. There is a subsection of scholars (and framers) of international law who believe that the provisions of the various human rights instruments have, in their totality, taken on the identity of *jus cogens*. The Universal Declaration of Human Rights is said to be particularly applicable.[47] Three of the most respected authorities in the field state that "many of the policies about human rights would appear to be so intensely demanded that they are acquiring... not merely the status of 'international concern,' but in addition that of *jus cogens*...."[48] Again, the lack of state compliance and the pervasiveness of national laws and practices that contradict the Universal Declaration and the other instruments would suggest that the broad consensus required for *jus cogens* is absent.

As illustrated by this breadth of opinion concerning the actual corpus of international customary law, the definition of positive peremptory norms has also proven elusive. A particular challenge in deferring to customary international law to settle rights conflicts lies in proving that the customary norms exist in the first place. Proof of their existence may perhaps be determined through studies of state practice, through the observation that states do indeed understand themselves as observing certain norms because of a legal obligation, and through evidence of constant and uniform usage of the norms as accepted elements of state law.[49] As with efforts to develop a hierarchy of fundamental human rights, the vagueness and ambiguity of *jus cogens* has stymied efforts to derive from it clear guidelines for the resolution of rights conflicts.

The actual attempts, in and of themselves, to create hierarchies both of "fundamental" rights values and of customary norms may do additional damage to endeavors to adjudicate between women's rights and those to the free expression of religious belief. As has been suggested above, many of the rights and norms most crucial to women's survival are only secondarily reflected in the most common lists of high-priority human rights and norms.[50] The real issues in the rights conflict are obscured by the inherently gendered nature of international and domestic human rights law, and by the fact that the great majority of rights-related jurisprudence stops at the front door of the home.

The fundamental human right to life, as it is claimed by the makers of some lists of absolute rights, is primarily understood to refer to due process – a prisoner is to be safeguarded until, if warranted, he or she is put to death. The fundamental right not to lose one's life in an extrajudicial killing is not applied to the innumerable (because they are unreported) instances of dowry death or "honor killings." Domestic violence is a primary concern of women, and appears nowhere on lists of basic human rights and freedoms. The same is true of sexual violence. Could the right not to be raped ever be derogable, or qualified?

The religious element within some commonly accepted fundamental rights is rarely addressed. For instance, the fundamental right not to be subjected to apartheid, as claimed by Ajami,[51] does not refer to gender apartheid, to the systematic discrimination against women that includes their segregation from mainstream society, the limiting of their civil liberties, and officially sanctioned teaching about their basic mental and/or moral inferiority. Such gender apartheid is most often perpetrated with the support of religious teaching. If basic apartheid were indeed considered a fundamental right, it would trump the right to propagate a discriminatory theological teaching.

The oft-claimed fundamental right to property is not understood to include women's rights to inheritance of family property, but rather for men to keep their property safe from confiscation – through severe taxation, extortion or force – by governments and other individuals. The fact that women are prevented by custom, law, and especially by religious teaching from inheriting property that is genuinely their own is not considered an abrogation of the basic right to one's property. The right not to be mutilated in the name of religion, which Special Rapporteur Krishnaswami has described as a non-derogable human right,[52] is rarely applied to the practice of female genital cutting, so often defended on religious grounds. One social philosopher has written that the strongest candidates among human rights for the category of absolute are those that speak to "a right to a higher kind of respect, an inviolate dignity, which as a broad category includes the negative rights not to be brainwashed, not to be made into a docile instrument for the purposes of others, and not to be converted into a domesticated animal."[53] The concept of *pativratya*, or appropriate Hindu wifehood, is arguably this exact phenomenon – the intentional (and religiously supported) transformation of independent girls and young women into persons whose sole reason for living is to complement their husband's existence and to meet his every need.[54] If the retention of one's individuality, self-determination, and basic moral agency is indeed a fundamental human right, in the case of *pativratya* it is trumped by the right to the free exercise of religion.

Domestic versus international standards

In the absence of international consensus on a hierarchy of rights claims or of peremptory norms, efforts have been made to develop other legal means to resolve conflicts between religious rights and women's rights. The fourth such strategy has been to define better the relationship between national legislation and international obligations. Article 27 of the Vienna Convention on the Law of Treaties states that, "A party may not invoke the provisions of its internal law as justification for its failure to perform a treaty."[55] National laws are to be secondary to treaty obligations. When applied to the conflict between women's rights and those to the free expression of religion, this legal precept is challenged on several fronts – state accountability according to the Women's Convention, the role of third parties in demanding rights protection, and the role of religious law in domestic law.

Lawmakers are of two minds on the question of how (or whether) international laws become incorporated into states' legislation. One theory holds that, upon the signing of a treaty, international law automatically becomes part of domestic law without any other formal act of incorporation. A second theory holds that international law is only a part of domestic law when it completes that state's formal process of adoption as positive law.[56] Added to the mixture is the variety of guidelines in the various instruments as to the requirements for state compliance. The undertakings clause of the Women's Convention (the clause outlining the responsibilities that states undertake in signing the treaty) is located in Article 2. In general, it requires States Parties "to ensure" compliance by their governments and "to take all appropriate measures" to effect "the elimination of discrimination in all its forms" by "any person, organization or enterprise" and "to modify or abolish existing laws, regulations, customs and practices" that interfere with the elimination of such discrimination. This undertaking clause effectively obligates States Parties to a dual system of compliance. Signatories undertake obligations of both means and ends – obligations to enact intentional and specific means to achieve certain goals, and obligations to simply achieve those ends in whatever manner is deemed appropriate. The obligation of result is specified in the first paragraph of Article 2 (which is almost identical to the general undertaking clause of the Race Convention) while the obligation of means is outlined in the seven specific subsections of Article 2. States Parties are effectively given their choice of these means, but are also given the overarching responsibility to be diligent in the implementation.[57]

The text of the Women's Convention contains no "liability offenses" – no measurable scale or criteria of what is entailed in actual compliance with the instrument. States Parties are simply required to be diligent. It would seem that the drafters of the Convention, understanding that all discrimination against women can never be eliminated, chose to outline the methods they thought most helpful to the endeavor. The Convention, therefore, does not list every single acceptable method of eliminating discrimination. Because the criteria for compliance are somewhat open ended, so also are the criteria by which to judge states' responsibilities and progress. "Appropriate measures" to end discrimination against women may be defined in myriad ways by the States Parties. The international community is charged with having the last word as to what is "appropriate," yet it is required always to be sensitive to the legal, political, and social reality of the state in question.[58] The international community, through CEDAW (the Committee on the Elimination of Discrimination Against Women), is implicitly charged with corporate diligence in seeing to the elimination of discrimination against women. As has been noted by one commentator, individual states rarely petition the international community for help in complying with their own treaty obligations, such as those involving women's rights. States do advocate vociferously on their own behalf, however, when they perceive a particular treaty as having potential economic or political benefit.[59]

In effect, the language of the Women's Convention does not charge States Parties with responsibility as much as accountability. Responsibility entails liability for breaking a law; accountability involves offering explanations of rights abuses and practical methods of redress. States are not actually liable for private acts of discrimination – states themselves are not the offending agent. Rather, Article 2(c) holds States Parties accountable for those acts once they have happened, accountable for changing the prevailing social conditions so that the rights abuse does not happen again, and accountable for punishing private violators. If the state in any way justifies or accommodates the offence, then the state does become responsible, responsible for its own lack of diligence in preventing or correcting such private acts through the political and legal methods it has at its disposal.[60] Those methods are themselves vaguely understood by states, and will vary greatly depending on the political or religious climate. One scholar of human rights law has suggested that states might punish religious organizations that perpetuate discrimination against women with a removal of tax-exempt status, government grants and subsidies, or with civil and criminal penalties.[61] This remedy would hardly be possible in those states where there is no effective separation between religious institutions and the state.

Additionally, there is no domestic accountability for any treaty provision to which a States Party has entered a reservation. If a state wishes to sign and ratify a treaty but anticipates difficulty enforcing a provision (or has no desire to see such a change), it may file a reservation to that item and be exempted from all accountability. States retain the power to decide which treaty obligations they wish to be responsible for.

Third party action

The role of third parties in responding to cases of human rights violations is another unsettled area of international law, but a fifth possible route to eventually ensuring state compliance with treaties and with redressing rights abuses. The International Court of Justice provided an important contribution to this question in its 1970 *Barcelona Traction* decision.[62] There the Court suggested that the basic enjoyment of human rights by citizens of any state is important enough to create obligations *erga omnes*. In the words of the Court, "all States can be held to have a legal interest in their protection."[63] Following on *Barcelona Traction*, the International Law Commission found all states to be jointly required to ensure universal compliance with a certain number ("albeit a small one") of international obligations.[64] The *Barcelona Traction* decision may be particularly responsible for the growing acceptance among states of the idea that each has a legitimate interest, even a right and obligation, to protect citizens of every state from significant human rights violations.[65] Appropriate remedies for such rights violations are not yet commonly agreed upon. The same is true for the list of rights that are significant enough to be of mutual interest to every state. The *Barcelona Traction* decision clearly separates rights that create obligations *erga omnes* from those that do not. The decision does not, however, enumerate those more significant rights. It suggests only that they be firmly rooted in international law, and not simply be claims or goals.[66] In short, the international courts have suggested to states that they participate in ensuring rights enjoyment for each other's citizens, which is a positive development for both women and religious believers. The courts have not, however, provided explicit guidelines for third party intervention. The same problem of vagueness obtains in this situation as with the question of which rights are fundamental or *jus cogens*.

The most firmly entrenched challenges within domestic law to international obligations are those in states whose constitutions defer to personal status laws (as in Kenya and India) and those whose legal system and positive laws are firmly rooted in religious law. Kenya and India find themselves needing to reform their basic constitutions or be in continual violation of treaties such as the Women's Convention. Although Kenya has yet to make changes to its constitution, it joins Tanzania, Zambia, and other states in enacting specific items of legislation particularly aimed at dismantling discriminatory personal status laws. The international treaties hold States Parties accountable for bringing all domestic law into conformity with their obligations under international law, and for creating new domestic legislation to counteract discriminatory practices based on religious teaching. States in every region of the world already circumscribe religious expression in order to ensure particular human rights (India, for instance, has outlawed untouchability). States are not empowered to direct religious authorities on issues of doctrinal interpretation, rituals, and other matters. They are empowered to interpret how the various rituals, practices and teachings may be inconsistent with international (and domestic) law, and are responsible for resolving those inconsistencies.[67] State sovereignty is not compromised in such an approach, since states have willingly become parties to the particular treaties.[68]

A number of states persist in asserting that religious law must take precedence over both domestic and international law – that its divine origin gives it unquestionable pre-eminence. This opinion is a difficult one to counteract. There is little or no common ground for discussion of the issue; the criteria are based on profound religious belief rather than commonly accepted international legal standards. One statement to the United Nations reads as follows:

> The Government of the Islamic Republic of Iran has stated that Islamic law is founded on the very original concept that divinity reigns supreme and divine law is pre-eminent to human law. The [Universal] Declaration is genuinely secular in its theme and essence and, as such, differs from Islamic law in its origin. There may be similarities or even perfect compatibility on some provisions, in particular those that meet the condition of *jus cogens*, but the original perceptions remain widely apart.[69]

International treaties are certainly not founded on the concept that "divinity reigns supreme." Some states have joined together to write their own international human rights instruments, ones that they craft to reflect their particular religious perspective. The Cairo Declaration on Human Rights in Islam states in its first article that, "All men are equal in terms of basic human dignity and basic obligations and responsibilities, without any discrimination on the grounds of race, color, language, sex, religious belief...." The Cairo Declaration repeats in Article 6 the assertion that women are equal to men in human dignity, but clearly does not ascribe to them equal rights. In some states, international (secular) law is portrayed to women citizens not only as inferior to religiously based rights instruments but as an evil tool of "westernism," a threat to the true liberation offered to them by their religious tradition.[70]

Individual citizens in States Parties may choose to exempt themselves altogether from the protection offered by the Women's Convention by choosing a religious tribunal to correct a human rights violation. The Convention can be invoked by the citizen of any States Party, however, if that country offers no alternative to religious tribunals or if its domestic legislation is based in religious law.[71] In the end, international law can only be implemented domestically through state agency. Governments themselves must be committed to bringing religious law into conformity with international obligations. Outside states or organizations can encourage compliance, yet the state will be most successful if its government is supported in the endeavor by broad political support and well-informed local networks of citizens.[72]

The problem of enforcement

A sixth point of focus in the international legal community's efforts to reconcile religious rights with those to non-discrimination concerns the difference between the recognition and the enforcement of rights claims. This line of reasoning suggests that states may grant unconditional recognition of the validity of a particular rights claim with only conditional guarantees of its enforcement. In this way the actual right is always held to be morally justified, although its exercise may not be. As Joel Feinberg has written, "a person can maintain a right to X even when he is not morally justified in its exercise, or others are justified in not according it to him. Lack of moral justification for exercising a right does not entail (even temporary) nonpossession." Feinberg adds that while one may have a particular duty in response to the justifiable right of one's own or of someone else, one might also have a stronger moral justification for not acting upon it.[73] In the case of the conflict between rights to free exercise of religion and rights to non-discrimination, Feinberg's assertion upholds the right of a person to have certain (discriminatory) religious convictions, but not to enforce them. A woman's right to equality would not invalidate the other's right to freedom of religion, although it would invalidate (or even criminalize) the exercise of that religious belief.

Several United States Supreme Court decisions have been modeled on just this differentiation between faith and practice. Two such decisions from the last century have been used more recently in India to substantiate courts' findings. In *Davis v. Beason* the US Supreme Court found that, "laws are made for the Governments of action and while they cannot interfere with mere religious beliefs and opinions, they may with practices."[74] These words were quoted with approval in the case of *State of Bombay v. Narasu Appa Mali*, whose justices held that polygamy may not necessarily be viewed as integral to the Hindu religion.[75] Supported by another American decision,[76] a Madras court has ruled that the freedom to practice one's religion, although claimed by the Indian Constitution to be an absolute right, is not absolute in and of itself but is tempered by the other rights-related provisions of the same Constitution.[77] These decisions would seem to uphold the Political Covenant's claim that the possession of a religious belief is a non-derogable right. They would also suggest that such a right of possession is quite different from the very derogable right to act upon one's religious belief.

In so separating faith from practice, the courts and conventions place religious believers in a difficult situation. Faith and practice may be legally separated with relative ease, but this is often not the case for the believers themselves. Such persons are welcomed to have any theological perspective, yet not to act it out. Many religious teachings include, as an integral component, the mandate to act. Faith involves practice – certain understandings of what it means to *be* faithful, or to *have* a belief, incorporate rules of *how* to be faithful, which require certain actions. A conservative Christian, whose interpretation of certain biblical texts teaches him that women are of lesser social and spiritual value than men, may refuse – or be unable – to act otherwise at home and at the workplace because it is contradictory to his religious beliefs. While the legal issues of belief and practice are separable, the situation is different for many religious teachings. Believers are not helped to a resolution of conflicting religious and secular legal demands but are invited to a kind of spiritual cognitive dissonance.

Legal precedents – when courts decide religious matters

Court decisions themselves, such as those described above, are a seventh area to which the legal community has looked for guidance in resolving conflicts of rights claims. There is a growing body of cases in international courts of human rights based on women's claims for equality before the law.[78] In some of those cases the role of religion is not explicit yet may well be a factor. The plaintiffs in *Johnston v. Ireland*,[79] for instance, challenged the Irish government's prohibition against divorce and remarriage partly on grounds of freedom of religion. That state is overwhelmingly Roman Catholic and applies much Catholic social teaching to its policies concerning family and reproductive issues. In Peru, also a largely Catholic country, the plaintiff in *Ato del Avellanal v. Peru*[80] challenged Article 168 of her country's Civil Code as being incompatible with certain non-discrimination provisions in the Political Covenant. Article 168 of the Peruvian Civil Code stated that only men could represent matrimonial property before courts of law. The courts of Peru decided against the plaintiff. The Human Rights Committee of the United Nations later upheld her complaint and required the Peruvian government to reform its Civil Code to comply with those provisions in the Political Covenant that mandate equality before the law and equal protection of the law.

The fact remains that secular courts have rendered numerous decisions on what is acceptable religious practice. The savings clauses of the various human rights instruments give them that opportunity, for the sake of morality, public order, and so on. For example, in *Saifuddin Saheb v. State of Bombay*[81] a Justice of the Supreme Court of India wrote that practices springing from religious belief may justifiably be circumscribed on "humanitarian grounds, and for the purpose of social reform." He followed with examples of restrictions on *sati* (widow immolation) and the dedication of young girls to temple prostitution. Several Indian cases have been described above that question the importance of polygamy to the practice of Hinduism. Other courts' decisions render the practice downright illegal.[82] Some secular courts have circumscribed religious practice not with arguments concerning public well-being or morality but through interpretations of specific sacred texts. One Bangladeshi court interpreted for itself a passage of the Qur'an to support its decision to award custody of a boy to his mother even after he was seven years of age (contrary to some schools of Muslim teaching).[83]

The best-known instance of such a foray by a secular court into the interpretation of religious texts is the *Shah Bano* case in India.[84] The case concerned the amount of maintenance required to be paid to a woman whose husband divorced her after many years of marriage. The Supreme Court of India held that, in order to prevent the woman from becoming indigent, the former husband was responsible for continuing maintenance payments even though the timetable for such payments under Muslim personal status law had expired. The Court referred to the provision in India's secular Code for Criminal Procedure, which requires the prevention of destitution. The Court also interpreted Islamic law, concluding that there existed no discrepancy between the provisions of the secular code and those of *Shari'a*. The Court's interpretation of a verse of the Qur'an, accomplished without the permission of (or assistance by) Islamic jurists, enraged many in India's Muslim community. The tremendous public protests that followed convinced the Court to reverse its decision and defer to popular understandings of Muslim personal status law concerning maintenance, abandoning its interpretation of the Qur'an and its reference to provisions against destitution in the secular criminal code. Probably under pressure from Muslim clerics, Shah Bano herself repealed her request for continued maintenance. The Indian government soon capitulated to more pressure from the Muslim community and enacted the Muslim Women (Protection of Rights on Divorce) Act of 1986, which stipulated that a divorced woman's relatives and Muslim charitable organizations are to see that such women do not become destitute. The Act was a tremendous victory for those Muslim men who wished to be absolved of financial responsibility for former wives. The Act granted them the secular right – to accompany their religious right – to pay maintenance to former wives only for a period of roughly three months.

Despite the Indian government's capitulation to pressure from a religious group, some scholars and activists concerned with human rights and religion have suggested that secular courts continue to interpret religious teaching for themselves – that they seek out verses or theological positions within that religious tradition that may settle the conflict in question.[85] And yet, the anger of some in the Indian Muslim community is not difficult to understand. Most (if not all) of the various religions would take great offence at having their sacred texts exegeted by those outside their tradition, particularly with the intention of using the findings as part of a legal decision against their interests. Sacred texts can be read by any literate person, but are not as easily understood. First, the texts are rooted in a religious history – theological, chronological, and soteriological – that must be well known by the interpreter in order to understand the verses in context. Second, religious groups understand the texts to have their greatest meaning on a level that is accessible only to those who believe in their sacredness. The element of faith is crucial to true understanding. That an outsider should claim to have the ability to knowledgeably interpret a religious tract is insulting. By the same token, though, the resolution of the conflict between women's rights and rights to religious expression may well reside in the reinterpretation of religious texts, reinterpretations that permit social and theological breadth and growth. That effort of reinterpretation, however, should be made by members of the religious groups themselves, and not by secular courts of law.

Conclusion

The focus of this chapter has been those secular courts of law, and efforts by the international legal community generally, to use the various means at their disposal to resolve disputes between competing rights claims. Such a survey of legal remedies points to some potential for legal resolutions to the conflict, but also to significant deficits. Regarding "fundamentality," the circumstances of particular rights conflicts can shatter the finest articulation of fundamental principles and norms. Formulas constructed in the abstract to ensure a lasting framework for resolution of conflicts may crumble when faced with concrete situations that defy attempts at categorization of rights values or reliance on treaties. Religious laws within the same tradition differ widely according to region, class, ethnicity, race, the political system of the particular state, and so on. Understandings of gender, influenced by these same factors, are just as diverse. Static methods of resolving rights claims will not translate from culture to culture, religion to religion, city to countryside, and so on. Legally, conflicts between women's human rights and rights to free expression of religion are best resolved on an (albeit time-consuming) case-by-case basis, rather than a pre-established hierarchy of claims.

The inconsistency between many precepts in international law and those in domestic legislation continues to be a stumbling block in legal efforts to resolve the rights conflict. Many states resolutely refuse to adapt their legislation to meet international criteria concerning women's rights (and, to a lesser degree, religious rights). Religions within states become accountable to that country's international obligations – and through no effort of their own. Most were not party to the decision to sign and ratify the treaties. It becomes particularly important, therefore, that certain rights guarantees be incorporated into national legislation, where states have greater opportunities to enforce compliance by all sectors of society. One possible route of reconciliation between international and national norms is the persistent encouragement of domestic courts to draw from the Women's Convention and other treaties in their decisions. Perhaps, through the setting of legal precedents, legislative reform can be eased into place.

One commentator on women's rights has suggested that states' religiously based reservations to the Women's Convention be viewed not as conflicts with religious law itself but with national legislation.[86] The aim of such an approach is to de-problematize religion; simultaneously, states would be encouraged to create better domestic legislation concerning women's rights and to demand compliance with it. Particular religious traditions, such as Islam, would no longer be singled out for reproach (many reservations have been made, after all, on the basis of *Shari'a*).

Religious law is at the root of much inconsistency between national and international rights norms, however, particularly in regard to women, and thus it should not be de-emphasized by those wishing to encourage domestic change. Religion, as long as it is an impediment to women's rights, should remain firmly problematized. In this way only will pressure for theological change be applied to religious leaders. As was suggested in Chapter 1, reinterpretation of religious law itself is the very best method of resolving conflicts between women's rights and those to free religious expression. This is something that secular legal systems are not empowered to do. The more persistent the attention paid to religious interpreters of sacred law, the better.

The conflict between women's human rights and rights to free expression of one's religion are occasionally cast by the legal community as a conflict between rights to equality and to liberty. This is problematic as well. This categorization may further complicate efforts to resolve the conflict. There exists the strong possibility that states and regions will create hierarchies between the two, constructing their own unyielding frameworks that may differ from those of other regions, and prevent the case-by-case assessment that such conflicts merit. In addition, hierarchies of specific equality claims may arise that will privilege some of them and delegitimize others. Already, racial equality appears to be more highly valued by the international community than gender equality. Some observers of the scene now write that racial equality has earned the status of *jus cogens*.[87] Gender equality certainly has not. There is every reason to believe that a focus on issues of liberty and equality will force an unrealistic sense of objectivity on the debate between women's rights and religious rights, diluting the underlying rights issues specific to individual claims, disempowering both claimants, but especially women.

The fact remains that human rights law, as a method of redress for rights conflicts, is not available to all people. Illiteracy, ignorance, political corruption or disarray, cultural or religious taboo, the disapproval of family members, and other factors prevent persons from accessing their state's legal system, especially women. Even for those states whose domestic law and whose compliance with United Nations instruments is ideal in terms of religious women's rights, the gaps and loopholes outlined above frequently eviscerate any chance for real redress. Legally, the human rights construct is significantly compromised in its ability to secure human rights for religious women, making change within religions all the more crucial.

3 Theological Challenges to Religious Women's Rights

And do you not know that you are (each) an Eve? The sentence of God on this sex of yours lives in this age: the guilt must of necessity live too. You are the devil's gateway: you are the unsealer of that (forbidden) tree: you are the first deserter of the divine law: you are she who persuaded him whom the devil was not valiant enough to attack. You destroyed so easily God's image, man. On account of your desert – that is, death – even the Son of God had to die.

Tertullian (c. 155–c. 255), *De cultu feminarum* 1:1[1]

This chapter will contrast the human rights notion with the theological positions of three of the world's major religions. Volumes have been written about each; these pages will provide a brief overview of equality and women. While each of these religious traditions contains a broad spectrum of interpretation on every social and religious topic, and the fullest compatibility with human rights norms for women, those positions that contribute to the conflict between religious freedoms and women's rights will receive particular attention. The chapter will demonstrate that in some religious communities the rights notion is so different from essential theological beliefs that its moral authority is eroded and the construct itself is disabled as a tool for securing religious women's rights. Alternately, the human rights idea can be so modified to adapt to religious teachings that the idea of gender equality is lost and the rights construct, as some religious communities employ it, is again unable to promote women's actual rights.

Islam

In some strains of traditional Islamic thinking there exist two complementary sets of rights, those accorded to humans (*haqolnas*, or *hakk-al-nas*) and those pertaining to God (*haqol*, or *hakk-Allah*). All law is intended to enhance the flourishing of humanity.[2] As part of the created order, humans do not have rights against, but rather duties towards, the creator ("Islam" means "submission"). Muslim law consists of both edicts of positive law (*wad'i*) and divinely imposed obligations (*taklifi*).[3] When people are wronged by other individuals – when their property is stolen, for instance – Islam does incorporate an understanding of a claim held against the transgressor by the victim. This "subjective right," or *hakk*, is implicit in such relationships with other persons or with property. Such rights may not be waived or transferred; they are the rights of husbands over wives, fathers over children, neighbor over neighbor, and so on. Some other rights may be renounced but not transferred, such as claims against persons responsible for defaming, assaulting, or insulting. There are no unanimously recognized criteria for deciding which rights belong to which category, but the potential abuse of such established rights is uniformly condemned.[4]

Human beings have worth and value by the simple fact of their existence, but each individual's particular merit is determined by the level of his or her faithful submission to Allah. If one is a member of the *umma*, the worldwide community of Muslims, and has entered into a contract, as it were, with God, then one becomes eligible for the entitlements that come with submission. Many rights are not intrinsic to human beings but are contingent upon their acts. Rights do not inhere in one's simple existence; they are purchased by living in accordance with the precepts of Islam.[5] As such, rights are not rights at all but privileges accorded by God to those who will become parties to the religious contract.[6]

In some strains of Islamic thought and practice there is a tradition of removing the concept of equality (and also freedom) from the physical sphere to the seclusion of the metaphysical. A contemporary Muslim thinker justifies this intentional "spiritualizing [of] what is currently seen as a secular value," saying, "it is only by spiritualizing the struggle for equality that it will capture the imagination of the ordinary human being, who, in the ultimate analysis, remains deeply spiritual."[7] This reinforcement of the dichotomy between the physical and the metaphysical is troubling to those who care about religious women's rights. What can be justified metaphysically can be more easily denied physically. One suspects that some attempts to spiritualize campaigns for political, social, and religious equality might be efforts to relativize their claims, to remove the teeth from such efforts so that no credible threat can be made against sexist institutions.

A majority of Muslim clerics – even the very conservative – assert that there exists a fundamental equality to all humanity based on the fact of their common origin in Adam and Eve.[8] The 1981 Universal Islamic Declaration of Human Rights (UIDHR) states that all persons have equal human value. In traditional Muslim thought, women and men are held to be equal in their "transcendental purpose," their quest to live a life of sufficient submission to Allah to merit salvation. Surah 2 of the Qur'an is interpreted not as stating that men and women are equal, but that women shall have all rights in proportion with what is "equitable."[9] (The varying interpretations of what is "equitable" in different communities result in vastly different levels of rights enjoyment for Muslim women.) According to one *hadith*, what makes individual persons superior to others is their "righteousness," the extent to which they conform their lives to the teachings of (orthodox) Islam. Allah accepts with equal merit the religious practices of men and women; the prayers and fasting of a woman are of equal value to those of a man.[10] Women's particular observances (e.g. strict interpretations of *purdah*) are often viewed from outside Islam as involving much more personal compromise, and "righteousness" as being more physically and materially costly to women than it is to men. The idea that the metaphysical plane of equality is the only valuable one disserves women. It instructs them that their spiritual equality with men is the only category of equality that is important; simultaneously it instructs them that the physical observances they must make in order to be "righteous" will be equally valued, while minimizing the fact that these religious practices give them an inferior quality of physical life. Equality and blessing in metaphysical life can confer upon women material lives of subordination and inferiority.

A tendency exists in some Muslim theories of equality to view the issue as one having integrity by category. Equality is achieved when all Muslim men are treated in exactly the same way, with the same standards, enjoying the same rewards for the same acts of devotion or service. Women, also, are to be treated in absolutely equal fashion under equal circumstances with other Muslim women. The same is true for other categories of persons, including Jews and Christians, those who follow all other religions, apostates, and so on.[11] Again, inequality for women and non-Muslims becomes justified under this scheme. All comparisons are made within groups, not across boundaries. Women and men do not have to be considered as practical equals to one another, and women continue to have substandard criteria for rights enjoyment.

Conservative Muslim clerics are today unlikely to state publicly the view that women and men are simply not of equal human value, and that gender equality is unacceptable. Rather, they assert that the discriminatory practices delineated in the *Shari'a* do not violate the principle of equality but reinforce it. True equality is actually evinced in practices and beliefs that may appear to subordinate women to men; in fact, these teachings are the very essence of equality. That this perspective is plausible to many in the Muslim world is a testimony to the pervasive belief that practical inequality is a part of the natural order of things. As a result, individuals will simultaneously voice support for the idea of total equality and for the inferior status of women and non-Muslims.[12]

In the case of women's equality this disjuncture is supported largely by the idea that women have an essentially different "nature" than men. That nature is then stereotyped and sentimentalized. Different natures are taught to necessitate different rights and obligations. Women are said to have intrinsic temperamental differences, ones that complement men's abilities. Men are rational and hard; women are emotional and tender. Women have naturally different roles in society because of these differences – they are suited for the compassionate work of maintaining a loving and healthy home atmosphere.[13] They are not capable of judgeships and governing positions. Women who challenge this essentializing of male and female natures are accused of destabilizing society and tearing at the "natural" social fabric. One Muslim scholar summarizes this perspective as "men have to lead; women have secondary roles in certain areas. This is integral to God's plan. It is part of His perennial wisdom."[14] Challenges to the revealed wisdom of God are, of course, discouraged.

Such holy wisdom is the justification for Egypt's reservation to Article 16 of the Women's Convention – religious precepts that the reservation's text proclaims "may not be called in question."[15] The "complementarity" between husband and wife that it describes is rooted in the notion that men's and women's natural temperaments require women to supplement – to play a supporting role behind – men's roles in marriage. Such "complementarity" is the only guarantee of "true equality between the spouses." Fouad Zakaria writes that the reservation's language is founded on the belief that a woman "completes" a man, "and adds a delicate and sensitive touch to his rationality." Men, he adds, "confuse factors resulting from women's social and economic conditions, such as their lack of independence, low legal status and persistent feeling of insecurity and inability with the 'essential nature' of women."[16] The religiously and socially constructed subordination of women and the emotional and psychological ramifications of that subordination are used as proof of women's essential inferiority to men.

Specifically, the false dichotomy between (female) sentiment and (male) reason reinforces the understanding that practical inequality is a part of the natural order. The notion of the "complementarity" of rights also creates some bizarre "rights" for women, such as the "right to chastity" (as articulated by Abu'l A'la Mawdudi, a Pakistani cleric).[17] While women's chastity might be thought to complement men's virility, their "right" to chastity serves men's desire for virgin daughters and faithful wives, and a lack of sexual autonomy for all women. Similarly, a woman's "right to live with her husband" complements a polygamous man's desire to avoid supporting several different households. A woman in such a marriage would enjoy the "right" to no alternative but to share her quarters with the other wives and, in the many regions with housing shortages, to remain in her husband's house after he has divorced her.

Some of the more conservative clerics respond to international legal standards for gender equality by equating such equality with women's promiscuity.[18] These claims serve a double purpose – the deepening of popular anti-western sentiment, and the reinforcing of traditionally discriminatory practices. A member of Morocco's Council of Religious Scholars has said, "For us, women are equal to men in law, but they are not the same as men, and they can't be allowed to wander around freely in the streets like some kind of animal."[19] Milder critics of gender equality point to a "crisis of values in the West," a disintegration of family life. Writes one Malaysian rights activist,

> [I]n . . . liberal democratic societies the desire for equality between the sexes has, in some cases, led to a subtle, sophisticated imposition of uniformity. That there are temperamental, apart from physical, differences between the sexes that militate against the creation of a unisex society is something that is arrogantly brushed aside by dogmatic advocates of sexual equality. There is an unwillingness to try to understand that the man–woman distinction, a certain degree of differentiation in roles, may be fundamental for the psychological well-being of society.[20]

"Uniformity" of human rights enjoyment, a "unisex" level of receipt of justice, would seem to undermine the very differences between men and women that keep society in balance. Conservative Muslim apologists for practical inequality point to inevitable social and moral disintegration of society (as evinced in the west) as proof of the inadvisability of gender equality in the physical sphere.

Two particular Qur'anic verses serve as the foundation for the theological justification of women's inequality. Surah 2:228 declares that "Women shall have rights similar to the rights against them, according to what is equitable; but men have a degree [of advantage] over them and Allah is Exalted in Power, Wise." According to Surah 4:34, "Men are in charge of women because Allah hath made the one of them to excel the other, and because they spend their property (for the support of women). So good women are obedient (to Allah), guarding in the secret that which Allah hath guarded."[21] An ancient yet still authoritative interpretation of this verse, by Al-Tabari (838–870, CE), reads as follows:

> In saying that men are the protectors and maintainers of women, God Almighty establishes men as the guardians of their women in all that which entails discipline and restraint and for which they are duty bound to God and to their husbands. That is, because God has given more to the one than to the other. God has given more to men because they bequeath women with dowry, provide them with their needs and supply them with adequate provisions. God Almighty has therefore endowed men with superior gifts and established them as the protectors and maintainers of women; who must obey them in all affairs of their lives.[22]

A modern commentator, Asghar Ali Engineer, suggests that Surah 4:34 places men above women simply because they earn and provide for them, and that if women were to provide for men they themselves would become superior. If both should earn equally, they would be equals by Qur'anic standards.[23] Al-Tabari's interpretation of the verse is another instance of conservative scholarship that essentializes male and female "natures" based on humanly constructed social realities.

There exist as well a number of traditions attributed to the Prophet Mohammed and early proverbs that are derogatory to women. Says one tradition, "A woman approaching from afore or from behind is a form of the devil." According to one proverb, "Women are defective in understanding and religion." Says another, "Women have been omitted by God from His mercy." The first Caliph, Hazrat Abu Bakr, is reported to have said, "One who consults woman for his affairs would humiliate himself," and "obedience to women makes one enter hell." To the second Caliph, Hazrat Umar, are attributed the words, "Seek refuge from God from the worst of women and be on your guard from the best of them." The fourth Caliph, Hazrat Ali, is recorded as saying, "Let not women remain in one state and trust them not with money. Leave them not with anything but managing the children, if you at all let them. What they desire brings you to destruction and ruins empires. They forget good and remember only evil. They always indulge in lies and persist in insolence."[24] Thus, the first decades of Islam saw the perpetuation of pejorative teachings concerning women by the most influential leaders.

Some of the most significant Muslim interpreters of twentieth-century rights initiatives have continued this harmful, negative sex stereotyping. Sultanhussein Tabandeh's *A Muslim Commentary on the Universal Declaration of Human Rights*[25] was delivered by its author to every Muslim representative to the 1968 Tehran International Conference on Human Rights. Tabandeh describes the UDHR as "a masterpiece," also claiming that "most of its provisions were already inherent in Islam."[26] Yet the rights accorded to women in that instrument he found to be quite at odds with Islam. Arguing that women should be restricted from obtaining a divorce, he noted that women are touchy, hasty, volatile, imprudent, gullible, and, thanks to their powerful sexual desire, easy victims of virile men. Women are made for household chores and childcare, while men are designed for warfare, wage-earning, and so on. Women's limited intelligence makes them unsuitable for (even incapable of) problem-solving and long-term planning. Because they are "timorous-hearted" and physically weak, they might run away from battle and therefore must be kept from it.

Abu'l A'la Mawdudi, an influential Pakistani commentator on rights and Islam, argues firmly in his *Purdah and the Status of Women in Islam*[27] that female nature is tender, submissive, sensitive, impressionable and timid. Women's function is to bear and rear children. Women lack the firmness, willpower, and ability to offer unbiased, objective judgments. Women's education, therefore, should be focused on instruction in childrearing and the maintaining of a pleasant and peaceful home.

Ayatollah Javad Bahonar, a close associate of Ayatollah Khomeini and briefly prime minister of Iran, is the author of an article that speaks directly to a fundamentalist understanding of women's intellectual capabilities.[28] Because men are physically larger and stronger than women, he writes, they have larger brains than women. Men's brains have a greater capacity to deal with "thought and deliberation," while women's brains have a large section "related to emotions."[29] Women are therefore better able to express tenderness and nurturing, and are best suited for child-rearing. Because a significant portion of women's brains are devoted to the emotions, women are ill-suited for work outside the home, which requires abilities for planning, perseverance, coolness, even hard-heartedness and connivance. In a portion of the article devoted to statistics regarding female physiology, Bahonar notes that "a man's brain weighs 100 g more than a woman's." He concludes that "differences in physical structure are reflected in the mental capacities of the two sexes."[30]

Every religious tradition has sacred texts, traditions, practices, proverbs, and interpreters that are derogatory to women. They also have others that advocate gender equality and innumerable strengths in women. Islam is no exception. As a religious tradition it is particularly rooted in the authority of its holy book, the Qur'an. This text provides many examples of divine revelations that honor and respect women, even suggesting in places that they are equal in all value to men.[31] Conservative interpreters select for emphasis those passages that place women at a disadvantage, while exploiting the authority of the Qur'an to support their own views. The *Shari'a* is said by many of these scholars to be lifted directly from the Qur'an.[32] In fact, the Qur'an is not a law book but instruction on the qualities of God; there is little legal advice to be gleaned from it, but rather theology. The Qur'an's two major themes are the oneness of God and the inevitability of judgment. Only three percent of the text concerns the law. One third of those verses, or one percent of the Qur'an, pertains to the family. Another one percent of the total text concerns what might be described as a "civil code."[33] Marriage, divorce, inheritance and ownership of property, and veiling/seclusion are the four most substantive Qur'anic topics relating specifically to women's material lives.[34] What few verses exist concerning these items are lifted by interpreters interested in the continued subordination of women and are codified into unbending regulations. The impression of holy sponsorship makes them difficult to challenge.

Concerning marriage and property issues, the Qur'an is interpreted by conservative clerics to permit women only one husband at a time, while men may have up to four wives simultaneously. Men may compel their wives to remain in the home and to be covered from head to foot if and when they leave the home. Women may not marry outside of Islam; men are allowed to marry Jewish or Christian women. If women disobey their husbands they may be beaten and/or deprived of maintenance. Women may not travel distances without their husbands' permission and, if the husband so chooses, may not walk locally without a chaperone. Women inherit only one-half of the portion that comes to men. Their testimony in court is valued at one-half that of a man for purposes of compensation; sometimes their testimony is rendered completely invalid.[35] Men may divorce their wives by *talaq*, the simple repetition of a divorce formula, while women must be able to name particular circumstances and prove their case in court. (Different schools of jurisprudence establish different criteria for divorce, such as mental instability, conversion to another religion, etc.) Upon divorce, men are granted custody of all children after infancy. These pre-modern stipulations (some of which had been abandoned in various countries, some of which were maintained) have been revived to form the backbone of the personal status laws that, in some countries, supersede more favorable secular laws regarding the same issues.

While the Qur'an presents a variety of possible interpretations regarding women's equality and autonomy, it also presents blatant contradictions for those who would codify its precepts. Differing schools of religious law and thought and differing processes and outcomes of *ijtihad* have resulted in differing practices in various communities. Women are, according to the sacred text, allowed to own property and manage their own businesses. Some *Shari'a* rules reflect this teaching. Other *Shari'a* stipulations assert the very opposite, calling for seclusion at home with financial management solely in the hands of male relatives. Similarly, *talaq* is permitted by the Qur'an but condemned by the Prophet, while one *hadith* reveals that women may pronounce *talaq* as well.[36] In general, the earlier verses of the Qur'an (those revealed in Mecca) are more favorable to women than the later ones (those received in Medina). The first generation of interpreters claimed that the later verses necessarily abrogate the former ones. Some contemporary reformers hold that this position can and should be reversed, that jurists have always reformulated *Shari'a* in light of new insights and historical contexts.[37] Some contemporary traditionalists seem to want to retain the ability to choose which contradictory Qur'anic verses will be made normative, without establishing firm rules regarding dating, knowing that the teachings they prefer are located throughout the text. They claim that the reformulation of (conservative) traditional interpretations is not possible.

Another debilitating issue for Muslim women's rights enjoyment is the fact that women are often portrayed as temptresses by traditionalists. Those same clerics who write that women naturally are intellectually inferior, affectionate, nurturing, and incapable of the connivance and tough-mindedness required to bear real responsibility may also teach that women are conniving, dishonest, heartless seducers who must be kept in check. To connect what might appear to be contradictory traits, these interpreters name the culprit not as the individual, simple woman, but the raw power of female sexuality. Women are encouraged to be ignorant of their bodies. Those who are ignorant are considered more pure; those who are more knowledgeable are considered "less worthy."[38] Women's sexuality is considered too harmful even for women to be aware of. Sexuality is mystified and mythologized, both for women and for men; the ability to interpret women's physical and sexual selfhood is retained by clerics who use it as a tool to subjugate women. "The whole Muslim social structure," writes Fatima Mernissi, "can be seen as an attack on, and a defense against, the disruptive power of female sexuality."[39]

The best interest of all persons (or those who desire salvation, which is to say all Muslims) is served if the power of women's sexuality is firmly controlled. Veiling and seclusion prevent women from being seen or experienced by men to whom they are not directly related. Women are incapable of participating in the public sphere; they are effectively rendered invisible. Men, their virility leaving them incapable of self-control, are prevented from becoming passive victims of women's sexual power.[40] The Arabic word *fitna* has two meanings, "social disorder" and "beautiful woman." Women are debased as the literal embodiment of destruction and disorder. Women are "*fitna*...a living representative of the dangers of sexuality and its rampant disruptive potential."[41]

The seclusion of women (*purdah*) has economic implications as well, for the man who is able to keep his wives and other female relatives isolated at home (and out of the workforce) is considered to be financially enviable.[42] Some women, therefore, proudly experience their own seclusion as a sign of their family's prestige. Many women who are veiled do so proudly as a badge of ideology or faith. Many embrace it as a way of insuring that men will leave them alone if they are in a public place.[43] Others oppose veiling because it removes any necessity to require men simply to respect all women in public places. The burden and responsibility for men's virility is borne by women. Men (and women) are taught that if women do not cover themselves, they deserve the harassment, fondling, or violence that occurs. Men are not required to respect women's privacy or bodily integrity, women are required to earn it through compliance with various tools of social control. In a similar fashion, polygamy is said to be necessary in order to discourage prostitution.[44] Men are so powerless in the face of female sexuality that they cannot be expected to have only one sex partner at a time. Again, women who live in polygynous households pay the price for this flattery of the male libido and absolution of sexual responsibility for men.

Religious leaders, in general, do not openly advocate clitoridectomy and infibulation, but these practices thrive in many (mostly North and West African) Muslim countries. Because women's sexuality is portrayed as being so destructive, clitoridectomy and infibulation are tacitly understood to help contain its power. The procedures are effective components in the wider pattern of women's subjugation.[45]

In the opinion of Fatima Mernissi, a Moroccan social scientist, Islam is not so much opposed to women as it is to the "heterosexual unit," to a relationship based on real and fulfilling love and enjoyment that might take a man's focus away from Allah while leaving him emotionally vulnerable to another person's welfare, hopes, and concerns. The whole Muslim social order, she writes, seeks to prevent intimacy between men and women, especially between wife and husband. Its conventions work to create emotional distance between them. Sex is considered a polluting act; men are taught to recite certain devotional phrases during sex in order to take their minds off their partners and fix them on Allah. Mothers are the only women to be actually loved, at the intentional expense of wives. Young wives and their mothers-in-law are pitted against one another from the beginning. Seclusion leads not to diminished sexual curiosity but to much greater estrangement, misunderstanding, and conflict.[46] True emotional and physical intimacy would have the ability, perhaps, to create antagonism toward the religiously based allocation of all real power to men.

As this book's final chapter will discuss, contemporary Muslims are engaged in a variety of approaches to ensuring women's rights within an authentically Islamic framework. At deepest issue is the question of what it means to *be* Muslim. Traditionalists point to the Qur'an and *Shari'a* to prove that what "the West" calls subjugation is actually at the heart of women's true equality, human value, and chance for salvation. Reformers say that Islam incorporates in its center a radically different ethic for women's practical rights enjoyment; it is *the* authentic ethic towards which all faithful persons should move. Their quarrel makes clear that having the power to interpret religion brings tremendous power in the political, social, and economic spheres of the lives of faithful women and men.

Hinduism

Hindu perspectives on human rights generally, and on gender equality, can be understood only in relation to the central feature in Hindu cosmology: *dharma*. "*Dharma*," according to one Indian philosopher, is "the law and order of the entire universe."[47] Another describes it as "the stillness of many tensions held in perfect balance."[48] Possible English translations for *dharma* include "duty, law (a seamless combination of law in the sense of the law of gravity, natural law, and law in the sense of paying taxes, cultural law), justice, right, religious merit, and finally, religion."[49] For the purpose of considering human rights, equations of *dharma* with natural law will be unfitting in three important aspects: *dharma* incorporates no emphasis on individualism, it emphasizes obligations rather than rights or rules, and its precepts cannot be universalized as true for every human being. *Dharma* is specific to persons according to stage of life, social group, sex, family connections, and so on.[50] *Dharma* is the immutable, universal law of nature that sustains all of creation; it is the source of spiritual and material well-being. It is ultimate reality in cosmological terms and individual duty in personal terms.

The Hindu religion teaches that the universe is a multi-dimensional reality, that all things – tangible and intangible – exist on multiple levels. Because of this perspective, Hindu thought makes no room for the absolutizing of any particular value. The importance of any value does not reside in its abstraction but in its context, a notion that is antithetical to the western concept of human rights, designed as they are to refer to something permanent, immovable, and absolute, applicable to every human being in every time and place. Universalization of rights values verges on anathema, while contextualization of social justice criteria is imperative. In traditional Hinduism, no value or right can be universalized or absolutized as valid for every person or era. The Hindu universe is on the move, cycling downward through the *yugas*, or epochs. At any moment in time, individual human beings may be glimpsed in their temporary station, as their souls also migrate along with the passing of time. Time is not linear; it is not progressing forward but around. Therefore values, ideals and concepts do not progress or retain their value but also cycle into new phases, new contexts. What was true and good in one era may never be so again.[51]

It follows, then, that for Hindus there are also many levels of truth. There is a basic, overarching unity to the concept of truth, but even spiritual truth is revealed to different individuals in very different ways. Hindu thought rejects the notion that, within a society, people (even co-religionists) might have the same vision of reality or a common perception of truth. That perspective stands in sharp contrast to those of Islam, Christianity, and Buddhism, which teach that a total unity of perception is indeed possible and should be sought. As one scholar has described Hinduism, "If there are many levels of truth and all are valid, there are many levels of rights and all are valid."[52]

Certain precepts central to the Hindu religion also serve as stumbling blocks to any easy accommodation of Hinduism with the liberal human rights notion. The idea of "the accident of birth" is alien to Hindu teachings on the soul's rebirth and on *karma*. Human beings are born to a very specific station (and gender) according to deeds performed in their past life. The context of one's birth is never accidental. Social inequality, therefore, can be perceived as both legitimate and deserved. Human beings are not understood to be equal in their basic value as persons. Past action determines current miseries or joys. Hardship is earned and, it is implied, not to be pitied. Orthodox Hindus temper criticism of this perspective with reminders that every individual – and certainly those born into much suffering – has the opportunity, through good actions, to earn a better birth in the soul's next cycle of existence. There is always equality of opportunity to improve one's lot.

Because the liberation of the soul (*moksha*) is the goal of all existence, it is imperative that the effects of all past *karmas* be undone, while not incurring new karmic debts to be paid. This can only be accomplished if a person performs the duties and functions of whatever station in life she finds herself. Compliance with a certain set of status-based social boundaries becomes strongly required, while the inability to change one's station is strongly suggested (or recommended, if one does indeed wish salvation from the cycle of rebirths). This perspective also recommends that one's life is not to be focused on the extraction of desirable material goods; rather, one must acquire and use only as much as will exhaust past *karmas*.

Without the performance of the dharmically assigned rites, classes of individuals could be responsible for the crashing of the universe. Intense pressure exists to uphold one's ritual responsibilities, along with a profound belief in mutual dependence for the continuation of the world. When duties are performed, order is maintained and the critical tension that balances the universe is kept in stasis. Rights claims that challenge human conditions perpetuated by *dharma* threaten the stability of the cosmos. Relationships are governed by duties, rather than rights. In the words of one Indian writer, "The only right conceded, be it to an individual or a group, is the right to compel the concerned parties to perform their duty."[53] The concept of *dharma* creates tremendous pressure to conform to social expectations.

Different rights are therefore attached to the different stages of birth and rebirth, rendering invalid any understanding of universal rights applicable to all people at any given time. In addition, the rights consistent with one's status bring obligations, and refusal to perform these duties means the forfeiting of all rights. The western view of inalienable and inherent rights as divorced from any obligation or duty is antithetical to this Hindu concept of *dharma*.[54] The Indian philosopher R.C. Pandeya exemplifies a contemporary traditional Hindu perspective on rights. He has written that all "unearned" rights, those that accrue to a person without appropriate "effort," violate the law of *karma*. They are "amoral," he writes; "natural rights become no-rights." One may not accord

> the same set of rights to people who work for it and those who do not. People whose conduct and position are not effective enough to lead them to such an achievement would also invoke these rights merely in the name of their humanity. This would, in effect, give rise to misplaced and undeserved expectations leading ultimately to perpetual tension in society.

The supreme duty, according to Pandeya, is "knowing oneself." Presumably, when one knows one's true self, one will never perform duties or insist on rights outside of one's appropriate station in the dharmic order.[55]

Hindu teaching differs radically from human rights theory on the concept of equality for, thanks to *varnadharma*, what is fair is very often not what is equal.[56] Human beings have innate qualities that determine their station; there is no single human "nature." By western criteria, individuals viewed thus are not equal at all, simply by virtue of being human. The remedy for any inequality of class or gender is the individual's righteous actions during his or her lifetime.[57] If a person lives according to the duties of *dharma* and the righteous practices of *karma*, she or he will be reborn into a better situation. Inequality in any particular moment is only transitory. There will always be practical inequality as long as individual souls are still at different points on their journey towards *moksha*. Remedies to physical inequality are senseless expenditures of effort, since the cycle of epochs and rebirths is intended to bring all living things towards the same endpoint, equal in blessing. Traditional Hindus claim true equality as a cornerstone of their religion because of the "equality of opportunity" that all have to obtain self-enlightenment, to pursue liberation of the soul from the cycle of rebirths. In the words of one Hindu scholar, "the opposite of equality is not hierarchy but order, and the opposite of dharma (duty) is not right but license."[58] Whatever rights accrue to an individual are acquired and not natural, the result of that person's actions or status.[59] One American author sums up the traditional Hindu perspective on equality as follows:

> Hinduism does not hold that all are created equal. Nor does it hold that individual needs, voluntary associational membership, and socio-economic class are central to what it means to be human. These are not, and could not be, the basis for rights. All rights are essentially the privileges of duty to be what one is, socially marked by proper maintenance of the ritual obligations which concentrate, preserve, purify, and perpetuate soul energy in accord with the hierarchy of the spiritual–material cosmos. While all humans have, in some measure, this soul energy, they have it in different degrees. Hence a structural inequality is fundamental to Hindu anthropology and society. To deny this, in the Hindu view, is both an empirical and spiritual failure.[60]

The personal qualities and legacies of the many Hindu gods and goddesses, as they are portrayed in the sacred texts of Hinduism, are considered examples to observant Hindus in every age and station. They embody the essential qualities appropriate (or dangerously inevitable) to different classes of people. As with the texts of many religious traditions, a variety of perspectives on women can be supported. Hindu scriptural references can be used to prove that women must be accorded the highest esteem or be treated as chattel. In each age, traditionalist Hindu lawgivers have interpreted the texts as saying that the "soul energy" of women is less than that of men, that women are farther from *moksha* than men.

As in Islam, holy texts and recorded sayings include phrases that continue to be damaging to women's dignity and efforts at equality. While many modern practitioners dismiss their veracity, traditionalists continue to assert their divine authority and importance, and their lingering effect through the centuries has been decidedly negative. "Indra himself hath said, the mind of a woman, brooks not of discipline....Her intellect hath little weight" (Rig Veda XIII.38.17), says one of the earliest and holiest texts, as well as "With woman there can be no lasting friendship: hearts of hyenas are the hearts of women," (Rig Veda X.96.15). The Precepts of Manu say of woman, "She should do nothing independently even in her own house. In childhood subject to her father, in youth to her husband and when her husband is dead, to her sons. She should never enjoy independence." The same text instructs that a woman who is not obedient will be reborn as a wolf, that a wife's virtues are responsible for the "heavenly bliss" of the husband and his ancestors, and that women who are widowed are the spiritual cause of their husbands' deaths. Their punishment must be to remain unmarried; otherwise, they forfeit their opportunity to take their place next to the husband in heaven. Much social control is exerted over women through threats of negative soteriological consequences.

Scriptural models of behavior for Hindu women focus almost exclusively on their roles as wives. "Womanhood," *per se*, is absent; "wifehood" is central. Women are not independent beings but exist solely in the context of their relationship to their husbands. Marriage is the key to salvation for women, and the focal point in their earthly experience. Traditional Hinduism has taught that marriage is the only sacrament available to women; an unmarried woman who dies was believed to turn into an evil spirit. The virtues extolled for women are all based on their relationship to their husbands – loyalty, submissiveness, and dependence. Women are depicted as weak and needing governance, existing primarily as enablers of male satisfaction, and as a means for men to acquire sons.

There is a also a strong strain in Hinduism of seeing women as temptresses, seductresses, luring good men away from spiritual pursuits, away from salvation. They are accomplices of evil, enticing men away from the straight path of righteousness. Unlike Islam, the stereotype of women's sexuality is not that it makes men incapable of self-control and so must be removed from the sphere of males, but that lusting women themselves will become predatory and so must be controlled.[61] Women's bodies are considered ritually polluted by sexual intercourse, while men's bodies are not likewise pollutable. The purity of women's bodies is of ultimate importance, and so must be protected by men even at the expense of women's personal freedom and autonomy.[62] These perspectives are evident in sacred literatures such as the Dharmashastras and the epics, but they also prevail even in the thought of the more recent reformers, such as Ramakrishna. Women are to be kept under close watch, to be pacified and won over with gifts of clothing and ornamentation, lest the negative side of their nature appear and they cause havoc. Women's tastes and deepest concerns are portrayed as being vain and shallow. Women are also understood, even by some contemporary modernizers, as having essentially different natures than men, natures that necessitate different sets of rights categories.[63]

The religious ideology that is to shape all honorable women's lives is called *Pativratya*, in which a woman reveres (and serves) her husband as a god. *Pativratya* is described by the residents of a small village in Karnataka as follows:

> A woman should realize that a man marries to continue his family line by getting sons. He should pay his debt to society, to his ancestors, and thereby ensure the spiritual well-being of his soul. The wife as Pativrata should be his true helpmate by helping him in every possible way to achieve his goals in life. She should never think that she has an existence apart from her husband. His needs should be hers. She should become one with him in every sense of the word.
>
> A Pativrata always eats whatever is left after her husband has eaten. Even if she was happy in her parents' home she should not think of it in her husband's house. If a woman as much as imagines the good life other couples are having or stops to watch other couples enjoying each other's company, the husband has a right to kill her as she was not completely true to him. Obeying the command of one's husband without question is a mark of virtue and good conduct. She should never be inquisitive. She should never be arrogant. Even a slight indiscretion on the part of the wife towards her husband is a crime and is unbecoming of a Pativrata.
>
> Pativrata will be happy to die before her husband. Dying in his own hands is an added privilege for her because thereby she surely reaches heaven. A Pativrata burns herself in the funeral pyre of her husband as it is not worth living after her husband's death. She never expects any concern or consideration from her husband. He does not have to pay attention even when she is in pain. It does not matter whether he is true to her or not. A Pativrata knows that her salvation lies in her devotion to her husband and to him only. She never even looks at another man. She believes *Pati pratyaksha devatha* (Husband is the living God).
>
> A true Pativrata has extraordinary powers which she accumulates by doing austere services to her husband. She can, for example, turn stone into food, turn gods into children, and bring dead husbands back to life – just as the wives of great sages did. She should listen to stories of great Pativratas in her spare time so that she will be inspired by them.[64]

A woman's reputation also is earned according to how well she trains her daughters to be similar Pativratas. There is very strong social pressure for women to perpetuate this ideology.

The great Pativratas are three revered heroines of Hindu scripture, Sita, Savitri, and Parvati. They remain in a hallowed, separate sphere from the likes of Damayanti (who planned a second marriage for herself) or Kunti (who enjoyed the company of men before her marriage and secured sons for herself by someone other than her husband). The triumvirate of truly virtuous women all placed their husbands' honor and happiness above all else on earth. Two of them died for their husbands, while the third journeyed to the land of Death and reclaimed her spouse for the living. They are uninterested in anything outside of their domestic affairs. They are chaste and submissive, they rarely engage in the distraction of emotional reciprocity, they suffer silently and never complain, they are uncompromising in their self-sacrifice.[65] At many Hindu weddings today the bride is told, "God's grace and may you be another Sita."[66]

Some of the Hindu goddesses present fuller representations of female nature. Saraswati (the Goddess of learning), Durga (the Goddess of power and protection), Kali (the Goddess of power), and Lakshmi (the Goddess of wealth) are strong figures indeed. The most popular of the group, Kali, is also known as the Goddess of destruction. She has a variety of moods and powers; she is often quite terrifying and requires appeasement. Around India stand many temples that are specially dedicated to her worship. But the bold qualities of these goddesses are interpreted to mean that women in every age are power-seeking and dominant; their natures are essentially destructive if not kept under control. The goddess' powerful characteristics are used against women to further disempower them. They are not translated into culturally acceptable modes of behavior for real women, but rather into caveats against women's innate destructiveness. True femininity is always equated with submissiveness and vulnerability. When it comes to women's possible empowerment, the mythological frameworks and the social/theoretical frameworks are considered to be unrelated, as if they existed on different planes. "The consequence," writes Roop Rehka Verma, "is that despite very lofty conceptions of womanhood in some metaphysical frameworks and mythological constructions, when it comes to view the woman as a reality on the ordinary plane of life, the perspective becomes narrow and partial."[67]

Just as the *yugas* of human existence are understood to disintegrate into more and more suffering with the passing of time, so do many scholars believe that the situation for Hindu women has deteriorated steadily since the beginning of Hindu civilization. The sacred texts of Hinduism portray women in increasingly passive, self-sacrificing ways with the advent of time. Even the same character will have different qualities emphasized, appearing educated and headstrong in one of the Vedas, then meek and compliant in a later text.[68]

In terms of education, personal independence, the practice of religious rites, the possession and inheritance of material goods, the incidence of child-marriage (thought to ensure that the bride is a virgin and that even the youngest girls become wives before their own death), the ability to remarry when widowed, and so on, women's quality of life has only declined. With the passage of time, greater and greater restrictions have been placed upon women by interpreters of the scriptures, effectively stripping women of whatever limited power or self-determination they may once have had. Religious sanction for particular social conventions has left girls completely in the control of their fathers, and wives in the hands of their husbands. Arranged, polygamous marriages ensure that every female is married, often at a very young age. The death of the husband may leave dozens of women permanently widowed, some as young as eight years old. Because the Hindu religion teaches that women may marry only once, these girls and women, unable to inherit property, become extremely vulnerable. A relative may care for them; prostitution or starvation are among the alternatives.

Independence for women has been discouraged in a number of ways, both religious and secular (the boundary is often negligible). Formal education has been said to lead to immorality – women would be enabled to write letters to men outside the family, encouraging liaisons with them. Literacy has also been taught to be a direct cause of widowhood, prompting girls and women to decline the opportunity for education even when it was presented. The ban on widow remarriage is reinforced in most contemporary schools of Hindu thought. It is said that if widows could remarry, women would kill their husbands in order to do so.[69] Others revive teachings from holy texts, such as those from the *Srutis* which state that men's deaths are the fault of their wives, who have failed in their spiritual practices to ensure the husbands' longevity. The widow, therefore, must practice austerities for the rest of her life in order to turn bad *karma* into better *karma* for her own next life.[70] In some regions, widows are made to shave their heads, wear a particular widow's uniform, give up pleasant clothes and all jewelry, and/or be secluded, since these women are considered polluting or inauspicious to view.[71]

Some centuries ago, great pressure came to be placed upon women to accept religious, rather than civil, rites of marriage. With a Hindu ceremony came a variety of practices that reemphasized women's role as the property of males while reinforcing their social powerlessness, particularly through preventing them from inheriting property. Secular marriages, while carrying fewer restrictions on inheritance, were legally construed to limit the privileges of the woman's daughters. Although recently passed laws (such as the Dowry Prohibition Act) prevent inheritance restrictions and the formal transfer of money at the time of marriage, brideprice, dowry, and various limitations on inheritance happen all the time. Dowry deaths (both murders and suicides) are increasing in number. Remarriage remains a stigma for women and property inheritance quite difficult.[72] Although women are legally permitted to vote, many refuse to do so, bowing to pressure from male relatives or internalizing religious messages of intellectual and social inadequacy.

Progressive Hindu women writers betray a strong sense of frustration with the complacency they identify in some of their co-religionist sisters. Special little rituals that only women may perform, the culture-wide adulation of motherhood, and other practices are viewed as "pedestalizing" elements of the continuing social control of women, elements that women themselves choose to accept rather than expose. Women, these writers believe, are made to feel that they have traded their freedom for real and benevolent security, that they are privileged to have such an opportunity and wise to have made the choice.[73] Religiously based social conditioning has pacified them, convincing them that their secondary status is indeed divinely ordained. More than a few scholars have wondered if the caste system can be eliminated without a thorough dismantling of Hindu teachings, so intrinsic is it to the religion's understanding of how the universe is ordered. Similar challenges will likely be faced by Hindu women who wish to reinterpret their tradition and construct a more liberating place for themselves in it.

Unlike Islam, Hinduism[74] does not go to great lengths to formally separate women for different "rights," but its religion-based undervaluing of women contributes to what is effectively a different standard of rights enjoyment. Positive religious laws do not codify discriminatory standards, as in Islam; rather, discriminatory traditions have been sanctified in secular government through personal status laws. These "family laws," concerning marriage and divorce, wills, guardianship, adoption, financial maintenance during and after marriage, and so on, form the backbone of many women's real experience of rights legislation. These personal status laws remain in the hands of both religious and secular authorities, and effectively eviscerate any rights protections accorded to women in the Indian Constitution.[75]

Christianity

Christianity is sometimes said to be the progenitor of the modern human rights concept, because of its deep influence on the societies in which the Enlightenment was spawned. This assertion is exaggerated.[76] While Christianity certainly wielded much philosophical influence on the evolution of the rights notion, the differences are fundamental. Christianity, for instance, shares with classical and liberal humanist perspectives the idea of natural law. Yet the classical view made no room for the transcendence that is essential to the Christian belief system. The liberal humanist view does incorporate a deeply transcendental element. It is based, however, in a deistic notion of the metaphysical, which assumes a radical autonomy for humanity. If there is a divine element to the universe, it exists completely separate from the human sphere and does not act in human history. The firmly theistic position of Christianity, on the other hand, centers on human dependence upon and relationship with God. Human beings have autonomy only within the boundaries of their response to God's particular covenant. Locke invoked a picture of humanity as inherently self-sufficient rather than dependent; he portrayed the individual as social by necessity, while Christianity understands humanity to be social by nature, called and drawn to mutual relationships with God and with other persons.[77]

Christianity and "the west" are not synonymous, of course, yet the relationship of the Christian tradition to the human rights concept is complicated by the fact that the philosophical foundations of human rights are western. Basic understandings of the person, of the state, and of the integrity or dignity of individuals (as such ideas inform the popular use of the human rights concept) have been molded by the Christian worldview that simmers below much of the western political and social tradition. With the passing of the centuries, Christianity has split into different factions, each with varying theological positions concerning the moral role of the individual, of the state, and of relations between the two. Particularly since the sixteenth century, Christian theology has become the home for numerous political ideologies. The human rights notion, a relatively modern invention, has been refracted through these different perspectives, and there is today no single Christian understanding of the concept.

A strong emphasis on human rights in contemporary Christian theology is considered erroneous by some writers from across the denominational spectrum. The most conservative Christian commentators have been reluctant to dismiss entirely the notion of rights, or at least not in print. While traditionalists in other religious communities often see the human rights idea as inconsistent with central ethical principles in their religion (employing a relativist standpoint), Christian traditionalists do not. After all, the human rights idea (as it has developed in international law) was created in the philosophical, legal, and religious setting of majority-Christian countries. Rather, they view human rights as something dangerous to the church, as something that is co-opting the church's real message, mission, and purpose. They consider the ethical principles of Christianity as being molded into new shapes and modified into a new entity. These foundational ethics are taken away from Christian understandings and recast in secular humanist terms. The problem is not that the central ideas and ethics of the human rights notion are foreign (as the religious relativists claim) but that they are being improperly employed; they are manipulated and transformed and misinterpreted, supplanting the true Christian message. If anything, the moral assumptions of human rights are dangerously familiar.

Max Stackhouse, for instance, warns of a new "piety...centered on the Great God Freedom." He is worried about reductionism, about the reducing of Christianity to freedom and other human rights principles. He writes, "Freedom has become the core of our...creed....The end, the goal, the highest standard and noblest vision for humanity, for society, and for civilization, is Freedom." As some Muslim and Hindu commentators also note, this stance is not appropriate because it is not a religious way of living. It is, rather, the substitution of a human ethic for divine commandments. Stackhouse concludes that, in the debate on human rights, "the Judeo-Christian traditions of the West confront one of the greatest challenges of the modern age." Human rights might be a proper creed, but only if they are properly embedded in the Judeo-Christian doctrinal framework. In other words, the central principles of the human rights idea must not be morphed or changed but interpreted in strictly Christian ways.[78]

Edward Norman is another conservative Christian commentator. He has written that there can be no "Christian view" of human rights, and writes vigorously against what he considers the secularization of Christianity by advocates of human rights. He views the leaders of many churches as identifying the church with the moral claims of western liberalism. They are guilty of a reduction of the Gospel to contemporary ideology. Christian doctrine is being reduced to human rights rhetoric, which is a sign of decay, not of progress. What is needed is the separation of the absolute concern of the Christian message from the relative concerns of culture – quickly – before Christianity is absorbed in toto by a different ideology, that of human rights.[79]

If some Christian conservatives are worried that the Christian tradition will be absorbed by or reduced to human rights rhetoric, Jacques Ellul and other conservatives are concerned that the church will not absorb and promote enough the rights notion. It is even required as an item of faith to do so. Human rights come from God through Jesus Christ, therefore if humanity is to enjoy human rights it is required of the church, and uniquely the church, to articulate and secure them. John Warwick Montgomery, meanwhile, is an example of the many conservatives for whom it is crucial, if the human rights idea is to be valid, to root rights in the Bible. The Bible has ultimate authority for such thinkers, and its teachings are normative. If human rights are to be a valid concept, they must be noted in the Bible, and if human rights are indeed in the Bible, then they are commanded to be observed. Montgomery, happily, finds human rights to be mandated in the biblical literature. The promotion of human rights, then, becomes a central act of faith for Christians.[80]

The teachings and acts of Jesus as recorded in the Gospels portray him as departing radically (and intentionally) from traditional perspectives on class, gender, ethnic and race equality, as well as from pejorative attitudes towards various religious groups and people with disabilities. Many liberal and progressive Christians understand Jesus to have preached a total equality of human value, as all persons are made of the very same essence (regardless of visible differences, they are all *imago dei*) and so are equally loved by their creator, God. Jesus' showing of respect, compassion, and justice towards those whom his opponents viewed as having lesser human value was greeted with horror (and sometimes violence) by those contemporaries, who rightly understood that this challenge to the prevailing social hierarchy was a threat to their privileged status in the community. Much of their discrimination had been justified by religious interpretation. The first communities of Jesus' followers sought to live out his teachings on radical human equality, continuing such shocking practices as women's religious leadership, the abandonment of local purity codes (through which many persons, especially women, had been marginalized), and an equal sharing of personal belongings so that none would be in want.

The earliest New Testament literature reflects this new articulation of human equality. Paul's Letter to the Galatians includes the classic (in its origins, baptismal) formula of Christian equality: "There is no longer Jew or Greek, there is no longer slave or free, there is no longer male and female; for all of you are one in Christ Jesus" (3:28). Race and religion, economic status, and gender divisions are erased by the saving act of Jesus' death and resurrection, which returns humanity to its original unity of value, triumphing over sinful, humanly constructed hierarchies. Jesus and Paul are to be understood as proclaiming an equality that is not to exist solely on a spiritual plane, but that is to be manifested in the details and institutions of daily life. Full equality is a spiritual feature that is intended to have equal potency in the lived world, to cross the border between the inner and outer life, the spirit and the world.

The New Testament literature that succeeds Paul's epistles provides evidence that, as time passed after the life of Jesus, there was growing discomfort with the bold new social relationships within the communities. As the religious movement spread to different regions, local discriminatory customs were accommodated, most likely in order to help facilitate conversions. The Household Codes of the deutero-Pauline and pseudo-Petrine letters reinstated a hierarchy of human value. Slaves were the lowest members of society. Above them were children, then women, and then free male adults.[81] On the issue of equality, Christianity has continued to adapt, theologically, to the different cultures to which it has spread. Certain biblical texts and local traditions are used to support fullest human equality; in other periods and regions different texts and traditions are used to legitimate deepest inequality. The emergence of a middle class in (largely Christian) European society, a class that advanced its own interests in no small part by producing its own ideology of equality and liberty, helped institutionalize the liberal notion of human equality. The Christian tradition, in its more progressive interpretations of equality, influenced significantly the development of this principle. The understanding of equality within human rights instruments resonates strongly with earliest Christian teachings on the topic. Many contemporary Christian communities, however, continue to ground their claims for inequality in theology and biblical exegesis. The poor and the disabled are said to be less valued by God, and punished by God with their afflictions. Persons of color and those from different cultures are said to be inferior to majority races and cultures, less favored by God. Somewhat like the Hindu concept of *karma*, Christians sometimes interpret personal hardship or physical difference with the will of God, superimposing divine approval on inequity, disability, or discrimination. Because hierarchies of human value simply exist, they are said to be a part of the divine social order, rather than the products of human discrimination (in Christian terms, of human sin).

Varieties of textual and theological interpretation regarding equality affect no group more than women. There are two contrasting traditions in Christianity regarding women, each supported by biblical passages and theological frameworks. The first is a theology of subordination. Its understandings of human origins are rooted in the second chapter of the Book of Genesis, in which God is depicted as creating a helper and companion for Adam, the first human being. Women are therefore supplemental, complementary to the male, created to assist him, never to lead or to have full autonomy. Since the male is naturally the head of the completed creation, patriarchal social relationships are considered the appropriate reflection of the natural or divinely created order. Men are to rule, women to serve obediently. If men's rule is unjust or violent, women are to suffer quietly and, through the example of their piety and graciousness, passively lure their husbands towards a kinder disposition.[82] The interpreted primacy of original man over original woman was articulated for the new church by the author of the deutero-Pauline Letter to the Ephesians: "Wives, be subject to your husbands as you are to the Lord. For the husband is the head of the wife just as Christ is the head of the church, the body of which he is the Savior. Just as the church is subject to Christ, so also wives ought to be, in everything, to their husbands" (5:22–24). This prevailing metaphor, that Christ (male) is married to the church (female), has served for two millennia to entrench patriarchal gender relations within families and between sexes. The following quote by American fundamentalist Jerry Falwell captures a contemporary manifestation:

> God Almighty created men and women biologically different and with differing needs and roles. He made men and women to complement each other and to love each other. . . .Scripture declares that God has called the father to be the spiritual leader in his family. . . .Their wives and children want to follow them and be under their protection. The husband is to be the decision-maker and the one who motivates his family with love. . . .He is to be a protector.[83]

The theology of women's subordination is further supported by, as one theologian describes it, "various insinuations that woman is, in fact, morally, ontologically, and intellectually the inferior of the male. Her subordination is not merely one of social office, but of actual inferiority. She is less capable of independent life in all respects than the male."[84] Furthermore, one of the first acts of the first woman, Eve, was to bring sin and suffering into the world. Women, therefore, are not only less capable than men at exercising independence but are even downright dangerous when permitted to try. Because a woman brought all that is evil or fallen into the world, women can justly be punished by subordination and suffering. The blaming of woman for society's ills justifies the perpetuation of her subordination.

This constructed image of women embraces an odd dichotomy. Women are considered to be superior to men in an heroic ability to withstand suffering and to practice virtues such as devotional piety, chastity, humility, and self-denial (traits that those who wish to control women might well want to promote). Simultaneously, however, women are said to be morally inferior to men. They are incapable of self-control, their emotions overtake them as they give in to their passions. They are willful. Lest they bring shame or harm to their husbands or male relatives, they must be kept under tight control. Women are associated with the body, with irrationality and lowliness, while men are associated with the mind and reason, with rationality and a higher order. The mind must control the passions of the body as men must control women. As in strains of Hinduism and Islam, women are temptresses to men, leading them away from moral propriety. Men should not be held accountable for their own appetites but may censure and control women for interesting them in the first place.

Continuing the dichotomy between women's higher and lower moral natures is teaching concerning Mary, the mother of Jesus. While Jesus, who is both human and divine, is believed to be sinless, the church has had trouble reconciling how a sinless person could be born of a fallen human being. Mary, therefore, has been taught to be sinless herself. She is held up to women as an alternate role model for Eve, the mother of all women. Mary was able to uphold her primary duty to produce offspring, but did so without dirtying herself with sexual relations. She was pious, self-giving, and morally pure. She is "proof" that women can be capable of (and required to adhere to) the better side of their moral nature, rather than its underside.

The theology of subordination has received strong ratification from Christianity's most important shapers, particularly in the centuries before the Enlightenment. Augustine interpreted his own deep struggle to be chaste as meaning that the embodied souls of women are naturally seductive in a way that men's are not, causing women to be more morally dangerous than men. He did not call women's nature inherently evil, but emphasized the fearfulness of their powerful inborn potential to corrupt. Augustine, therefore, could understand women's spiritual souls to be equal to men's, while their embodied souls were lower in the hierarchy of value. Aquinas went further, writing that women are not only innately subordinate to men, but are irreparably deficient expressions of human nature. He held this opinion not on the basis of Christian interpretation but because of what he knew of Aristotle's views about the roles of women and men in procreation.[85]

With the Enlightenment, popular Christian understanding of human nature returned to *imago dei*, all humanity being in the image of God. Following the creation story of the first chapter of the Book of Genesis rather than that in the second chapter, philosophers and theologians saw humanity as created in a single divine action, and not in complementary steps. Both women and men were designed jointly as the head of the created order, and to share dominion over the rest of creation. By the nineteenth and twentieth centuries, this theology of equivalence prompted the more progressive churches not only to preach equality but also to attempt to make it a reality in society. Writes one theologian, "The old theory of embodiment and sexual division as a fall into sin and subordination is eliminated. The sin of domination and division arises, not through embodiment, but through entry into social arrangements of civilization which distort the original order of nature into a hierarchical order of privilege or servitude."[86] This shift in thinking was accompanied by a new emphasis on the building of the Kingdom of God – of the salvation of the current world that exists in addition to the perfected one that is to come. The Christian social movements that emerged often included gender equality among their goals or assumptions.

The theology of subordination, however, remains alive and well in the majority of Christian denominations and churches. Personal status laws in largely Christian countries, such as restrictions on divorce, abortion, and adoption, tend to circumscribe the rights of women more so than men. Some Christian feminists in developing countries report that various aspects of indigenous culture – even indigenous religions – are being valorized and revived by male traditionalists to enforce patriarchal norms rather than sanction more progressive Christian practices. At times Christianity is circumscribed; at others, it is incorporated into the project, such as in those communities in India where menstrual taboos from the Hebrew Bible have been revived (ostensibly, from several thousand years ago in the Middle East) to support subordinating local Hindu customs regarding ritual purity for women.[87] Christian feminists ask questions of their own tradition similar to those of Muslim feminists – how can the originally liberating perspectives of women in the religion be re-appropriated in the present? Alternatively, were ancient practices or teachings actually liberating in the first place?

How can conservatives come to understand the religion's major prophet or founder as supportive of gender equality? Is patriarchy essential to the religion or has the tradition simply become structured along patriarchal lines? While there are important exceptions within some schools of thought and practice, the theology of subordination still bears heavy influence in the lives and faith communities of many Christian women.

Conclusion

Patriarchy in religious practice is retained by choice. Each of the traditions under consideration has ample theological, cultural, and textual resources to ensure gender equality, and a host of reformers at work to see that they are employed. However, as the discussion in these pages attests, there exist in these religions considerable historical, textual, theological, and traditional resources with which to substantiate the disempowerment and marginalization of women. With these resources conservatives are able to rationalize women's exemption from a variety of rights norms, and to insist that their own arguments are untouchable because of their divine source. The incompatibility of religious perspectives with certain rights norms goes to the deepest level – to the basic metaphysical foundations of religious belief and of the rights notion, and to fundamental criteria for social justice. In communities such as these, resistance to the rights construct may be so great as to render it useless in the struggle for women's human rights.

4
The Question of Relativism

> It is a small matter to starve to death, but a large matter to lose one's virtue.
>
> a Confucian aphorism of Zhu Xi, supporting a ban on widow remarriage

Appeals to moral relativism have posed a significant challenge to the human rights construct in its brief history. Relativism has been triumphed effectively by apologists for patriarchal ideology to suggest that the rights construct (particularly as applied to women) is an inappropriate (even colonialist) intrusion into the theological integrity of religious communities, who should enjoy a human right to free religious practice. Relativists' arguments for the superiority of their moral/ethical codes, the history and immutability of their traditions, and their source in the divine, are both powerful and effective. On these grounds governments or communities have exempted themselves from adhering to some or all rights categories. When relativist claims are made on the grounds of religion (as opposed to culture or to morals generally) the challenge is especially potent because of appeals to divine will and the force of claims to religious freedom. Relativism regarding gender is also especially potent. As shown in the previous chapter, factions within various religions argue that women are a different category of person from men and so in certain circumstances are required to have different criteria for rights enjoyment. At their worst, claims for religious relativism may further compromise women's rights if rights discourse is employed by communities to actually substantiate instances of gender discrimination.

Relativism

Regarding human rights, the "normative" relativist perspective (in the terminology of Fernando Tesón)[1] understands each of the world's cultures to be of equal ethical and political worth. All moral evaluations are said to be culturally conditioned, therefore the particularism of the origin of all morals, ethics, and values limits their validity solely to the religious, cultural, and social context in which they arose. This being so, normative relativism holds that it is impossible to establish any valid cross-cultural norms for evaluating and comparing moral values; each moral system must be regarded as having equal legitimacy.[2] In the field of human rights, normative relativists claim that no transnational legal or ethical standards actually exist, *ergo* there is no single mutual criterion for judging human rights practices cross-culturally. Human rights standards vary according to national tastes and idiosyncrasies, and what is considered a human rights violation in one culture may be perfectly legal behavior in another. Transnational normative judgments must be precluded by respect and tolerance.[3]

The very concept of human rights is therefore claimed to be invalid by some relativists. Human rights, they note, are grounded in natural law theory, itself a culturally specific tenet. The international instruments lack legitimacy for many peoples simply because they were drafted without their perspective or with the input only of their foreign-educated elites. The human rights idea has no commonly shared philosophical foundation sufficient to afford a uniform interpretation of rights in the international community. To assume such a common foundation would be to impose values and legal structures upon countless peoples to whom they are not autochthonous. The universalist approach is said, by proponents of normative relativism, to center on the "fallacy" that human rights exist independent of culture, value systems, and ideology.[4]

The employment of the relativist stance by religious conservatives is likely to be the more moderate "metaethical" relativism (Tesón's terminology again), which asserts that no objective standard of judgment of moral norms can be created in a multi-religious context, only within and for a specific religio-cultural or regional setting. Moral terminology is said to lack meaning cross-culturally, making it altogether impossible to discover moral "truth" on a wider scale than one's particular sect. Their perspective, however, involves an interesting twist on relativism's primary claim. In their writings, these conservatives appear *not* to agree with the idea that all moral/ethical systems are of equal worth. If so, they would be required to give some consideration to gender equality or any other moral claim proposed by rights activists. Inherent in religion-based relativism is the notion that moral systems are decidedly not of equal worth – that a particular one is superior. In short, those who claim exemption from rights norms on the basis of incompatibility with religious practice are unlikely to assert that the very concept of a human right is invalid in their belief system, since simultaneous claims to the firmly legislated right to freedom of religion are their very best defense.[5] Rather, in any conflict of rights claims, they variously assert that freedom of religion must take precedence, that their own religion is the best guarantor of human rights, or they construct an alternate rights scheme (such as the Universal Islamic Declaration of Human Rights).

Governments and organizations claiming a relativist perspective without appeals to religion are more likely to suggest that the kernel of the rights idea is incompatible with concepts foundational to their society (normative relativism). These concepts often include the primacy of duty to others (rather than rights claims demanding responsibility and accountability from others), and the corporate identity of tribe or family (rather than the individualism said to be inherent in the rights notion).[6] Religious self-exemptions stress the central importance of religious practice in individuals' and communities' lives, the social and spiritual harmony and balance of these communities, the time-honored, inherent systems of value and justice within the tradition, and the soteriological implications of deviation from divinely mandated practices.[7] These are held up as infinitely more worthy of respect and protection than whatever particular rights claim is immediately, temporarily at issue. The very idea of a human right, however, is usually not at issue.

Religious relativism presents an extraordinary challenge to the human rights idea. The appeal to divine sanction, the basic right to free religious exercise, and the sometimes blurry line between having a belief and the legitimacy of acting upon it have brought the most profound of questions to the practice of securing rights. In particular, the denial of women's rights in the name of religion is arguably the single greatest challenge to the whole notion of human rights because of the assertion that women have essentially different "natures" than men. There is, therefore, no single, mutual nature to all human beings. There is no basic, common humanity, but several forms of human beings whose inherent stations, expectations, value, and duties are different and are made so by divine will. The central assumption of the human rights notion – that there is a common, invaluable element to every human being that signifies radically equal worth and deserves equal protection – is rendered toothless. In a subtle contradiction, states or communities may claim that they have a "human" right to religious freedom, while using that right to proclaim that, in essence, there is no such thing as an unqualified "human" right. Challenges to this dichotomy are sometimes rebutted with allegations of cultural insensitivity (as was declared by some majority-Muslim states when non-Muslim states objected to their *Shari'a*-based reservations to the Women's Convention)[8] or religious persecution (of which Saudi Arabia has accused Amnesty International for its critique of their rights record).[9]

Even the "dignity" language, popular among some western rights advocates as both the source and protected end of all human rights, is used by some religious critics to undermine the rights project. Women, they say, are equal in dignity to men, but that dignity is best protected by ensuring that women's "special nature" is supported.[10] A life of dignity for women may have very different practical criteria than that for men. One Sudanese critic of appeals to relativism describes his preferred way of arbitrating conflicts of rights claims as "the principle of reciprocity": I won't condone for you any act or condition that I would not accept for myself.[11] Many authentically religious perspectives, however, legitimize very different treatment for women. Men are expected fully to condone many acts or conditions for women that they would not accept for themselves, and women are expected to accept different criteria for men. Such situations are understood to be completely just and "natural." Human rights schemes that are founded on the idea of different natures are made into accomplices in a larger project of disempowering women, preventing them from acquiring resources, independence, autonomy, or participation in institutions of political, social, economic, or religious power.

The charge of ideological imperialism that undergirds calls for relativism is something that must be taken seriously in every instance. Non-western critics of rights schemes repeatedly refer to international norms as new tools for colonization – if western powers no longer literally run the governments of states in the global south and east, then the rights idea gives them an opportunity to control legal, political, and social affairs from United Nations headquarters in New York and Geneva. It is post-colonial recolonization. The heavy promotion of civil and political rights by the United States and its allies reflects, say these critics, the employment of the rights notion for the maintenance of American hegemonic power. Nawal El-Saadawi and other supporters of human rights have spoken against western governments' use of the rights idea to implement economic and political agendas that further their domination in particular countries.[12] Others have noted that the international rights regime supported by the United States encourages the accession to power in other countries of leaders who will be supportive of US interests, while it disables potential challenges to the American project of its increased economic dominance.[13] One Malaysian activist has written that "the UN is neither willing nor capable of protecting human rights *qua* human rights ... (that the UN) is nothing more than an instrument of the U.S. and other Western powers, (with the result that) national sovereignty is the only way of safeguarding the human rights of the masses which are now threatened by a powerful state (the U.S.) in a unipolar world."[14]

Similarly, the inherent charge of theological imperialism contained in religious relativism – of foisting different metaphysical ethics and systems of value upon other traditions – is sometimes described as evangelism from afar. Writing from a Hindu perspective, Bithika Mukerji warns of "insidious and infiltrating influences" beneath the surface of international rights schemes, "a penal code for policing the ethical standards of various nations."[15] Indeed, there are few people who would deny that the idea of human rights is politically, culturally, and theologically rooted in western liberalism and the Judeo-Christian tradition. Those who do undertake dialogue on conflicts between rights norms and religious traditions find themselves balancing considerations of imperialism and religious integrity, historical injustices, and current indignities. At deepest issue, in the words of one legal scholar, is whether or not universalism and pluralism are mutually exclusive.[16]

Some religious relativists employ a particular stereotype of women to support their claim that, on religious grounds, they deserve different (inferior) rights standards: women are the guardians and transmitters of culture and religion. As such, they need to remain especially observant of religio-cultural traditions, lest they not be passed on to the next generation. In the words of a conservative American Christian woman, "A woman's nature is simply, other-oriented.... To the traditional woman self-centeredness remains as ugly and sinful as ever. The less time women spend thinking about themselves, the happier they are.... Women are ordained by their nature to spend themselves in meeting the needs of others. And women, far more than men, will transmit culture and values to the next generation. There is nothing demeaning about this nature: it is ennobling."[17] In the former Zaire, for instance, women were prohibited from wearing western dress, while no such restrictions existed for men.[18] As one African woman has written, "Women must act as mediators between the past and the present, while men see themselves as mediators between the present and the future."[19] Women are taught to consider themselves honored to be communicators of traditional religious values. It is so important and specialized a task that it requires women to be separated from any foreign influences that could warp the purity of these values that their "female nature" enables them to communicate. It is important, therefore, that women be less assimilated into the wider society.[20]

Special "protections" need to be provided for women, who are entrusted with the honor of the family and the faith. One rationalization for veiling in Islam has been that unveiled women are unable to think straight and so "become a source of evil." They thus become a national weak spot – the means by which an enemy might infiltrate and destroy a society.[21] As Marie-Aimée Hélie-Lucas writes,

> Being the guardian is so central to the threatened identity that it is also identified as the weakest point, the most vulnerable to be protected from alien influences. Being the guardian is being a potential traitor who should therefore be closely watched. Laws should be codified which clearly fix the private sphere as central to protection of the threatened identity, bind women to their role of guardians and prevent them from any possibility to fulfill the dark part of their natural mission, to show the other profile of their Janus face, prevent them from betrayal and the destruction of the community – national, religious, or communal.[22]

Appeals to religious relativism have been quite effective in preventing rights norms from being applied to women in some communities. The relativists' arguments, however, are far from airtight. The following sections will offer a critical analysis of religious relativists' categories of self-exemption from endorsing religious women's human rights.

Theological breadth

The very idea of relativism in human rights points to the great mitigating factor in the relativists' own argument: relativism exists *within* religions. If self-exemptions are made from rights standards in the name of freedom of religion, so can such exemptions from various practices be made within religions. In each of the so-called "world religions," the range of beliefs – of theological underpinnings and of rituals and practices – is very broad. Central symbols, confessions of faith, or foundational cosmologies (such as *dharma*) genuinely gather a far-flung –

even global – community together into what truly is a single religious tradition. Beneath this top layer, however, exist multiple strands of interpretation and practice, each claiming its own authenticity and authority. Persons in the same religious tradition may worship and live in very different ways – they may even have different deities or messianic expectations. Therefore, claims to "the only way our religion is" or "our religion teaches one thing" regarding a certain topic are rarely – if ever – correct. Religious women and their supporters have as a first counter-argument to such claims for relativism in human rights the fact of religious breadth, enhanced by numerous examples of practices whose validity and enforcement vary widely depending on region, class, or religious sub-group.

An examination of Hindu practices in India shows how diverse that tradition actually is, how much theological and practical variety it encompasses, and its potential for flexibility and progress regarding women's rights. Those conservatives who insist that Hinduism permits only one particular practice or lifestyle have their own religious tradition as the best evidence of their personal selectivity.[23] As with "Indian culture," Hinduism encompasses an overarching cosmology that is shared by and accessible to all Hindus. Meanwhile, in its particularities the tradition presents its own best evidence of its great breadth of belief and practice.

There are a handful of ancient sources of Hindu law with varying instructions regarding widow remarriage, property inheritance for women, and other issues. Among their many provisions, each provides particular boundaries on the social control of women, women's access to financial resources, the trading of women (via marriage), the reproductive capacity of women, and agricultural production by women. Region matters: the southern, Dravidian regions have always been more open to sources such as the Dravida school of the Mitakshara family law, the Dayabhaga, and others more favorable to women.[24] In Kerala (among other places) several castes are matrilineal; the roots of their practice are in the Marumakkathayam school. A few southern states have created government legislation to amend Hindu property provisions so that they will be more favorable to women (an interesting boundary-crossing by the public into the private). The local mores in much of South India permit Hindu women to work freely in the fields, enjoy relatively fewer restrictions on their mobility, and have better chances at inheritance than North Indian women. However, those same local mores are also very locally generated: among the Kottai Pillaimar of

Tamil Nadu, for instance, *purdah* for Hindu women is so severe that they are kept within a walled fortress.[25]

Purdah for Hindu women exists in many parts of India and in many different manifestations, often in response to the characteristics of *purdah* practiced by Muslim neighbors. As among Muslims, the ideal of purity is the intended object of protection. For Muslims the purity relates to notions of women's modesty, to a family's honor, and to women's sexual inaccessibility. Among Hindus, *purdah* is more likely to protect caste purity – to remove women from opportunities to mix their "blood" with men of other, particularly lower, castes. Again, family honor and sexual inaccessibility are key, but the notion of caste adds a particularly Hindu and religious function. In Madhya Pradesh, some Hindu communities expect women to pull their saris over their faces when they go out or when they meet respected males even in their own homes. In their natal villages, however, they need not adhere to this "*purdah*" at all.[26] In other regions, including in cities, some families will not permit their daughters and wives ever to leave the house, not formally as a practice of *purdah* but very intentionally to preserve their purity. All in all, Hindus practice – and Hinduism encompasses – a wide array of types of *purdah*, while some communities observe no restrictions of any kind. In practice, there exists no single or authoritative set of boundaries on Hindu women's movement and relationships.

The same is true of other practices, many of which are referenced in religious laws that conservatives portray as incontrovertible. The vast majority of castes, for instance, permit widow remarriage, in spite of the existence of authoritative ancient texts that forbid it. In many areas it is common for childless widows to remarry, but less so for widows with children still in the home. The widowed mothers themselves may not wish to remarry if they fear mistreatment by a second husband of their existing children or their loss of any rights to inherit the first husband's property. The same breadth of interpretation exists concerning divorce, with many communities permitting it in spite of the popular understanding that seminal texts forbid the practice. By the same token, cousin marriages are permitted in some parts of the country, even though the practice is usually looked down upon as "Muslim."

It is not only region, but also class that matters: wide variations exist in what is considered to be (and practiced as) "authentic Hinduism" based on a family or community's income and economic standing. The process of "Sanskritization" is widely considered to have negative impacts upon women's rights enjoyment. As families strive upward in terms of social standing, they sometimes adopt customs that they believe set the upper strata apart from others, including bans on widow remarriage, the introduction of child marriage, restrictions on women's movement, employment, and dress, and so on.[27] Ironically, in many Hindu families that are able to achieve greater economic standing the adherence to "orthodox" Hindu customs wanes. Younger generations find themselves with more education, more options, more employment, and more social freedom. The situation is different for lower class families even if they do not actively strive for higher social standing. Families that need the paid employment of every member just in order to survive do not have the option of practicing *purdah* or remaining unmarried after the death of a spouse. Even the husband-worship (*pativratya*) that is expected of Hindu wives in many parts of the country is not present among Dalit women, the lowest on the caste and income ladder. They are more likely to resist and even fight back any violence in their own family. It is a kind of violence that they are more able to repel, rather than the ever-present physical threat of caste-related violence.[28]

In short, Hinduism in India is not a monolithic tradition but a religion with many different interpretations and practices. Religious law and regional and family customs vary substantively. Hindu traditionalists who proclaim that the religion permits only certain practices, attitudes, and ways of life are easily shown to be selective and particular in their own presentation of the tradition. One western observer has described two indigenous Hinduisms, or two particular strands of Hinduism, each of which begets many modified schools of practice. One he describes as interior looking, rigid in social form, separate, exemplified in the caste system and unequal male–female relations, and cultivated by communalist groups such as the Jan Sangh and Rashtriya Sevak Sangh. The other has many ethical principles in common with liberal humanism, and stresses tolerance of diversity, openness, respect, and "the cosmic validity of all forms of worship."[29] Individual religious leaders are working to create what one Hindu scholar calls "new and refreshing theologies" to counter "the stifling ethos of classical theology."[30] The blanket acceptance by non-Hindus of some of the most reactionary policies that are proclaimed as normative by conservative religious communities is both inaccurate and damaging to efforts to secure rights for women.

Similarly, religious customs and interpretations vary widely in the global community of Muslims. The practice of *purdah* reveals much on this score. Many scholars of Islam (both Muslim and non-Muslim) now agree that *purdah* is a pre-Islamic cultural practice, not even Arabian in its origins but probably derived from one of the early communities to which Islam spread (most likely Persia). The Qur'an's strong injunction that women and men be modest in physical appearance does not contradict the practice of *purdah; purdah* can be understood as one (extreme) interpretation of the Qur'anic mandate to cover oneself appropriately in public. Veiling and seclusion are not, however, a part of the Prophet's original revelation. Consequently, *purdah* means very different things in different parts of the *umma*. In some regions a woman is considered to be appropriately modest because she wears a headscarf and clothing that covers her arms and legs. In others, women are inappropriate if they wear, in public, anything less than a sheet covering them from head to toe with a mesh screen in front of the eyes through which to see. In other regions, women are considered appropriately dressed even if their arms, legs, and hair are exposed. Often, the difference in interpretations of the injunction to be physically modest depends on the culture of the society (whether or not variations on the practice are indigenous) or the political, social, and economic goals of those in power. If women are needed in the workforce, restrictions regarding *purdah* are eased. If power is being sought or retained through appeals to conservative religion, the qualifications for *purdah* are strengthened. Advocates for women's rights insist that *purdah* conflicts with the Women's Convention in several important ways. Specifically, *purdah* excludes women from economic and political participation, violates the principle of gender equality, and perpetuates negative stereotypes that hinder the advancement of women.[31]

Meanwhile, some Muslim women find *purdah* to be positive, even liberating.[32] Seclusion means that they are freed from outside jobs that are grinding, repetitive, or simply a burden. Their seclusion is a proud, public confirmation of their rise to the middle class, and their ability to get by without women's contributions to family income. Veiling also means that, when on the street or in the market, they need not fear harassment or violence from male passersby. Some women, of course, view seclusion and/or veiling as important elements in the expression of their personal faith.

Similarly, the practice of female genital cutting predates Islam. No Qur'anic verses refer to it, although in one saying of the Prophet he is recorded as receiving holy advice to advocate the removal of only a small portion of the clitoris *if* the procedure is to be done. Even this *hadith* leaves open the choice of whether or not to "circumcise."[33] Clitoridectomy and infibulation are practiced in more than 20 African countries, as well as Malaysia, Indonesia, southern parts of the Arabian peninsula, Pakistan, some communities of the former Soviet Union, the United Arab Emirates, Oman, Bahrain, South Yemen, Peru, Brazil, eastern Mexico, and among Australian aborigines.[34] Few scholars would assert that the practice is a mandated ritual within Islam. Many Muslim communities do not perform the procedures, while numerous non-Muslim ones do. Sudan, whose majority (and governing) population is Muslim, outlawed female genital cutting in 1946, although the practices remain quite prevalent. Clitoridectomy and infibulation have achieved, in some regions, the status of a genuinely religious rite of passage, an unquestioned and important component of female "modesty."

Nahid Toubia has written that the primary reason for the perpetuation of the practices is marriageability – a socially constructed criterion for gauging and insuring the sexual "purity" of women at time of marriage.[35] Like *purdah*, even if clitoridectomy and infibulation are pre-Islamic and non-Qur'anic, they have come, over the centuries, to take on the aspect of a religiously meaningful act, thanks to manipulated theology and bad sociology. As such, advocates for the end of these practices would do well not to dismiss them simply as cultural holdovers but to investigate what they mean, religiously, to those women and men who support them. The most productive strategy would be to treat them as religious rituals (while still educating others as to their non-religious roots), and simultaneously pointing to the great breadth of interpretation within Islam as a challenge to their validity and importance.

A similar breadth of interpretation obtains regarding women's ability to vote. Some Muslim states have long permitted it, others more recently have legalized it (Yemen, for example); others still, such as Saudi Arabia, staunchly refuse women the right to vote, and all of it in the name of Islam. Access to abortion and contraception also is very different for women in different countries. As Marie-Aimée Hélie-Lucas writes,

> Both are legal in Tunisia; both are enforced on women in Bangladesh together with sterilization for both sexes; contraception is allowed but abortion forbidden in Pakistan. Algeria has forbidden both for a long time (from 1962 till 1974) in spite of a *fatwa* issued a year after independence by the High Islamic council in Algiers; it finally allowed contraception when our annual population growth rate had reached 3.5, threatening the wealth and privileges of the ex-socialist bureaucrats who by then had turned into a classical bourgeoisie owning the means of production. All these countries claim that they defined their population policy according to the spirit of Islam. In each country, people and certainly women are made to believe that the rules enforced locally or nationally reflect the spirit of Islam and

> are injunctions of God that Muslim states apply in their legislation. Moreover, the official discourse implies or eventually states that these laws are Islamic.[36]

Abortion and contraception, therefore, are practiced in a great variety of ways in the Muslim world, with each understanding proclaimed to be religiously authoritative (although often interpreted on the basis of the economic and political needs of states).

Even religious communities within the same region and state vary widely in their practices. Indian (Sunni) Muslims, for example, may follow the Hanafi, Shafi, Hambali, and Maliki traditions (the first two are the most prevalent), while Indian Shiites follow the Ismaili and Ithna Ashari schools. There are substantive differences among each, and also among the ways the individual traditions are interpreted in local communities. Additionally, studies of Muslim practices throughout the country have shown that *Shari'a* is consistently overridden by local social custom.[37] In India, *Shari'a* was not invoked as a basis of law until the beginning of the twentieth century, with the evolution of concerns for community differentiation and identity (and this after some centuries of Muslim rule).[38] Perhaps this relatively recent introduction of the authority of *Shari'a* contributes to the fact that it so often takes second place after local custom. *Shari'a* is not the single authoritative source that religious conservatives often portray it to be, and as a result there is a wide variety of "religious" practices amongst Indian Muslim families.[39]

Sometimes this may do a positive service to women, as when divorce (including triple *talaq*) is stigmatized in the local culture and thus discouraged because of the whole family's perceived loss of social standing.[40] Sometimes the relative absence of legal authority does a disservice to women, as in the fact that very few Muslim families follow the rules of inheritance for women. Some communities, for instance the Gujar Bakarwals, make small compensation by giving women movable property such as animals as part of their dowries, saying that this nullifies any claim to other family property. Other communities, such as the Meos of Rajasthan, claim that because they will take in married daughters if their husbands are absent, this removes any claim to inheritance. In the end, most Muslim inheritance practices are just like their Hindu neighbors', whatever the local custom may prescribe.[41]

Consequently, as with Hinduism, region is a very important variable in the way Islam is practiced in India. Certain overarching prescriptions to do with the basic structure of family life are understood as important to Muslim families throughout the country, yet there is great variety in actual practice thanks to the social conditions through which the various tenets are filtered.[42] In general, local Hindu norms have strong influence in Muslim families. The great majority of Indian Muslims are converts from Hinduism, and most converted not as individual families but as whole caste groups. Group conversion resulted in greatly reduced pressure to drop Hindu rituals after conversion, since there was no new need to differentiate oneself religiously from one's neighbors, and because the whole community continued its collective, culturally local memory of "how to do things."[43] The Hindu notion of caste remains a particularly strong influence on the sensibilities of those Indians who have converted to other religions, especially regarding codes of personal and collective purity.

While most Muslims in India are strongly patrilineal, some Keralite Muslims are matrilineal (the Moplahs), in keeping with the practices of their Hindu Nair neighbors. These families have adopted the practice of dowry and abandoned the giving of *mehr*. Husbands move into their wives' natal homes and are not expected to inherit property or maintain their wives. Among other Keralite Muslims who are patrilineal, men inherit property in accordance with standard Islamic law and bring wives to live in a house of their own.[44] Strong local Hindu custom concerning joint family living has also been shown to influence the practice of Muslim neighbors; the Karkhanedars of Delhi, Muslims in Dharwar, Karnataka, and those in eastern Uttar Pradesh closely observe the local custom of joint family structure. One Indian researcher of family practices has concluded succinctly, "Muslim family norms in India correspond closely to those held among Hindus," and *local* Hindus at that, given the breadth of religious interpretation in that community as well.[45]

As with Hindus, class also plays a strong role in how families and communities interpret religious instruction. While not appropriately called "Sanskritization," the same upward social striving occurs among Muslims. As with Hindus, the same irony obtains, as upper class families loosen restrictions on women's movement, education, and employment possibilities, while lower classes tighten them in order to heighten their perceived respectability.[46] Other studies have shown that fertility rates for Muslim women are related not to religious teaching but to education levels and socio-economic status.[47] Further studies have revealed that commonalities of education and class are the basis of commonalities in family life and that neighboring Hindus and Muslims of the same economic stratum have more in common with each other than they do with their co-religionists in the same region.[48]

The influential presence of Islamists in India suggests that there may be a movement towards the centralizing of religious law, particularly though emphasis on *Shari'a*. The effect may be to counter the regional, slightly syncretistic way that Muslims currently structure their family and social relations. Or it may not. Imtiaz Ahmad has written that introduction of *Shari'a* as a monolithic and all-encompassing body of law "often . . . results in the displacement of one set of heterodox principles by another set of practices which are equally heterodox." Ahmad continues,

> Far from promoting strict adherence to elements of the sharia, Islamization has allowed the different Muslim communities in India to either legitimize local customs and practices or to reconcile them with sharia. It has, in other words, allowed the Muslim communities to have, and to project, a truly Islamic image of themselves and yet continue to remain an integral part of the cultural complex in which they are embedded.[49]

Long-held local customs that have come to hold religious significance are, it would seem, strong and elastic enough to continue, despite any attempt to homogenize them. The presence of a great variety of Muslim traditions and practices will continue to be the norm.

In sum, the reality for Indian Muslim women in terms of religious instruction for family life is quite the same as that of Hindu women. For both communities there are a number of schools of law from which to follow, laxity in levels of adherence, numerous ways to interpret them, strong influence from local and regional culture, and similarly strong influence from neighboring religions (often it is all a big blend of local culture and religions). Religious traditionalists who assert that Islam prescribes a single set of practices, attitudes and lifestyles are simply incorrect, both in theory and in practice.

A similar disparity exists among predominantly Christian countries, where differences of theological perspective (and the extent to which religion is intentionally separated from national policy-making) make for very different scenarios. Both abortion and divorce, for instance, are legal in the United States and Great Britain, while in predominantly Roman Catholic Latin America abortion is largely illegal. Divorce is newly legal yet abortion is not allowed in the Republic of Ireland.[50] Local culture exerts as significant an influence upon Christianity as it does Hinduism and Islam. In parts of sub-Saharan Africa, for instance, formal western marriage ceremonies are seldom performed. Christian couples live and have children together – with the approval of their clergy and religious community – in a way that would be considered anathema to some Christians in other parts of the world.

In some liberal Protestant communities, women are permitted not only to be ordained as ministers but also to hold leadership positions within dioceses and denominations. In Catholic, Orthodox, and conservative Protestant denominations and rites women are either permitted a modest amount of leadership or are outright banned from it – both literally and figuratively. Females may not be allowed to hold leadership positions within the communion, or may be fully prevented even from approaching the altar during worship, so deep is the antipathy towards women as either secondary humans or the historical conduit of evil.

Efforts by conservative Christians in every country to counter the rise in the number of women in the workforce by proclaiming that the entirety of their existence should be in the home are manifesting the same controlling dynamic as Hindu and Muslim seclusion. In other Christian communities, meanwhile, women are permitted sexual and reproductive rights, are permitted to move freely and are encouraged to work. Some Christian communities understand men to be the "natural" leaders of families and municipalities (in accordance with their interpretation of certain biblical passages), while others view women as equally qualified for leadership in any setting (in accordance with their interpretation of the same or other biblical passages).[51]

The fact of theological breadth in all of the world's religions, therefore, is a first and very defensible response to religious relativists' claims for exemption from international rights standards. Advocates for women's rights may see the issue as an opportunity to exercise personal *choice* in the matter of religious practice – to decide for oneself which rituals, scriptural interpretations, and theological perspectives should be adhered to. Such choice making is not, however, possible for some of the world's women (see Chapter 6 for a fuller discussion of the issue). Furthermore, conservative religious leaders may defend their positions by saying that certain persons alone have the authority to interpret which actions and beliefs comprise an appropriately religious life, and that the very concept of theological breadth is contrary to their religion's teachings. The simple assertion of theological breadth, then, may be perceived as a challenge to the defenders' freedom of religion.[52]

Selectivity in interpretation

A second argument against claims to religious relativism (and one closely related to the notion of theological breadth) is the fact of the selectivity exercised in determining which practices will be authoritative, and for whom. Indeed, the issues that today are called human rights abuses for women are not new – they existed long before the international legal community reached this particular consensus on what to call them. But some of the most discriminatory or disempowering religious practices gain legitimacy because they are genuinely old and because they are selectively maintained. For many women the problem is not that they are living under religious law, but that such law is being selectively retrieved from a corpus of time-worn practices and applied to them with the effect of keeping them disempowered.

Islam happens to offer the clearest examples of selective application of gender-discriminating religious law, simply because the tradition is, in many locations, so formally legalistic. As numerous commentators have noted, *Shari'a* continues to be interpreted in its most traditional, retrograde forms when the subject is women.[53] Earliest (and therefore, to conservatives, the most authoritative) Islamic law contained no references to economic endeavors such as banking and insurance. "Islamic" ways of practicing these things have since been constructed, but conveniently without the tempering of authentic *Shari'a* injunctions against usury, huge profits, monopolies, and the required financial redistribution of the *zakat* tax.[54] Business matters have been fully accommodated to the globalizing business world in order for Muslim men to compete for self-enrichment in global capitalism.

Legists also have selectively interpreted ancient injunctions on modesty for men and women. The original instruction is the same for both sexes – a lowered gaze in public, avoidance of ostentatious displays of jewelry or wealth, appropriate covering of the body with clothing, and so on. Contemporary teaching on its significance, however, has placed the burden of a whole society's "modesty" literally on the (covered) heads of women. Where older interpretations no longer serve a government's particular needs, traditions are again selectively reinterpreted. For example, the *hijab* currently sponsored by Islamists in urban parts of some countries as an ancient and authentic tradition is actually a new creation. This particular form of dress for women (a large scarf covering the hair and shoulders, and a full-length coat over trousers or dark stockings) permits them enough physical dexterity with which to work but covers so much of their bodies as to further entrench conservative notions of the corrupting potential of women's bodies. One Iranian-born scholar calls the *hijab*, "a quite novel and contemporary ensemble, deployed as a uniform."[55]

Great selectivity of interpretation is also employed in the terms under which women are married and divorced. Some schools of legal thought permit a woman to include in her pre-nuptual agreement a prohibition on her husband's taking another wife while still married to her, plus a right to "persuade" her husband to divorce her in the event that she wants to end the marriage. This option is rarely made known to women.[56] Women are similarly given partial information about their financial future after having been divorced. The common understanding is that women will be returned the dowry (*mehr*) that they brought to the marriage, and be modestly maintained by their former husbands for the period of the *iddat*. Another, more favorable practice, one derived from *Ayat* 241 of the Qur'an, is called *mataa*. It requires a man to make reasonable provision for his divorced wife (perhaps in a lump sum or continuing payments) without a time limit such as the *iddat*. Conservative Sunni legists, when reminded of this teaching, assert that it was only ever meant to apply to the very pious, and not to the general population.[57] In fact, women have in this injunction a solid argument in the religious courts for greater financial compensation after divorce. Again, it is an option that is rarely made known to women.

Even the most firmly entrenched religious practices can be selectively modified when economic interests will be served. For instance, in Bangladesh women from rich households are permitted to leave their homes and travel (alone if necessary) to a city for several days in order to conduct business in court, and the action is deemed to be responsibly within the boundaries of *purdah*. Poor women who wish to leave their homes for several hours to attend a meeting are called *bepurdah* – "not-purdah." As one scholar notes, "Clearly, tradition is a human creation and the interpretation and enforcement of tradition is at some person's or some group's discretion: in many cases, the discretion of the rich and the powerful."[58]

Westernization

Appeals to religious relativism are, in many cases, simultaneously supported by and supportive of movements to remove "western" influences from particular societies. Westernization is said to lead to a loss of religious integrity[59] – the more western the society, the further removed it must be from the practice of "true" religion. The roots of various movements to dewesternize extend far beyond religion, although integrity of religious practice is sometimes proclaimed to be the goal. Modernization and westernization are often conflated, creating a kind of double standard in those states that dearly wish to enjoy the positive aspects of modernity, urbanization, and industrialization while consolidating political power through appeals to traditional religion (for instance, the Muslim Brotherhood in Egypt). As will be discussed in the next chapter, efforts to modernize the public realm while dewesternizing the private inordinately affect the rights of women.

Westernization, rather than modernization, is very particularly understood as the culprit in some traditionalist religious movements. These communities resent what they consider to be forced cultural homogenization and the unspoken assumption that the process is both natural and inevitable. One Indian Christian scholar has written of communities' employment of traditionalist religion to quell their "qualms of conscience" regarding their appropriation of "Western lifestyle, consumption, economic practices, and English language."[60] Conservative, "authentic" religious practices can assuage negative feelings about the appropriation of foreign ideologies, especially if that appropriation is, on certain levels, experienced as enticing, strategic, or enjoyable. Another conservative religious response to perceived westernization is couched, subtly or not so subtly, in nationalism, such as the Hindutva movement in India. A comprehensive, conservative religious identity is identified as the nation's bulwark against foreign policies that are perceived as disempowering and marginalizing the country as a whole.

Another kind of double standard obtains when governments select which western elements to retain (for the sake of building their own power base) and claim as religiously indigenous, and which to jettison as imperialist holdovers. The very institution of the nation-state, for example, is western in origin but uncontested in dewesternizing efforts.[61] Human rights are sometimes said to be western, at other times claimed as autochthonous, although usually with different criteria than in the international instruments.[62] In the end, alternative "religious" rights schemes continue to borrow heavily from the west.[63]

A complicating factor for women in the dewesternizing process is the lingering resentment of many men and women of the paternalistic, imperialist "improvements" for women made during colonization. Cultural and/or religious customs for women that differed greatly from those of Europe were belittled or outlawed (such as *sati*); countries were considered to have become more "civilized" when certain religious customs for women were discarded. Today, religious conservatives in and out of governments call for a return to many traditional practices or modes of dress for women as part of a triumphant vanquishing of the last vestiges of forced westernization (such as veiling). Women are the human currency in these efforts to reassert non-western paternalism. In a particularly ambiguous situation are those women who approve of efforts to remove all traces of colonialism and to celebrate religious pride and independence, but who resent the loss of status and rights enjoyment that such a return to traditional practices would entail. While they support the practice of religion as a kind of popular resistance, they realize that the terms of that resistance mean that they themselves will pay for it.[64] Religious women everywhere pay for societies' dewesternization if that process includes self-exemption from women's rights norms.

Political uses of religion

Arguably, what is religious is, by its very nature, inherently political. Another factor in some appeals to religious relativism is the intentional political uses of certain rights infringements for women that are made in the name of religion but whose ultimate aim is the consolidation of secular power. Religious and political communities everywhere are responding to societal forces far beyond their own borders. For instance, the globalization of capitalism has, in some regions, promoted deterritorialization and alienation. The consequent uprooting – physical, psychological, and political – can make traditional religion an attractive focus for national attention.[65] The further entrenchment of political, military, and economic power in particular countries deepens senses of insecurity and inferiority. In some regions what follows is a search for national and communal identity that finds its most influential leaders among conservative religious authorities, ones who frame the search for identity in three ways: "identity as threatened; identity as a process of 'going back'; and, identity confined to the private sphere."[66] As a result, *Shari'a, dharma,* and "biblical morality" become political ideologies in support of religious nationalisms and communalisms. The institutions of the family and of education frequently become new proving grounds for the validity of religion as well as foci for national policy,[67] with immense consequences for women's rights enjoyment.

Some critics of the political use of Hinduism in India point to what they see as the government's blatant promotion of one particular strand of the religion as authentic. This project is independent from the intentionally communal Hindu political organizations but services their agenda nonetheless. Through official and popular mention in text books, and so on, the government promotes, "the Brahmanic Darsanas which accept the sanctity of Vedas as the legitimate Hinduism. As a corollary the modern Hindu accepts the Upanishads and Brahma Sutras and the theology of the Advaita Vedanta as synonymous with Hinduism." Meanwhile, anti-Brahminical sects and other movements are subtly but officially de-emphasized, as the state sponsors a particular version of Hinduism to suit its own interests for power consolidation.[68] For at least a decade before the electoral triumph of Hindu communalism, the state was pouring support into communal activities. Conservative religion was used as a convenient brushfire, a distraction from government initiatives that were sure to be unpopular, such as cutbacks in social services, falling real incomes, and financial assistance to owners of large industries and agricultural businesses.

The current revival of traditional religion in some communities has strong political and economic foundations. Within societies, calls for all-inclusive practice of conservative, traditional religion sometimes reflect internal struggles for power or influence. Rural and petty-bourgeois persons are largely behind appeals for "Islamization" (the Zia al-Haq program in Pakistan, for example); this same economic stratum also lends great support to Hindu nationalism in India and to "Christian" politics in the United States. They are built on genuine religious sentiment, but they are also naked political movements, attempts to consolidate group power. In each case, personal access to political and economic power structures can be improved when religion can be manipulated. Religious practice is accessible to all; it can aid in improving one's social standing and legitimacy, and can serve as a tool to gain access to economic and political strata that are higher than one's own.[69] Again, women's rights enjoyment is often compromised as traditional religion is employed for social and economic self-improvement by certain sectors of society.

The case of the Christian Coalition, the Moral Majority, and similar groups in the United States is important to remember, if only because it serves as a reminder that politicized religion is not the province only of poor countries and non-Christians. The Republican party in the United States became a strong ally of rightist Christian groups during the campaigns and presidency of Ronald Reagan not because of flagrantly sexist policies of its own but because the organizations promised to deliver many votes. Republicans were able to use the social and theological rhetoric to appeal to non-wealthy conservative voters whose own financial interests were to be significantly disserved by Republican policies. George W. Bush has similarly allied himself with the Christian right.

Many Muslim commentators have noted the skillful use of the very concept of *Shari'a* as a tool to build the power of the *ulema*.[70] Women in particular are used to construct a sense of group cohesiveness that can be manipulated by those who govern. A focus on women's piety also serves to distract populations' attention from real issues, such as political repression, insurgencies, widespread poverty, and the privileges enjoyed by a small elite.[71] In the words of one Saudi woman,

> When governments impose a certain set of beliefs on individuals, through propaganda, violence, or torture, we are dealing not with culture but rather with political expediency.
>
> The claim that such practices are cultural is dangerous, if not racist.
>
> When a woman walks down the street in Saudi Arabia without a veil and the Mutawwi'in (religious police) flog her, this is not cultural, it's political. Who gave permission to the Mutawwi'in? The government. They fear that women will try to change things, and they'll lose their political power....
>
> The status of women in the Middle East is deteriorating, not because of Islam as some claim, but because of political repression.
>
> Islam is being manipulated. In the Middle East, as everywhere else, men would do anything to preserve their power and authority.
>
> In Saudi Arabia, the veil is just a form of oppression, a way for men to say they have power over women....
>
> In the Middle East, men have chosen to exploit Islam for their own interests, not out of piety or fear of Allah. But elsewhere men have used other religions or ideologies to achieve personal political gains.[72]

In the words of Moroccan scholar Fatima Mernissi, "if women's rights are a problem for some Muslim men, it is neither because of the Koran or the Prophet, nor the Islamic tradition, but simply because those rights conflict with the interests of a male elite."[73]

Three methods in particular have been employed by Islamists in order to reshape the individual's relation to society. The first is an emphasis on the *umma*. The second is the creation of, and emphasis upon, non-religious activities and services that bring people together, help them identify their interests as being mutual, and relocate their focus for personal problem solving from secular to religious resources. The third is the public identification of a common enemy, a "them" who is opposed to "us."[74] Muslim fundamentalists capitalize upon rapid urbanization and its resulting social and economic fallout, upon common disaffection with state authority, the experience of colonialism, and the pressures of being dependent upon the world economic system.[75] Islamist organizations run schools, clinics, and social and sports clubs both to make up for government lapses in these areas and as sites for reinforcing their ideologies. Recruits to Islamic groups are often "young, male, urban, modern-educated, lower to middle class," as James Piscatori reports. The poor, unemployed and uneducated also sometimes find Islamist rhetoric appealing, but may have experienced less instability due to economic restructuring since they never had much to lose.[76]

Harsh boundaries are constructed as to who and what are enemies of the faith. In some areas disagreements emerge within the religious leadership, and various Islamist anti-government groups compete with one another in advancing virtually the same agenda. Government, however, remains the primary target of Islamist disapproval. As Piscatori explains, "Islamist movements are a 'second-order reaction.'" They are "not so much a reaction to the failures of modernization ... but ... a reaction to the failures of leaders – religious as well as political – to deal with those failures," such as when "leaders respond ineptly or uncreatively to the increasing economic difficulties and deterioration of public services."[77] Islamic leaders use the economic distress caused by structural adjustment and liberalization programs to support their movement for increased power in society. As Valentine Moghadam says of the economic downturn in Jordan, "Poverty, inequality, unemployment, and challenges to the patriarchal gender contract have been singled out by Islamist movements as reasons why existing states are no longer viable and why Islamic codes need to be reintroduced or strengthened." However, "no Islamic movement or state has been able to adequately address or resolve the economic crisis, or to suggest an alternative to economic restructuring and globalization."[78]

Manipulations may happen in the opposite direction, however. Not only do religious organizations seek to capitalize upon political causes, but political parties occasionally seek to co-opt the agendas of conservative religious groups, viewing their organizing potential as an enviable complement to their own movement. Arguably, this was the case with recent Republican political campaigns and the American Christian right. Such was the case in Algeria with the FIS, which originated as a religious movement but was transformed into a political one by actors who sought to harness its power for their own project.[79] The existence of multiple and sometimes competing projects within the umbrella term "Islamization" points to an important similarity that it shares with globalization. While each would appear monolithic in form and intention, introducing consolidation and unification to a large process and population, in reality both Islamization and globalization are composed of significant "contradictions, volatilities, and disorder."[80]

Globalization's impact on conservative religious movements is not limited to majority Muslim or Hindu societies or to countries whose populations are largely being disserved by the process. In the United States, for example, which is commonly thought of as reaping the gains of the current economic and political processes, conservative Christians have seen their organization and power grow. The increased economic conservatism in the 1970s and 1980s in the United States, Canada, and Britain, and the resulting shifts in the global economy, provided theological conservatives with more political capital. While fundamentalist movements in poorer countries are significantly a response to the negative effects of societal restructuring, in the United States such movements are significantly a response to restructuring's spoils. Christian fundamentalists are quite concerned to safeguard the social, political, economic, and religious power that they have acquired in the last four decades. A central campaign of conservative Christian organizations is a reduction in the size of the government. Having now reached the middle class, these religious conservatives do not want (because they do not need) spending on social welfare. They disapprove of many of the policies of the larger, more powerful, post-World War II governments, ones whose spending and court decisions may contradict their moral viewpoints.[81] The more powerful the government and courts, the more likely it is that important ethical decisions will be beyond one's control.

This sense of loss of control, of being subjected to social forces that one is powerless to suppress, is a feature shared with citizens of poorer countries. In many ways, conservative religious movements in wealthy countries are actually fanned by the same phenomena as those in poorer countries. Despite relative wealth, orderly economic and political institutions, civil liberties, and abundant resources, American fundamentalists fear instability and a loss of personal and global influence.[82] They are not incorrect. American power and hegemony have been reduced since the World War II (although it might not seem so to other regions of the world). Armed conflicts in Iran, Vietnam, Central America, Afghanistan, Iraq and other parts of the Middle East are experienced as symptoms of dwindling power. Although the United States has the largest national economy in the world it is challenged by those of the European Union, Japan and, increasingly, China. Far from being simply the causal agent in societal restructuring, the United States is *being* restructured, as both positive and negative trends reveal regarding education, health care, technology, the environment, and other systems.

To Christian fundamentalists the great adversary is not westernization but atheism, secular humanism, communism, and socialism.[83] Fundamentalists may enjoy high levels of participation in education, health care and technology, yet still feel distanced from what they sense to be "urban" or "foreign" cultural influences in each. "Biblical morality" is offered as an appealing alternative to the insecurities of transition, one that will provide cultural control, permanency, and ethical authority.[84] Globalized Americans, whatever their religious tastes, may experience modernization's underside – ambivalence, loss of community, demographic dislocation, the end of certain traditions, and a feeling of inauthenticity. The spending power of the dollar is lower than it was in the 1970s, so while American families can point to consistent wage increases over the decades they also understand, sometimes only viscerally, that they are less well off than they used to be. Fundamentalists organize politically around these sentiments, often framing them as issues of secularization, advances in science, uniformity in educational curricula, industrialization, and strong centralized government.[85] In the end, as Peter Beyer writes, the Christian right in the United States attempts "to limit the inclusive tendencies of the global system by asserting the exclusive validity of a particular group culture."[86]

They share this project, this response to transition, with Islamists, Hindu nationalists, and other traditionalist religious groups. Like them, they also endeavor to shape more than to limit the direction of modernization, industrialization, economic liberalization, and other processes. And like these other conservative religious movements, Christian fundamentalists place strong emphasis upon sex, the family, and the appropriate role of women. The family is proclaimed to be the crucial institution for the instruction and perpetuation of the legitimate use of the body. Beyer concludes, "If the United States is to regain its dominance in the world, its families must maintain a structure that consistently yields individuals motivated to channel their energies for the sake of their nation and not in pursuit of sensual pleasure.... Families, therefore, exist to foster necessary bodily control."[87] Nancy Ammerman writes, "The restoration of patriarchy in household and public life is the ideal." Strong men are needed to lead the family and the nation, while weak men are those who come under the influence of strong women. Ammerman continues, "the rhetoric of patriarchy and submission serves primarily as a normative counterweight to the individualistic and hedonistic ways of the larger society. The rhetorical contrast is between a secular world where people put personal pleasure ahead of family responsibility and a religious community where individuals accept their rightful and God-given roles and responsibilities."[88] Control over women, their sexuality, and their role in the family is crucial to the Christian fundamentalist project, particularly as it responds to prevailing societal transitions.

Martin Riesebrodt, a sociologist of religion, concludes the following:

> When we analyze fundamentalist ideologies in terms of their posited ideal social order, we find a consistent emphasis on patriarchal structures. The ideal family is the patriarchal family where the father is responsible for the public sphere (economy, politics) and the women for the private sphere (home, children). The economic ideal extols family enterprise and a religious integration of "capital" and "labor" instead of institutionalized class-conflict, "big business," and "big labor." The political ideal ascribes to the state primarily the role of a protector of the moral order, but otherwise eschews intervention into people's affairs. Private charity based on social, moral, and religious control constitutes the fundamentalist idea of brotherhood. It is distinctly opposed to the depersonalized structures of the welfare state. Therefore, in my view, fundamentalism is primarily a radical patriarchalism.[89]

Fundamentalisms and other conservative political uses of religion are structured on the acquisition or maintenance of power by groups whose strategy often involves the disempowerment of women. When rights norms for women threaten that disempowerment, relativist arguments are sometimes employed to safeguard the political project.

Religious developments

Exemptions from rights norms are occasionally demanded by religious leaders who insist upon the immutability of their tradition – their religion has been practiced in a certain way for many centuries and so any calls for change are inappropriate. This claim is false. No religion exists in a vacuum, pure, impervious to and unmodified by any outside influences. Religions are not hermetically sealed. Each has been influenced by other religions (some began as offshoots of other religions) or other cultures, and will continue to do so. What becomes adopted is chosen because of its appeal to members of the tradition. Calls from conservative religious leaders to live as "authentically" as possible often mean to live as "anciently" as possible, recovering the original practices of the religion. Scholars of human rights such as Rhoda Howard and Abdullahi Ahmed An-Na'im have asserted that a return to the life of five centuries (not to mention several millennia) ago, now that colonial powers are physically gone, is literally impossible.[90] Full exposure has already been had to very different ways of ordering practical and spiritual life. Different institutions and values have been fully adapted to local situations. There is no going back. There is also no way of knowing what past historical practices and attitudes were exactly like. In the absence of real data, selective interpretations are made (by those with the power to do so) to serve modern agendas.

Often a tradition's history becomes romanticized, idealized as a time when the religion was politically or theologically triumphant, enjoying an absolute absence of social or political problems. Conditions for women are often portrayed as having been immeasurably better. Even if they did not enjoy many of the liberties craved by modern women, the truly religious society offered them something much more to be desired: the loving support of an inclusive, comprehensive kinship system in which women, although the property of male relatives, led lives of perfect happiness since they wanted for nothing.[91] Fueling such idealizing of the past and such claims to immutability is fear of current change. "Movement and change," writes Fatima Mernissi, come to be seen "as social imbalance and moral disintegration."[92] Another Muslim scholar describes such essentializing of "ancient" religion as "Orientalism in reverse," something he views as "no less reactionary, mystifying, ahistorical, and anti-human" than basic Orientalism.[93] In the end, the defense of discriminatory practices in the name of a religion's immutability is completely unfounded, although as an argument against the appropriation of modern rights standards it is quite compelling. As one writer states, "It is the struggles of the present that create the myths; it is the reverence for the past that give [*sic*] them power and control."[94]

Religions change. No religion is practiced, or could be practiced, as it was either centuries or millennia ago. A last counterpoint to religious relativists is the ever-transforming face of religious practice, the fluid movement of transformation and evolution in religious perspectives. "The way it has always been" is hardly – if ever – true.

Conclusion

Self-exemptions from rights norms in the name of religious freedom include the implicit demand, "You have to respect difference." The answer to the claim is a resounding "Yes, but." Yes, the preservation of religious autonomy and integrity is extremely important, as is the freedom to live in accordance with one's deepest beliefs. But, for each case an analysis must be done of the theological basis of the claim, any political objectives behind the claim, and what women stand to gain or lose in terms of power because of it. The question is less one of moral universalism versus relativism between rights and religion, and more one of universalism within religious traditions – whether or not (and how) conservative religious leaders and followers may adopt indigenous theological positions that do not perpetuate the subordination of women. A forced homogenization of ethical principles is the last thing desired – both within religions and between them. Difference must be respected indeed, but it must and need not be at the expense of justice for women.

Just as each religion encompasses an indigenous framework for gender equity, the human rights idea has the same flexibility, the same malleability that perpetuates its relevance in different contexts. The universalist/relativist dichotomy is too totalizing, as Richard Wilson has noted, and does not permit different actors to manipulate the rights idea to suit the particularities of various social and religious contexts.[95] Such contextualization of rights discourse does not imply or require its relativization or clear the way for it to be made substanceless in the form of a "religious" rights construct that eviscerates all criteria for real gender justice. The human rights construct has relevance for (and so has been appropriated by) people in most cultures and religious traditions.[96] The various moldings of the construct to accommodate local history and experience, identities, beliefs, and modernities are testimonies not to the relativism of the rights notion but its breadth and elasticity.

If the human rights notion is to be of help to women subordinated in the name of religious ideology and practice, then the issue of relativism must be phased out of the ongoing conversation on religion and rights. This is not to deny the importance of questions of difference and universalism, but to acknowledge that the religions and the rights notion have enough breadth to accommodate religious women's rights in every context. As long as the discourse on religious women's rights has to accommodate "moral relativism" the conservative religious leaders will have the upper hand. The human rights notion has not, in more than fifty years in international law, erased or relativized the moral foundations of the religions and it never will. It does not have the power. In many communities, the introduction of moral relativism to the conversation will significantly challenge reformers' work. Supporters of religious women must move beyond the no-win relativism debate and encourage the many legitimate voices within each tradition that are already proclaiming that violence and subordination are not religiously defensible.

5
The Question of Privacy

O father you brought my brother up to be happy,
You brought me up for shedding tears,
O father, you have brought your son up to give him your house,
And you have left a cage for me.

Song of a Hindu bride[1]

Claims for exemption from human rights standards that are made in the name of the preservation of one's privacy are a powerful inhibitor of religious women's rights. The qualities of gender and of religious practice that create such a specialized "conversation within a conversation" in terms of relativism are also at play in matters of privacy. Often, religion is said to belong to what is most private in the lives of individuals and communities. It is literally a sacred area, where governmental and other regulations must not tread. Equally private, and therefore unregulable, are the home and the family. Religious women in some communities are thus doubly removed from the public, and from guarantees of rights protection afforded in the public sphere, while rights infringements perpetuated in the family in the name of religion become doubly beyond the reach of state protection.

The examples and arguments in these pages intend to show that while claims for separable public and private spheres are far from being airtight, appeals to privacy are tremendously effective in preventing some religious women from enjoying human rights. Informal and formal rights to privacy and to free religious practice trump other rights norms for women, and the rights concept *per se* is not only unhelpful in securing women's rights but can become an accessory in denying them entirely. Reasons include the embeddedness of the idea of privacy within the human rights concept, the fact that even those instruments that do guarantee rights protection in the home can be interpreted also to require states to protect injurious practices there, the unwillingness of States Parties to enforce the protections that do exist, liberal theorists' challenges to the reach of instruments into the family and home (an example of the lack of conviction with which even liberal governments approach existing protections), the power of formal and informal personal status laws, religious insistence on a public/private dichotomy, and the manipulation of privacy by states and religious communities to serve their own ends. In some contexts, the human rights idea is thus rendered ineffective in securing religious women's human rights.

Privacy and the human rights construct

The concept of human rights is a philosophical product of liberalism, and like liberalism, in many articulations, wedded to the notion of a public/private dichotomy. "Central to liberalism is the concept of privacy as a sphere of behaviour free from public interference, that is, unregulated by law," writes legal scholar Kate O'Donovan.[2] She describes the classical liberal perspective on the public/private dichotomy as follows:

> "Public" may be used to denote state activity, the values of the market-place, work, the male domain or that sphere of activity which is regulated by laws. "Private" may denote civil society, the values of family, intimacy, the personal life, home, women's domain or behaviours unregulated by law... Those areas such as the personal, sexuality, biological reproduction, family, home, which are particularly identified socially as women's domain, are also seen as private.[3]

Early theorists contributed to the nascent human rights idea the understanding of separable spheres differentiated by gender. In his *Second Treatise* John Locke excluded the family from civil society (i.e., formally constituted institutions and practices independent of governmental organizations). In the public realm, women were to enjoy nominal social equality with men, but in the private realm they were to be subordinated since men are "abler and stronger," as Locke put it. Such an arrangement, he wrote, had its "foundation in nature."[4]

John Stuart Mill later modified Locke's perspective, describing civil society itself as having both a public and a private realm. Women he portrayed as "separate but equal" – equally able and entitled to negotiate the public and the private but *choosing* to remain in the private realm and exert power and influence there.[5] Mill further reified the emphasis on individualism, writing, "the only part of the conduct of any one, for which he is amenable to society, is that which concerns others. In the part which merely concerns himself, his independence is, of right, absolute." Included in this inviolate personal sphere were "liberty of tastes and pursuits; of framing the plan of our life to suit our own character; of doing as we like subject to such consequences as may follow."[6] His sentiment is shared by many modern rights theorists and lawmakers,[7] who assert that legislation concerning human wellbeing should only be focused on the *common* good, lest it interfere with individuals' own beliefs about what is good for themselves.

The liberal emphasis on the protection of personal wealth, with a simultaneous insistence on non-intervention into personal (private) matters or curbs on the acquisition of wealth, creates an interesting elasticity in the notion of what is private and what is public. At times, all of civil society is portrayed as private,[8] as when the ownership of property is said to be a private matter beyond the management (but not beyond the protection) of governments. At other times, whole corporations become legally defined as "persons," bearers of "human rights" that governments are sworn to protect. Privately owned, publicly operated business ventures are given the ability to claim that certain governmental actions are abusive to their wellbeing. The prevailing emphasis on negative liberty in liberalism works to the advantage of those who wish their property or earning potential to be "left alone," but it particularly disserves women, as it enshrines the right to promote one's self-interest without fear of interference. Civil/political rights issues are framed in positive language – freedom rights to vote, to assemble, to speak freely, to acquire property. The rest involves the freedom simply to be left alone and enjoy one's privacy, leaving unarticulated many of the rights goals necessary for women or the legal and social structures needed to attain certain negative liberties.[9] Paternalistic language about women's special right to their own privacy (often subtly referring to safety, or the necessity for sensitive women not to have to endure the brusqueness of the world) serves to leave them out of public life. Meanwhile, formal "privacy" rights (to have an abortion, for instance) are often codified without providing any practical tools to actually implement them.[10]

An added component in the protection of the private life of the family is the heavy emphasis in human rights discourse on the civil/political sphere.[11] It is the sphere of most interest to liberalism, much more so than rights law concerning economic, cultural, and social issues (the acquisition and protection of personal property having been grafted into the category of "civil liberties"). In some societies women are overtly or subtly considered as property, transferred from one household to another in the marriage transaction; they become the epitome of privately held property.[12] For them, the liberal emphasis on the civil/political realm in (liberally inspired) rights discourse adds an extra step in their removal from the protection of much rights law. Even the strong emphasis in liberalism on political equality – the right of each citizen to vote – has been divorced from any consideration of broad gender equality, not to mention equality of race, class, ethnicity, or sexual orientation. Formal political equality is upheld simultaneously with egregious discrimination, thanks largely to the notion that politics is public while other things are "personal."

The dualistic thinking of a public/private dichotomy is part of a much wider complex of oppositional, essentializing stereotypes that are deeply embedded in liberal ideology. Locke's understanding of the rootedness of men's and women's characters in "nature" typifies a deflection of responsibility for social reality in the supposed face of an inevitable, just and true ordering of societies. It is a way of thinking that is not confined to liberalism, of course; it is quite prevalent in other political and social ideologies, as well as the theology, ethics, and exegesis of religious traditions. Religious women are again doubly disabled – by conservative religious ideologies that support the idea of their having a different "nature" and by human rights precepts grounded in a liberal tradition that leans on the same dichotomy. Both liberalism and religious ideologies support the notion that there exists a universal, natural, egalitarian, individualist order that beneficently promotes the common good. As Carole Pateman has pointed out regarding liberalism, this myth, in partnership with the public/private dichotomy, greatly obscures the subjection of women to men.[13] The contribution of religion only adds to the obfuscation.

The construction of dual realms, a public and a private, exists not only in theory or personal imagination. States effectively legislate into being the very existence of the household. The household is needed as an engine for economic production. The household is where a majority of the world's labor happens. Both the gendering that occurs within households and the state protection for the household as an institution are not incidental but intentionally constructed by extended families and governments to maintain their economic objectives.[14] The impunity that surrounds rights abuses in the home is bolstered by states' deference to the institution of the family and, on the transnational level, by their emphasis on institutional (rather than individual) compliance with international law.

Privacy and human rights instruments

Fortunately, the drafters of the Women's Convention succeeded in crafting an instrument that acknowledges no formal split between the public and the private. Article 2(e) requires States Parties "To take all appropriate measures to eliminate discrimination against women by any person, organization, or enterprise." The exact composition of "appropriate measures" is not defined, but the provision is generally understood to mean that governments are not considered immediately responsible for the acts of private agents; rather, they may be held accountable for prosecuting non-state actors who abuse the rights of women. Ostensibly, private organizations, including religious ones, may be required to give up certain state-granted privileges as a penalty for infractions under the Women's Convention, privileges such as tax-exempt status, government grants, and subsidies. States Parties are not given the discretion to intervene in actual doctrines and practices, only to place sanctions upon the religious organization's relationship to government. This measure assumes, of course, that there *is* a separation of religious and governmental institutions in the countries that ratify the Convention.

Intending, perhaps, to strengthen the ability of the Convention to address rights abuses in the family, the Committee on the Elimination of Discrimination Against Women (CEDAW) issued, in its General Recommendation 19 on Violence Against Women, a mandate for States Parties to take "appropriate and effective measures to overcome all forms of gender-based violence, whether by public or private act." Such Recommendations are not legally binding, but do provide important guidelines for interpreting the Convention. The Recommendation states,

> Family violence is one of the most insidious forms of violence against women. It is prevalent in all societies. Within family relationships women of all ages are subjected to violence of all kinds, including battering, rape, other forms of sexual assault, mental and other forms of violence, which are perpetuated by traditional attitudes.[15]

In response to family violence, the Recommendation requires States Parties to enact criminal penalties, legislation against acts of violence perpetrated in the name of "family honor," and programs to support victims of family violence, including incest. Multiple branches of governments' law enforcement are to be involved, including the police and the judiciary.[16] While the Women's Convention contains some vague language regarding the actual responsibilities of States Parties vis-à-vis non-state actors, it makes a stronger case on the issue than existing rights legislation. Some of those documents may be interpreted rather easily in favor of interfering in family abuse.

The Universal Declaration of Human Rights, for instance, forbids "arbitrary interference with privacy and the family" (Article 12). States are left to interpret for themselves what comprises "arbitrary" interference, yet permission is given to play a role in home-based rights issues in the first place. At the other end of the spectrum is the African Charter of Human and People's Rights which declares, in Article 17.3, that "The promotion and protection of morals and traditional values recognized by the community shall be the duty of the State." While one might laud the state's requirement to safeguard traditions and practices of great value to the society, the language has the strong potential to call for state assistance in preserving practices and attitudes that perpetuate the subordination of and discrimination against women. In contrast, the Women's Convention (Article 5) calls on States Parties to eliminate traditional social and cultural practices that perpetuate discrimination against women or stereotypes that undergird it.

Liberal critiques of rights protection in the home

The limited protection that the Convention requires regarding rights abuses among family members has not been supported by States Parties and even some liberal rights theorists. They protest what they view as the Convention's unsupportable foray into the private sphere, interfering with general rights to freedom of opinion, expression and belief. An example of a writer with such opinions is Theodor Meron. He describes the primary shortcoming of the Women's Convention (whose mission he does support) as "overbreadth." He is genuinely worried that Article 2 grants to States Parties the permission to restrict privacy and associational rights if such measures are necessary to prevent discrimination towards women. The Convention itself, he cautions, becomes a vehicle of discrimination against certain ethnic or religious groups, from whom it requires behavior that is offensive to tradition or theology. This premise, he asserts, contradicts other legislation that forbids discrimination on the basis of race or religion. Meron states that women's rights are certainly violated in the private sphere, sometimes to the extent of eviscerating real equality of opportunity in the public sphere (which, in his opinion, is the legitimate object of the Convention). But he then concludes the following:

> There is danger, however, that state regulation of interpersonal conduct may violate the privacy and associational rights of the individual and conflict with the principles of freedom of opinion, expression, and belief. Such regulation may require invasive state action to determine compliance, including inquiry into political and religious beliefs. Attempts to regulate discrimination in interpersonal conduct may invite abuse of the discretion vested in the State by the broad language of Art. 1.[17]

Meron concludes that all rights would be best preserved from the excesses of an intrusive government through non-legislated responses to women's inequality. Education and "appropriate governmental incentives" are his suggestions for avoiding the "excessive encroachment by the State into interpersonal relations."[18] Holding fast to the idea of a public/private separation, Meron asserts that the teaching in homes and religious (but not public) schools of sex stereotyping is genuine and protected religious behavior. However, where such stereotypes may serve to prevent women from equal participation in the public sphere, states are legitimately compelled to intervene. If private beliefs thwart public rights enjoyment, governments (whose responsibility is human rights promotion only in the public realm) may act.[19]

Meron is also concerned that the Convention's understanding of what is public and what is private is also overly broad. In an effort to formally define the true parameters, he looks to the US Supreme Court's decision in *Roberts v. United States Jaycees*.[20] He agrees with the Court's decision that what is "private" should be based on "the relative smallness of a relationship or an association, the degree of selectivity exercised, and the degree of seclusion from others."[21] His primary reference points would seem to be corporations and national service organizations. Of them he writes, "With regard to large and unselective groups there is a compelling public interest in eliminating discrimination and assuring access for all to publicly available goods and services, which include not only tangible ones, but also privileges and advantages." Regarding rights legislation he therefore concludes, "While certain private and interpersonal, associational relations would be insulated from the reach of the Convention, the activities of large private entities and of basically unselective organizations would be regarded as publicly available goods and services."[22] Meron's analysis is oblivious to privacy issues regarding the family and religious institutions, in which questions of selectivity, size, and seclusion have completely different meaning – if any at all.

Meron's arguments go to the heart of the fallacy of an actual public/private divide, and to the persistent relegation of women's quality of life to a realm beyond those of "legitimate" human rights concerns. Is it, for instance, harmless negative stereotyping that a girl receives at home if it does not eventually prevent her from having a job, although she spends a lifetime submitting to emotional and physical violence in the family home because she's been taught to believe that women deserve it? Meron's (and perhaps other liberals') position would not consider such abuse a human rights infringement of concern to governments or international legal bodies. Rather, it is an unfortunate circumstance that needs to be addressed in secular schools (which numerous countries do not have – a flagrant example of the inseparability of the public and private spheres). Meron completely misses what Liesbeth Lijnzaad describes as the "causal connection between discrimination in the private sphere and the existence of formalized discrimination in public life."[23]

The same point as Meron's is essentially made – and missed – by Joel Feinberg. As discussed in Chapter Two,[24] Feinberg understands that the proper emphasis in rights enforcement need not be on what a person believes (the private), but only on what he or she does (the public). Everyone has a right to religious belief in very discriminatory things about others, but not necessarily to act upon those beliefs. Attention, he writes, should be applied to recognition versus enforcement. In this way the actual right to freedom of belief is always held to be morally justified, although its exercise may not be. Feinberg adds that while one may have a particular (in this case, religious) duty in response to one's beliefs, one would also have a stronger moral justification for not acting upon it if the result would be the infringement of another's rights.[25] Persons always retain their right to have certain (discriminatory) religious convictions, but not to enforce them. In this way a woman's right to equality does not invalidate the other's right to freedom of religion, although it may invalidate (or even criminalize) the exercise of that religious belief.[26] While one might appreciate Feinberg's attempt to maintain the principle of religious freedom in spite of strong curbs upon it, religious groups recognize the very strongest moral injunction to require them to act on a belief. A belief held but not enfleshed is not a validly maintained belief, or is considered hypocrisy. Akin to Meron's blind spot is Feinberg's assumption that personally held discriminatory viewpoints can simply be confined to the private sphere, to personal sentiment, with no negative ramifications for the (legitimate) public sphere. He thus lends credence to the liberal notion that what is private is beyond the reach of the law, and that women's privately endured discrimination and rights abuses are completely separable from their public lives.[27]

And so liberal ideology can become a partner of the male religious traditionalists in preventing certain human rights laws and norms from being applied to women. Both liberalism and religious conservatism have a propensity to consider the family, as Susan Moller Okin wrote, "an inappropriate context for justice, since love, altruism, or shared interests are assumed to hold sway in it." At the same time, Okin writes, the religious leaders will also add that "the family is 'naturally' a realm of hierarchy and even injustice,"[28] and that what may indeed look like injustice is actually a manifestation of loving care. Such an understanding of the family is an excellent example of what Onora O'Neill describes as "relationships that institutionalize dependence." She adds that "institutions that rely too heavily on the self-restraint of the stronger cannot reliably avoid injustice." Ignorance, isolation, physical strength, sexuality, and economic control collude to further entrench women's dependent status within the family. O'Neill's suggestion that such institutions be restructured so that weaker parties get the power to refuse or renegotiate their circumstances is the aim of many religious progressives' attention on the private sphere – on the family – and is even more deeply resisted by their religious opponents.[29]

A particularly damaging position among liberal political theorists is the assertion that social inequalities for women in the private sphere "are irrelevant to questions about political equality, universal suffrage and associated civil liberties of the public realm."[30] Not only does a firm divide exist between the public and the private, they say, but it is actually an asset to women. If discrimination does exist for women in their homes or non-regulated associations (such as religious communities), such biases are legally, securely cordoned off from the realm of public participation whose benefits governments are sworn to protect for all citizens. Feminists (and others) refute this idea, arguing that particular forms of inequality cannot be isolated to a distinct realm of a person's experience. That realm is a non-existent construction in the first place; discrimination is discrimination, fluidly experienced in and negatively impacting every dimension of one's life. The mere assertion of a particular sphere designed to host "minor" inequalities such as the personal or the social serves to marginalize those who are consigned to it (women) and to preserve the power of those in the public realm (the realm that "really counts"), the power of those who there may perhaps choose to bestow such opportunities upon women as the exercise of civil liberties.

Both in liberalism and in religious ideologies there exists a tendency to ascribe to the private sphere an emphasis on intimacy, affection, emotional support and sexuality (all of which are the "natural" province of women) while the public sphere is one where "political man" can naturally express himself, dedicated as he is to collective concerns.[31] As one scholar puts it, "femininity and publicity are oxymorons"[32] – the feminine is to the private as the masculine is to the public: "natural."[33] The elimination of the public/private dichotomy is only marginally achievable without the deconstruction of many others, fully interwoven as they are. Together, such binaries play into patriarchal power relations. They reinforce a patriarchal worldview rooted in either/or dichotomies, the notion of superiority between gendered characteristics, and impermeable boundaries between such characteristics. The oppositional relationship is rarely so surface as "good/bad;" rather, value is accorded conditionally, depending on the objectives of those with power, as in "tough" versus "nurturing." Nurturing is portrayed as intrinsically female, sometimes weak, and sometimes positive.

Personal status laws

Joel Feinberg's suggestion that individuals be required to adapt certain ethical principles for use in public while practicing them quite differently in private[34] is a methodology already in use by numerous states around the globe. These countries have systems of national laws covering commerce and government, murder and theft, for common life and inter-communal relationships, but they defer to personal status laws, sometimes called family law, to regulate citizens' private affairs. These laws – sometimes formally written into codes, sometimes an unwritten part of "conventional wisdom" – are based in religious, regional, or tribal traditions. Because these personal status laws overwhelmingly deal with inheritance, divorce, marriage, remarriage, succession, adoption, and so on, they govern the total existence of the many women whose religious communities prevent their participation in public life. Some states, such as India, have secular laws covering the same issues, leaving the choice to individual citizens of which to follow. As many rights scholars have noted, that decision is often made only by the male head of household, and in favor of religious laws that blatantly privilege men and disempower women. India provides an excellent example of the discriminatory nature of personal status laws, and their ability to disempower women in the name of protecting privacy. India also gives evidence of the pervasiveness of family law, formal or informal, in secular democracies as well as "religious" or autocratic societies, and of the influence of personal status laws on secular judicial deliberations.

Today Hindus are governed by the Hindu Marriage Act of 1955, the Hindu Guardianship and Minorities Act of 1956, the Hindu Adoption and Maintenance Act of 1956, and the Hindu Succession Act of 1956. While outlawing polygamy, the Hindu Marriage Act's language is so vague as to leave undefined the process of actually getting married (while also privileging and recognizing one kind of marriage ceremony indigenous to certain upper caste North Indians). Men take advantage of this lacuna by engaging in nebulous rituals with more than one woman. Women come to find that they are actually in an extremely vulnerable position in terms of their rights to maintenance, inheritance, and custody. If a man is caught practicing such polygyny, or if he chooses to abandon one or more wives and make another woman his legal wife, the others face the stigma of being a mistress and the real possibility of destitution for themselves and their children. In the end, the provision against polygamy has actually harmed women, since previous personal status laws concerning marriage recognized the rights of multiple wives.[35] While women are denied equal rights in inheritance by the Hindu Succession Act (see below), which deprives many of financial independence or a basic livelihood, the Hindu Marriage Act (Sections 24 and 25), through twisted logic on the idea of equality, requires women in certain instances to provide maintenance to former husbands.[36]

Similarly, the Hindu Adoption and Maintenance Act contains "improvements" of dubious or qualified value to women, although it is lauded by many as the only adoption provision for any religious community in the country. Under the Act a woman can neither adopt nor place her child for adoption. The father (under the Hindu Guardianship and Adoption Act) remains the guardian of children. Mothers, however, retain guardianship over any illegitimate children, thereby absolving fathers of any responsibility for such offspring.[37] The Hindu Succession Act does provide for inheritance by women of joint family property, considered a tremendous improvement in Hindu women's rights at the time of its drafting. Unfortunately, male relatives still receive a significantly larger share of the property – whatever has been designated as theirs, plus a share of the father's property. Female offspring inherit only a portion of the father's share. In many families, the Act is disregarded altogether and women receive no inheritance whatsoever. As with the Hindu Acts described above, the Succession Act has served to homogenize the great plethora of Hindu personal laws on the subjects in question. In some cases this has meant that more favorable local religious customs have been overridden. For instance, some communities in Rajasthan once had more favorable marriage and divorce provisions for women.[38]

The affairs of Muslims in India fall under the jurisdiction of the *Shari'a* Act of 1937, the Muslim Women's Dissolution of Marriage Act of 1939, the Muslim Women's (Protection of Rights on Divorce) Act of 1986, and other, uncodified laws. The Muslim Women's Act of 1986, coming in the wake of the Shah Bano controversy,[39] effectively denies Muslim women the opportunity to appeal to civil criminal legislation for maintenance after divorce (in particular, Section 125 of the Code of Criminal Procedure). Muslim women are now entitled to only three months of maintenance after divorce – the period of *iddat*.[40] The Muslim Women's Dissolution of Marriage Act was intended to aid women in divorcing their husbands (and to deter them from converting to other religions in order to obtain a divorce). It provides nine grounds for divorce (insanity, cruelty, desertion, etc.), yet its legislation is rarely used. One study has found that 78.57 per cent of Muslim women are unaware of the law and its opportunities.[41] As one scholar of Indian Muslim law concludes, the Act "has not been in practice very effective."[42] Meanwhile, triple *talaq*[43] is practiced in some regions, and women's recourse is very limited. Muslim women share with Hindu women a ban (imposed by their respective personal status laws) on seeking divorce or maintenance through civil legislation if they have been married under religious law, rather than in a civil ceremony provided for in the Special Marriage Act of 1954. In reality, the provisions of the Act are made available to very few women by their families or immediate religious communities.

Christian women fall under the jurisdiction of the Indian Marriage Act, the Indian Divorce Act, and the Indian Succession Act. The Indian Marriage Act has been in force since 1872, and does not permit a civil marriage for Christians (effectively nullifying their opportunity to access the Special Marriage Act).[44] The Indian Divorce Act dates to 1869; it permits men to divorce wives on account of adultery, but requires women who wish a divorce to prove bigamy, cruelty, desertion or incest in addition to adultery. In North India, Roman Catholic tribunals that effect divorce proceedings have never bothered to convene, causing extended grief for the persons involved.[45] In 1990, a significant improvement to Christian personal law was introduced in the form of the Christian Marriage and Matrimonial Causes Bill, the Indian Succession Amendment Bill, and the Indian Christian Adoption Amendment Bill. The first bill contained provisions that would provide equal divorce criteria between women and men, and included the very important criterion of dowry harassment as a legitimate ground for divorce.[46] The bills were supported by all but a few Christian groups, yet the government announced it would not approve any change to personal status laws that did not have "unanimous" communal support, preserving the interests of the male church elite who opposed the measures.

Religious laws of personal status, in short, often serve to deny women their own agency in contracting marriages, ending marriages, having custody of children, remarrying, inheriting property, testifying in courts, getting an education, gaining employment, accessing health care, choosing or retaining their citizenship, or being economically self-sufficient. The power to make many personal decisions, to formally represent their own interests, and to be independent of male control is effectively denied them. States have, on occasion, placed limits on religious family law, but only when its own political and economic interests are at stake. For instance, civil servants of any religion in India are not permitted to practice polygamy under the Service Conduct Rules, perhaps to limit the number of benefits that must be extended to employees' families, or simply to honor the secular law against polygamy. (Because the practice is largely equated with Muslims in India, the restriction also may be a veiled attempt to exclude or dissuade Muslims from civil service jobs.) The practice of polygamy, therefore, has ambiguous legal status; it is illegal under secular law, but continues under the safety of rights to privacy in the free exercise of religion. The situation illustrates again the indivisibility of the public from the private, as the government extends privacy rights generally to religious groups in terms of family law, but rescinds them without flinching when it understands them to conflict with public service or its own financial interest.

Personal status laws for all three of these religious communities are holdovers from British rule – a result of British court officials' interpretations of nineteenth-century customs, interspersed with interpretations of foreign sacred texts and traditions by European judges.[47] Many conclude that the laws are terribly out of date and compromised in terms of religious integrity. In the current situation of simmering communal tensions in India, however, personal status laws are not being retracted but only further entrenched. To the religious leaders involved they often provide an effective tool for solidifying identity and uniformity within the community. For those religious groups that are numerical minorities they also help to counter fears of majoritarianism. But the personal status laws also serve as fodder for more communal strife, with some groups asserting that provisions within others' laws create an unfair, privileged status for them (so some Hindu men have said of Muslim men's right to polygamy). In the middle are India's women, for whom refusal to follow personal status laws (or whatever the community believes to be personal status law) can result in formal punishment that includes physical violence, and shaming tactics such as shaving the head.[48] The Women's Convention, while containing a clear provision for women's equality before the law in civil matters, does not make clear the status of women who face religious tribunals or secular courts that are applying religious law.[49]

In sum, the notion of separate public and private spheres has a strong presence in Indian lawmaking, in religious communities, and in families. As it is currently constituted, the dichotomy strongly disserves the interests of religious women's human rights. The notion of separate spheres is bolstered by the state's duplicitous assignment to itself of the responsibility to choose when to intervene in religious affairs, its abdication of responsibility for the human rights of women to the religious communities from which they come, and its formal legal support for patriarchal familial ideology. The dichotomy is firmly institutionalized and strongly defended. Somewhat ironically, reformers have found equality in the public sphere – at least on paper – to be a much more realizable objective than in the private.[50] Families and religious communities have the first and last word on women's actual rights enjoyment. Where they staunchly defend the ideologies of wife and mother, women's rights suffer, no matter what positive rights laws may exist. On the other hand, where families and communities and women themselves abandon this ideology and accompanying subordinating practices, women's rights may flourish even in spite of national institutionalized discrimination.[51]

Indian women suffer other rights abuses as a result of entrenched notions of a private sphere. The boundary between the religious and the secular is blurred when secular courts decide matters with a conscious appeal to religion. While one might wish that the courts would intervene in family affairs to assure basic human rights, in actuality, "the criminal law has been allowed to enter into the terrain of the family, but only on the terms set out by familial ideology," according to Ratna Kapur and Brenda Cossman. Legal forays into family life have not supported women's rights but patriarchal subordination. The result is decisions such as the one in *Surinder Kaur v. Gurdeep Singh*, in which the husband tried his wife for restitution of conjugal rights. The wife had taken a job away from home and refused to return to her husband, alleging that he had beaten her and put her out of the house twice, and that she feared for her safety. In finding in favor of the husband, the court's decision included the following: "According to Hindu law, marriage is a holy union.... It enjoins on the wife the duty of attendance, obedience to and veneration for the husband and to live with him wherever he may choose to reside."[52] Meanwhile, judgments rendered in favor of women sometimes have been based on their proven virtue – their demonstrated compliance with the ideology of the "good Hindu wife" – as examined in detail during the court proceedings. Whether they are the plaintiff or defendant, women's "honor" is often put publicly on trial. Kapur and Cossman conclude,

> Where a woman's sexuality is considered private, that is, guarded within the confines of the family, as a virgin daughter or a loyal wife, the criminal law may protect her. When women adhere to the norms of the good Hindu wife and/or daughter, she may receive some protection from third party intervention. But when a woman deviates from these norms... the law considers her sexuality to have become public, and thus, not to come within the purview of the protection of criminal law.[53]

In sum, the Indian Constitution's ambiguities about the secular and the religious, the public and the private, plus the government's role in maintaining the boundaries between them all, serve to further prevent the human rights idea from achieving them for religious women.

Similarly, some African states have constitutions that prescribe total equality in gender relations, religion, and so on, yet they defer to tribal or religious law and custom on personal status issues (Kenya, for instance). Because many women cannot read (especially in rural areas) and may not have access to television or radios, they also have no access to knowledge about their constitutional rights or to the ongoing debates about personal status issues.[54] Personal status laws are a fact of life in the global north as well, although they are differently structured. As noted earlier, Ireland's "secular" laws on divorce and abortion are drawn directly from Roman Catholic teaching.[55] In the United States, "privacy" matters are likely to be legislated nationally as well as regionally, by states or even municipalities. The political might of religious groups in various states has much to do with different states' laws concerning abortion, adoption, gay rights, euthanasia, domestic violence, and a host of other topics.

Privacy, religion, and states

Various conservative religious reactions to modernity, westernization, and debilitating economic and political transitions[56] have served to strengthen in many regions the public/private dichotomy, and in ways that strongly disadvantage religious women. If the whole of society seems to be changing in ways that individuals cannot control, a firm line will be reified between what the state or general culture can influence and what, in another world, temporal institutions and processes can never touch. Consequently, conservative religious movements have placed strong emphasis on the family and home. If the society seems headed down a terribly misguided path, the integrity of one's personal conduct may at least be preserved. Corporate life may be in tatters, but family life can still comply with holy norms. In the home, moral boundaries are felt to be more enforceable – if it seems impossible to influence all of science, educational systems, or social movements, one can at least make changes for the better in the smallest of social units, such as the family. In this way, too, the societal damage might one day be undone, for if children can be indoctrinated properly there is the chance that the future will bring the needed social, economic, political, and religious reforms.[57]

In substantially multi-religious or multi-ethnic countries, where members of minority spiritual traditions may feel threatened by the majority group's power to decide ethical issues, the private realm and personal status laws also sometimes come to be viewed as the last stronghold of real autonomy. Greater emphasis on traditional family practices is often the result. A country such as India provides a fine example of the fact that current revivals of retrograde practices regarding women are rooted in inter-communal insecurities or their historical experiences of colonization or subjugation. During Moghol rule, Brahmins were permitted decision-making power on issues of caste, marriage, and inheritance, but denied input on other areas of government. Such interpersonal or family matters came to be vested with even more significance for religious leaders, who in turn sought to load them with even more significance for their followers, there being no other avenues left them for power or decision-making. "Home" became the last stronghold of authority and autonomy. Later, western colonizers repeated the process, perpetuating the idea of a private, "important" sphere where indigenous leaders could feel they exercised power, while ultimate ability to govern remained in the hands of the British. Christian missionaries contributed to the situation by focusing on the inhabitants' "souls," on their private, or religious selves, as the realm of greatest importance. Governing power was, they taught, appropriately wielded by others far away.[58] Depending on caste and class, women's status was differently manipulated, as urban elites modernized their female relatives' quality of life to publicize their own agenda for "progress," and non-elites downgraded their female relatives' status to bolster their own claim to "tradition." Colonization served both to reinforce the notion of separate realms and to promote the manipulation of women as symbols of various male aspirations.

Both in multi-religious countries such as India and in states formally dominated by one tradition, religious leaders sometimes endeavor to retain their personal power by emphasizing the immutability of family law and of the private realm itself. Even in countries supposedly governed by religious law in all areas of life, the private realm is promoted as one whose adherence to traditional teachings is central to national integrity and worldly success. Marie-Aimée Hélie-Lucas writes of Islamic North Africa,

> Failing to describe identity in positive terms, as well as to promote any specificity in Islamic politics or Islamic economics, fundamentalists have only succeeded in identifying one area as the essence of Islamic identity: the private sphere. They therefore concentrate their efforts on Personal Law and on the family, which become the epitome of Islamic politics, a condensation of all other identities, and a place of refuge. Whoever challenges this refuge threatens all the multiple identities at once, as well as the essence of identity.[59]

The maintenance of the notion of "private" space becomes one of fierce focus for religious conservatives who need it, plus the personal status laws that govern it, for the maintenance of their own power in their communities. Women's lives again become the focal point in the consolidation of group identity.

The emphasis on the sanctity of the family and of personal religious practice conveniently obfuscates the fact that such private issues as succession and inheritance laws effectively regulate and control women's access to economic resources. Such resources cross all constructed boundaries between the public and private spheres, as well as women's access to the public sphere itself. Private injunctions have extremely public ramifications. Personal, "traditional" decisions about how family money will be allocated effectively decide which family members will participate in the wider economic world.[60] Some African laws on personal status, for example, require the eldest son of the deceased to inherit all land and other resources of monetary value. The practice thoroughly prevents women from ever receiving land tenure and therefore the collateral with which ever to apply for bank loans.[61] Financial and social independence and autonomy for women are tacitly curtailed while religious integrity and familial and cultural cohesiveness are loudly "protected."

Purdah provides a good example of how the boundaries of religious teaching, the public and the private become completely negotiable based on states' workforce needs, the survival requirements of the poorest, and the personal economic and social goals of the bourgeoisie. Donna Sullivan notes that

> ... in rural areas of Pakistan, cattle and vegetable markets are closed to all classes of women except those of the poorest classes. Fields are not regarded as public space except for women of the most wealthy landowning classes; this distinction reflects the need for women's agricultural labor. In urban centers, lower middle class women encounter the most severe restrictions on their freedom of movement. Women belonging to the Baluch and Pathan ethnic groups face particularly extensive restrictions, both within their traditional settings and beyond.

When states and families need the economic productivity of women, the religious boundaries of public and private become quickly renegotiated. Also renegotiated is the status and value attached to the relevant activities. As Sullivan concludes, "The shared feature of the public/private distinction in different social contexts is the attribution of lesser value to the activities of women within the private realm."[62]

That religious and secular leaders everywhere should make use of the idea of separate public and private realms when their own interests will be promoted stands out most clearly when one remembers that the religions themselves do not intrinsically encompass such an idea. As stated above, religions in general have a fully wedded understanding of the relationship between belief and action, and dismiss the notion that the two may be separated into different spheres of life. The post-Enlightenment project of the removal of religion to a private, personal sphere and the development of a secular culture to guide the public has, arguably, been an influential factor in those western societies (and their dominant religion, Christianity) most influenced by the Enlightenment. But the idea that religion can and should be shuffled off to a private sphere is not original to or desirable in many societies. For instance, the contemporary Indian understanding of secularism is not that religion is a private matter but that government should take a hands-off approach to religious practice generally.[63] Religious practice remains an extremely public affair. This fact is manipulated ironically by those governments that register reservations to human rights instruments in the name of religion on behalf on entire populations, millions of whom may not share the particular religious perspective. Religious belief is made to be a matter of public consensus, while defended in the name of privacy. Put simply, the public/private dichotomy is a false construction that is promoted in every society at times when certain dominating groups' interests will be served.

The issue of religious women's rights illustrates most pointedly the blurry, artificial line between the public and the private. Is education, for example, a project of the family or of the state? Is it an individual's right (or a family's) to decide how much education a person receives, given they have the income to pay for it, and to decide the ethical content of the coursework? The Taliban in Afghanistan have claimed, in the name of authentic Islam, the authority to drastically restrict women's education levels. Is overwork, spousal rape, beating, even murder permissible for married women under the veneer of religiously sanctioned gender hierarchy? What of the fact that states consider rape, beatings and murder to be governmentally prosecutable crimes? Is the practice of religion really a private matter or is it actually one of the most public – a group affiliation supported by states and sometimes manifested in state-sponsored taxes (*zakat*, or German taxes that support citizens' particular denominations), educational systems, and tax breaks for denominations or congregations? Some states that most vigorously defend certain religious practices in the name of privacy also officially mandate that those practices be observed by all citizens. Where is the public/private boundary in countries where individual religious practice is under the jurisdiction of government? Or where governments assert (as an item of faith) that the common good is based on every citizen's personal conformity to particular religious norms?

Whatever boundary may be claimed to exist is further eroded by states' frequent circumscriptions on the private, free exercise of religion. Statutes outlawing polygamy, the use of hallucinogens in worship or other spiritual observance, and the visiting of sacred lands are unexceptional in the United States, for instance.[64] There, laws also require people to pay taxes to support things that completely defy basic precepts of their religions, such as abortion procedures in public hospitals and the teaching of evolution in public schools. Financial support of armed forces and of corporations within the military–industrial complex is offensive to religious pacifists, as is the use of public funds to support the process of capital punishment. The legal availability of contraceptives is anathema to some, as is for others the positive legal status of same-sex marriages. Recently, an American couple was tried for the death of their small son; they had followed the precepts of their religion (Christian Science) that does not permit medical treatment, and denied him the intervention that easily could have cured his bowel obstruction. In innumerable ways, states' governments already defy the religious principles and invade the religious privacy of citizens. Consequently, arguments for the strict separation between "public" and "private" spheres are proven insupportable even among those countries that do not claim to base their legal systems and ethical mores in a particular religion.

The whole matter of personal status laws in secular states obfuscates public/private boundaries, as (public) governments authorize religiously based discrimination in (private) life. Liberal democracies such as the United States permit discrimination in employment among religious communities, allowing some groups to prevent women (and also sometimes gays, lesbians, and people of color) from becoming clergy or administrative leaders in religious communities. The "stained glass ceiling" is a fact of life for many women in traditions that do – at least nominally – welcome women's leadership. Liberal governments also permit communities to restrict their members' access to certain federally supported options to do with family planning, education levels, and employment opportunities. Most citizens would want governments to allot a certain amount of room for religious groups to exercise their ethical principles with integrity (the right to *choose*, for instance, is the genuine cornerstone of the abortion rights movement). However, with the exception of conscientious objector status for religious pacifist men, instances of publicly required compliance in individual believers' matters are disproportionately related to the quality of life of women.

Many religious women, if they wish to participate in the public realm at all, must first meet some private requirements, since it is by women's perceived behavior, both in public and in private, that whole families (or communities) may judge one another. Language about chastity, virtue, and honor is heavily weighted to insure conformity. For women in those Hindu and Muslim communities that require them to be veiled in public, the basic incoherence of the public/private dichotomy comes into sharpest focus. The veil is intended to insure that if women must go out in public, they remain in private space. A woman's essential privacy – her body, hair, face, perhaps all of them – are covered before leaving home, so that even though body, hair and face go to the market they can never be fully present. Some forms of veiling are so complete as to prevent women from being personally identifiable to anybody, rendering them anonymous, effectively invisible. They are out in public but not outside the "private," the secluded. Fatima Mernissi writes, "the veil can be interpreted as a symbol revealing a collective fantasy of the Muslim community: to make women disappear, to eliminate them from communal life, to relegate them to an easily controllable terrain, the home, to prevent them moving about, and to highlight their illegal position on male territory by means of a mask."[65] Veiling means that, when necessary, the private world may enter the public one without being compromised. The practice shows, however, how artificial, constructed, and porous are the boundaries between the two, as permission is given for islands of "privacy" to navigate the most public of spaces.

The religions introduce, as do no other categories, the question of the subjectivity of defining what is "harm." While most people would agree that physical violence is harmful, there is no such consensus on something like simply bad theology. A growing number of legal cases are creating a corpus of concrete decisions on the responsibility of states to redress harm done by non-state actors,[66] but the great test for religious women's rights must come from some kind of consensus on what comprises "harm." The closest language to date is found in the Declaration on the Elimination of Violence Against Women,[67] which in Article 1 defines violence against women as "any act of gender-based violence that results in, or is likely to result in, physical, sexual or psychological harm or suffering to women, including threats of such acts, coercion or arbitrary deprivation of liberty, whether occurring in public or private life." The inclusion of private life is important, but the language leaves open all specific interpretation of harmful acts. Negative sex stereotyping may well be called harmful, although religious conservatives might respond that it is crucial, helpful, appropriate socialization for women's successful participation in a culture.

Arcot Krishnaswami, Special Rapporteur to the United Nations on religious discrimination, once wrote that state "churches" (i.e., state-sponsored religious institutions) do not equal the state itself; they therefore can never be signatories to rights covenants and so may not be held accountable for rights infringements, even if they are religious groups specially endorsed by states.[68] What accountability could there possibly be, then, between official, even national, religious institutions to meet state-based obligations for human rights norms? Are states really free of any oversight of the rights records of the religions they supposedly endorse – that some states claim to be based upon? Advocates for religious women's rights insist that they are not. But the conundrum continues: if, as Article 17.3 of the African Charter of Human and People's Rights declares, "The promotion and protection of morals and traditional values recognized by the community shall be the duty of the state,"[69] what is one to do with the fact that many states are absolutely in line with traditional religious values that discriminate against and disempower women? Sometimes the state is not a woman's ally. In any situation, state non-involvement *is* involvement – declining to be involved *is* acting to offer consent to prevailing practices.[70]

The Universal Declaration of Human Rights, quite in line with normative jurisprudence in liberal democracies, prohibits "arbitrary interference with privacy and the family," (Article 12). It does not offer any definition of arbitrariness, however. States Parties are essentially left to their own devices to interpret what is appropriate participation in the private sphere. As numerous scholars have noted, even those states that claim to remain removed from the private sphere are quite proactive in it nonetheless. Governments do construct the very difference between public and private life.[71] Liberal states, as noted above, have a particularly strong heritage of policies designed to keep the state firmly out of individuals' lives. Others, those claiming to be based on religious laws such as *Shari'a*, for instance, may be just the opposite. In most countries, governments officially decide who is married and who is not, who is to be considered the (legitimate) child of whom and who is not.[72] States pass laws on matters such as abortion, encouraging a raging debate in the United States and other countries about how much privacy an individual should be allowed to maintain. Anti-abortion advocates (often social and political conservatives who decry, in theory, any state intrusion into the private realm) call the procedure not a matter of privacy but of murder, one of the few instances in which states must act to prevent a terrible crime. On the other side are progressives, persons more likely to prefer greater state responsibility in private individuals' experiences of poverty, violence, and joblessness, who in this case advocate for state non-interference in personal experiences. The situation points clearly to several ways in which states might intervene in the private: will it be concerning matters that are, on the surface, moral, including whether or not a zygote or a fetus is a person (which is also an economic and political question), or will it involve practical, largely economic and political, quality of life issues for children and adults (issues that also happen to be inherently moral)? In the end, support for or opposition to women's personal agency and power often are the basic lines of differentiation between opposing groups on any variety of issues, much more so than blanket allegiances such as "libertarian" or "radical." That same support and opposition to women's empowerment are also frequently the deciding factors in whether an issue is decided to be a public or private one.

No clear way has yet become obvious as to how the notion of the public/private dichotomy can be dismantled especially, in regard to the rights of religious women, without further endangering the appropriate separation of governments from religious institutions. One human rights lawyer has proposed that a change in "private" religious practices that disadvantage women might be achieved through states' withdrawing or withholding tax privileges given to the particular religious institutions.[73] Such government-sponsored "incentive" would hardly be realistic, however, in the many countries that claim a state religion. In addition, it would be a difficult tactic to defend, creating the possibility that governments will deny tax (and numerous other) privileges to religious and secular groups that they deem distasteful. The potential for the abuse of the civil rights of numerous institutions and their members is significant. In its more extreme form, it is inherently compromising of association rights, in addition to those to freedom of belief.

Conclusion

In the end, the rights of religious women meet a powerful deterrent in the confluence of conservative religious ideology and the liberal human rights idea, both of which are firmly rooted in the concept of separate and legitimate public and private spheres. The answer to the massive, important question of where state authority should begin and end has most often been answered with the word "home," and secondarily with the words "place of worship." The resulting public/private divide perpetuates the disempowerment of women, the denial of their access to resources, influence, independence, self-actualization and, sometimes, basic human rights.

The human rights idea was constructed, in part, with the hope of naming exactly which categories of human harm states are required to act upon, to construct a list of abuses that must never be out of reach of the law. One problem today is not so much that the list is not complete or sufficiently visionary (in spite of its vagueness), but that states have yet to back the idea with sufficient power. In some cases, perhaps, governments are reluctant to weaken the notion of a public/private divide because, as a state, it also finds it useful and wishes to maintain it. Governments, meanwhile, are largely led by male elites who may see potential personal disadvantage in any questioning of the dichotomy. And then there are the religious groups and their leaders who (accurately) see any dismantling of the public/private divide as a threat to their current method of holding on to some of their power. There is also fear, possibly, within the international rights-codifying community, that the only alternative to the perpetuation of discriminatory standards is the complete elimination of religion as a protected category in rights enforcement, or the complete erasure of any limitations on state regulation of personal affairs. Since there is broad consensus that neither is desirable, this worst case scenario is avoided by accepting the lesser evil of rights compromises in the name of gender and religion. Of course, the choice of interpretation is in no way so either/or.

6
The Question of Agency

Equality is not a Christian ideal... it is the nature of woman to submit.

Elizabeth Elliot *Let Me Be a Woman*[1]

As noted in the preceding chapter, the notion of human rights is a product of and is embedded in liberal ideology, which itself is inured to the idea of the primary importance of personal choice, including in the enjoyment of human rights. A frequent response to the dilemma of religious constrictions on women's rights is, "The only thing that should count is what women want for themselves." Disputes about which human rights should be applied to which people can be overcome, the thinking goes, by allowing the subject herself to decide how she wants to live her life. On the surface, this would seem to be an ideal solution, one that avoids cultural or religious imperialism and intervention, that circumvents abuses by the powerful within and among communities, and that honors the agency and integrity of the subject in question. However, when religion is a factor in women's choice-making about their enjoyment of human rights, the issue becomes very complicated. Religious perspectives intentionally instruct people about what they should want for themselves. This need not be a negative fact; religious teachings may encourage women and men to strive for social justice for themselves and others, for instance. Yet the fact remains that some religious women are instructed to choose against what would seem to be in their best self-interest – to choose against particular human rights norms.

The very concept of agency is heavily contested among feminists, subalternists, sociologists, scholars of rights, and others. At the heart of the debate are the boundaries and criteria of real empowerment, the effect of the individual's rootedness in her context, and the subjective, culturally located position of those who would assess others' agency. The questions that the term unavoidably raises – concerning independence of thought and action, self-actualization, desire fulfillment, the persistence of structural and systemic patriarchy, and so on – go to the heart of the most important issues regarding the participation of women in subordinating religious traditions. This study accepts the concept of agency, finding it not only helpful but also crucial to the discussion of discrepancies between religious practices and rights enjoyment. The case for women as deserving of both religious integrity and human rights is strengthened by the assertion that they are indeed agents, self-aware actors making intentional choices, within the boundaries prescribed by their community or outside of them. That their choices might be molded – and negatively so – by religious teaching does not prevent them from having agency, much as it does complicate the assertion that what they want for themselves should be the deciding factor in their rights enjoyment.

Some women are instructed, subtly or overtly, not to want what are considered human rights, autonomy in choice-making, and so on.[2] The human rights notion is challenged in its efficacy by such women's spiritual formation. Whatever their circumstances they are informed, both formally and informally, that they are agents; they are encouraged to see themselves as having a valid station and menu of choices. They are entreated in countless ways to embrace their agency (perhaps towards ends that meet the approval of others). The message that they hear is not, "You are a non-person, a puppet on a string," but "You are a person with decision-making and self-directing power; use it correctly." Such a message can be a tool for encouraging conformity with reigning religious norms. If freedom of religion is of vital importance (and this study assumes that it is), what is one to do with those women who genuinely choose rights-denying practices and theologies?

Choosing against one's self-interest

The opportunity to exercise personal *choice* in the matter of religious practice – to decide for oneself which rights, rituals, scriptural interpretations and theological perspectives should be adhered to – is not a native assumption or a practical possibility for women in some religious communities. Open canons for sacred texts, new interpretations, or the choice of whether or not to participate in certain rituals are not acceptable for anyone in their communities. In terms of religious interpretation and practice they simply have no choices. Meanwhile, some women embrace the idea of predestination, the divine selection before or at birth of those who will achieve salvation or enlightenment, regardless of a person's actions during her lifetime. Similarly, some understand each person's actions, choices, and situation in life to be fated, perhaps the inevitable outcome of the actions and choices of a previous life. Some theological constructions place women's agency within an even broader teleological setting, a kind of cosmic agency. Changing their material conditions may seem impossible. These women understand the suffering that they experience to be divinely mandated, deserved, or inevitable, and so choices to ameliorate their situation are not valid for them. Some may believe their daily "choices" to be inevitable manifestations of what is predetermined, and not at all a "free" choice.

As was noted above in Chapter 1, religion also affects the way in which human situations are perceived. Confinement, hunger, suffering, grief, and other negative states may have tremendously positive meaning, given the particular context (*purdah*, fasting, self-denial, etc.). Choices made in response to these religious understandings may, again, contradict those of persons who are judged to be exercising responsible agency, or choice-making that benefits their self-interest. Conversely, a person may endure intense spiritual suffering while also holding all the rights aspired to in United Nations instruments, and judge her own quality of life to be poor.

Reference already has been made to the opinion among some people that all necessary human rights are actually safeguarded by religion itself.[3] This is not only the perspective of certain religious leaders but of some women themselves. They genuinely have come to believe that their rights to inherit family assets, to the protection of their marriage, to the protection of their bodies and to life itself are secured by the teachings and practices of their particular religion. International rights norms and laws may be needed for those who do not subscribe to their religion and therefore have no such rights guarantees in their own communities. Certain women in every religious tradition genuinely believe that their religion guarantees all legitimate rights. In willfully – even enthusiastically – following those religious rights regimes they make choices that others deem against their self-interest. Some become the staunchest, most orthodox defenders of practices and theologies that discriminate against them.

Religious ideology has the power to shape or subvert all the "progress potential" of women who, by common standards of measure, should be enjoying a better overall quality of life. There are religious criteria for status that exist alongside material categories, and they may be more important to individual women, who will make choices to augment their religiously defined status rather than that defined by rights regimes. The religious source of information that is given to women and with which they make their choices contains a depth of power or authority simply by virtue of its religious origin. Sometimes women are intentionally or unintentionally given religious *mis*information, which negatively affects the choices they make regarding their own wellbeing. As wrong as the information may be, it still carries the weight of authority and women wholeheartedly choose to follow it.[4]

In every society the prevailing religions and cultures are powerful factors in shaping the tastes, attitudes, and ambitions of every person. Many individuals come to accept prevailing norms and practices as "natural" or "obvious" or "right" because they are the only things they have ever known. Many come to adapt their personal expectations and desires to match their reality. On one hand, real quality of life cannot be assessed simply by considering what an individual wants for herself or how she judges her own situation. Such a subjective welfarist perspective only entrenches the status quo, as Cass Sunstein has written, reifying the power of the various institutions (including religion) that have so strongly instructed members of a society in what to value in the first place.[5] On the other hand, a person's self-perception and personal desires are crucial components in any assessment of a woman's agency and level of rights enjoyment. A middle ground is inherently sought by the human rights movement, with its emphasis on both personal satisfaction and concrete criteria for social justice. The case of personal participation in religious community is one of the hardest of situations in which to establish that middle ground.

Amartya Sen has endeavored to separate the notion of wellbeing from that of agency, a helpful perspective when considering the influence of religious ideology on human rights. He writes, "it can be said that the well-being aspect of a person is important in assessing a person's *advantage*, whereas the agency aspect is important in assessing what a person can do in line with his or her own conception of the *good*."[6] In some cases, a person may have a very low level of advantage but a tremendous capacity to enact what he or she understands to be the good. A woman, for instance, may be required by her family and religious community to accede to a level of basic rights enjoyment that is terribly inferior to that of men in her community, simply because she is female. However, her own ability, simultaneously, to accomplish what she perceives to be "the good" may be extremely high – in fact, her positive agency may be a direct consequence of her low state of wellbeing. She may understand as supremely good her ability to be a model of piety, to practice self-denial, or to submit to a subordinate status in her community. The particular complication of religion in the question of agency, wellbeing, and human rights is that in no other context is negative advantage so likely to be so directly linked to what a person genuinely understands to be pursuit of the good.

Sen's conclusion is that particular conceptions of the good must be studied in detail, but that the validity of the individual's use of her agentive capacity is, in the end, to be evaluated by her alone. He writes, "The need for careful assessment of aims, objectives, allegiances, and so on, and of the conception of the good, may be important and exacting. But despite this need for discipline, the use of one's agency is, in an important sense, a matter for oneself to judge."[7] Framed in this way, what individual women want *is* what matters most. And yet, even if women have fully adapted their desires and expectations to comply with their subordinate positions, the fact of the subordination continues. Sen writes, "It can be a serious error to take the absence of protests and questioning of inequality as evidence of the absence of that inequality (or of the non-viability of that question)."[8] Yes, what women want matters most, *but* it must always be evaluated within the context of the particular religious and social norms that have so strongly shaped women's preferences, self-perception, and goals. This is not to say, however, that a woman's own level of satisfaction can be an objective marker if she has been taught to want and expect less. As Julie Annas writes, "[I]t is clear that desires which owe their nature even in part to the agent's reduced circumstances cannot adequately adjudicate questions of justice."[9]

Women who accept and internalize as natural the subordinating norms taught them in their religious communities may be so interwoven into those institutions that a critical perspective on their own situation and choice-making is impossible to achieve. The actors are completely embedded in the religious culture that has formed them; they and the culture are part of each other; they are fully enmeshed. Such embeddedness can make it very difficult to imagine alternatives.

As Pierre Bourdieu has pointed out, neither social structures nor particular agents ever are independent entities.[10] Each is deeply embedded in the other. Religious institutions and the communities they may dominate simultaneously create and reify the norms to which they cling. The religious values and truths of a community are the source, the process, and the result of ongoing meaning-making. The inspiration, the machine, and the product *are* the religious truths; they are perpetually revalidating themselves in what Anthony Giddens refers to as "homeostatic causal loops." He writes, "the structural properties of social systems are both medium and outcome of the practices they recursively organise."[11] In the end, persons in any society receive seemingly limitless reinforcement of norms and values, reinforcement that may make alternative views and critical appraisal of whatever is given as normative quite difficult to achieve.

Some religious women's menu of choices, however, may be extremely limited, or confined to options so inconsequential to real wellbeing that their status as a legitimate choice seems a cruel joke. It would be wrong, however, to conclude that such women have no viable agency. Religious women's choices may be small and the consequences of deviation (choosing wrongly) very steep, but the fact that observers may not like the range of choices or may feel that the entire scenario is unjust does not negate the fact that real agentive capacities are being enacted. One researcher of women's lives and rights enjoyment in Bangladesh concluded her study with the affirmation that, although her informants were subjected to a religious ideology that forced them strongly to deny their very physical presence in the world, the women maintained a genuine level of agency because of their "capacity to experience and interpret."[12] Indeed, women's agentive capacity can be lowered by religious ideology almost to a level of simply (but genuinely) experiencing the choices that others have made for them.

Even the most minimal of agentive capacities can offer, in context, the biggest social capital. On religious grounds in particular, the moral and affective obligation of women to be paragons of "virtue" is often rationalized as an exchange for physical protection from other men. "Symbolic capital," as Bourdieu describes it,[13] is earned by religious women through exhibition of "virtue" and translates into economic capital for men and women. Women's preservation of "the family honor," in some religious ideologies, is literally cashed in for highly valued marriages into and out of the family, for business partnerships, clerical opportunity for males, social prestige, and so on. Some women may accept the rationale that a truly equal exchange is being transacted – virtue for safety or a wealthier marriage – and that their choices are being freely and profitably made. The tacit contract, however, constructed by those who dominate, reinforces the submission and obedience of women to men in a scheme that not only reifies male power but also converts women's "agency" into male economic or social gain.

Concepts such as agency, autonomy, and choice-making might seem to be positive in any religious or cultural context, regardless of socialization. No matter what one's actual level of independent thought or decision-making may be it would seem natural that subjects would want it. However, studies made in different regions of the world have shown that concepts such as autonomy are actually not desirable to some women. One example of the complicated quality of autonomy and choice-making comes from the work of Patricia and Roger Jeffery in rural North India. They have noted that some women do not understand themselves to have more autonomy (in this context, most notably the right to freedom of movement) if they are, for instance, permitted to go to the market or shop for their own clothes. The women may perceive it, rather, as a loss of prestige, status, influence, or caring. What is understood by others to be a gain in terms of independence is experienced by their informants as a real social loss.[14]

The Jefferys also have found that autonomy, as it is commonly understood among western scholars and activists, is far from desirable to a good number of these informants. They do not want it at all. Autonomy is a negative concept to them, "unattractive and frightening." The interviewers write, "[I]ndicators of autonomy should include who controls a woman's sexuality and fertility, and her role in the allocation of economic resources."[15] The women's distaste for autonomy as it is thus perceived may be rooted partially in the fact that its correlate in Hindi (plus local dialects and concepts) is a decidedly pejorative term. But the women seem also to have internalized the local patriarchal arguments against women's self-determination.[16] Some of the Muslim women in the study asserted that land rights were not an issue of concern for them. They criticized other women who protested unfair land practices, and these condemnations by the accommodating women contributed to the inability of other, resisting women to form crucial allegiances.[17] In short, what religious women may want for themselves, or see as benefiting their self-interest, may be very different from that of outside advocates and from the criteria of human rights norms.

The category of religion thwarts the most common criteria for evaluating autonomy and empowerment. Control of one's own sexuality, freedom of movement, accessibility of information, decision-making, ability to inherit property, sense of dignity and ability to organize one's own affairs – each of these situations may be experienced by religious women individually, or by their whole community, as being completely a part of their everyday lives. They may know themselves fully to be actors, holders of opinions, participants in many events, in control of resources, and so on. They may understand themselves to be bursting with self-confidence and self-esteem and a sense of agency. They may genuinely receive the full respect of all who are around them. They may also be, at the same time, enduring extraordinary constrictions on every part of their lives due to religious ideology. Within their own worlds, they do have all the markers of empowerment and autonomy, and the respect that they have has been earned because of their willingness to perpetuate the traditional (or newly constructed) practices and attitudes that contribute to their subordination. In this way, religious women's power is shown to be a very different thing from religious women's status. Status, which is "a woman's overall position in the society," is quite separate from power, "women's ability to influence and control at the personal level."[18] Women may enjoy very high status in spite – *or because* – of their low level of power.

Many religious women's agency is negotiated not in "the world" but at home, where religious ideology governs interpersonal issues of power, conflict, and control. Research that relies solely on indicators such as educational level and even fertility rates as measures of agency and autonomy but do not examine intra-familial religious dynamics misses a major element in the equation. It is in the home-based religious ideology that a girl may learn that she deserves a lesser quality of life, and where she will learn to make decisions based on the "truth" of her spiritual and material inferiority. If a girl has observed throughout her childhood that her brothers get more food, that her hunger pains are uninteresting to her family, that she is not sent to school, and that the women she knows are beaten by the men she knows, she will likely come to have a lower estimation of her human worth in relation to her brothers'. Told all her life that she has the inborn abilities only to attend to a husband, raise children, and do housework, and seeing that this is also true for every woman she knows, she is likely to accept these messages as incontrovertible truth. Having been inculcated with the notion that women have special abilities, gifts and duties for self-sacrifice, she will endeavor to cultivate skills and a personality to match. As Hanna Papanek has noted, "if the process of socialization for inequality has been successful, most people will not perceive inequalities for what they are – or, if they do, will argue for their moral rightness."[19] Papanek writes, "[W]omen are taught to express compulsory emotions that are consistent with the idea of their superior spiritual or religious status."[20] Girls and women are not only taught that they are particularly forgiving, saintly, and self-denying, they also are expected to manifest these qualities.

One might well wonder why, if traditionalist religious ideology has been the source of strong qualifications on a woman's well-being, she would perpetuate harmful practices and theologies in her daughters.

Papanek's research names marriageability as a primary goal in the shaping of girls' attitudes and behaviors. In some societies women see no alternative to marriage as a way to the highest possible status and wellbeing,[21] and therefore practices that a mother may have experienced as particularly painful or unjust are repeated on her daughters if it will ensure marriage. But Papanek also identifies a kind of complicity in subordination that is centered on a need to personally validate one's own suffering by reproducing it in others. She writes,

> Those who have struggled hard to reach a certain place, a certain security, will often insist that others must undergo the same struggle... But this insistence requires an internal reversal, an acceptance of the justice and morality of a process against which one may have struggled earlier. Having done so, adult women confirm their complicity with a way of life marked by inequality. It is this complicity that is the sign of successful "secondary socialization," for it also marks the adult woman's acceptance of the fact that she sees no alternatives. She settles for "the honor of voluntary deference" as the only "path to honor" open to her.[22]

Papanek concludes that the situation cannot change until older women are convinced that their own self-interest must not involve the restriction of opportunities and of resource allocations for younger women. They must come to understand a refusal to reproduce subordinating conditions as having a very practical purpose in their own lives.

The benefits of participating in discriminatory systems

Some women participate in discriminatory religious systems not because they have no critical evaluation of them but because the benefits of participating in the ideology outweigh the costs of deviating from it. For these women it is the best way to get by at present, or simply to survive. Accommodating subordination is, to them, preferable to challenging it, and they make their choices accordingly.

Describing Algerian communities, for example, Marie-Aimée Hélie-Lucas has noted that women are portrayed as traitors, importers of "foreign ideology," if they lobby for the end of certain religious customs or for greater opportunities and autonomy. Some women will thus be deterred from questioning particular religious practices either because they fear the political or social consequences of being a traitor, or because they have come to believe the strong rhetoric from religious conservatives that their religious tradition is under siege and in danger of being eliminated.[23] Another North African commentator has named fear of vulnerability or of blurred boundaries as a motivating factor in some religious women's participation in their own subordination. The questioning of deeply entrenched and religiously defended limits on all aspects of one's life can be a frightening prospect. A possible loss of all rules and regulations could leave one in a nebulous social position that is actually worse than before, and even leave one vulnerable to physical attack.[24]

Writing from a Sudanese perspective, Nahid Toubia describes an acculturation process that begins in early childhood, with parental rewards offered for acceptance of practices such as clitoridectomy and infibulation, and with peer pressure. Girls who question or challenge social or religious norms are subdued by the women in the family, who will manipulate the girls' feelings and dependent status by shunning them or feigning serious illness until the girls come to accept whatever is at issue. Toubia writes, "Older women in particular are delegated to be the gatekeepers and internal security bodies in the women's section, and men need only keep a distant overview of the situation, confident that their wishes and instructions are being observed."[25] After marriage, much that a young woman might have hoped to change in her life is no longer conceivably negotiable. "When a woman passes through the experience of totally compromising on her own choices and accepts what was dictated and forced upon her, it is very difficult to maintain her self-respect unless she adopts these values as her own and pretends she has always accepted them,"[26] says Toubia.

"Conversion" to acceptance of what could not be surmounted becomes a survival strategy. Grace Akello, rejecting the reigning understanding of women's dignity in her native Uganda, writes,

> The deepest human motive is to seek the respect of others, and women will conform to the basest of obligations defined for them to have access to some respect.... To gain a sense of achievement, [a woman] must exert herself to prove that she is capable of fulfilling the demands of traditional society on womanhood. To be proud of her own existence she must have the approval of her society; *she must be proud of her own subordination.*[27]

Having been instructed by one's religious community to believe in certain roles, practices, and human value for women, some come to believe deeply that any discrimination they endure is not, in fact, discrimination, but the divine ordering of the world. Some may quell inner voices that contradict the religious teaching in an effort to eliminate the cognitive dissonance, and to avoid facing a challenge to their whole cosmology, one that threatens their total sense of identity, meaning, and security.

Accommodating subordinating theologies may bring material gain to women, or even actual rights and freedoms. They sometimes decide, therefore, that their best prospects, at least for the short term or given the entrenchment of certain social and religious customs, involve participation. They may gain "credits" when they participate in practices that seem to harm them.[28] They "choose against" human rights norms. For instance, in societies where dowries are given, many young girls approaching marriageable age actually crave dowry, since they understand their wellbeing to be directly tied to it. They do not organize against the giving of dowry as a thing that may turn them into commodities rather than human beings, or contribute to their neglect as girls and to domestic violence as wives. In their immediate context they judge that their welfare is best served by having a dowry – and the most substantial one possible for their families – so that they may make a better marriage.[29] Some of their mothers, acknowledging the unfairness to women in the different personal status laws' rules on inheritance, actively support the perpetuation of dowry. They see it as the only possibility at this point in time to pass on some of their own wealth to their daughters. For instance, interviews with women in working-class families in Cairo have shown their version of dowry (called *ayma*) to give them power and leverage in their marriage, security in divorce, and the leverage even to initiate divorce (the women want power, leverage, security). The fact that the *ayma* is processed under civil rather than personal law means that formal judgments are rendered relatively quickly and easily.[30]

Similarly, some girls (and their mothers) choose to cease their education before they "need" to – they "choose against" their human right to education. They do so before the family finances run out or the girl's productive labor is absolutely required, because the more education a girl has, the higher the dowry her family must raise in order to get her married. Other women decide that the expense is too great to justify further education since no practical improvements come to the girl or a family as a result of higher education. As one young woman puts it, "[I]f I were educated I would still have to work with cattle-dung."[31] In societies where marriage is compulsory and female wellbeing is directly tied to the match that is made for them, these girls are not wrong to focus their decision-making on whatever will improve their marriage prospects. Even clitoridectomy and infibulation are supported by some women if their status in the community rises significantly, if marriage is possible only by submission to the procedures, if wealthier marriages are more likely, or if performing the procedure on others results in increased symbolic and economic capital for themselves. Observers can rightly proclaim that women approve of genital cutting because they have been so deeply trained to serve male efforts at the sexual control of women, but the conversation needs to be taken to the next level to address why women think their own self-interest is enhanced by supporting it. If one wants to help end such practices, denying women's agency (as well as any religious meaning that might be applied) and dryly calling for human rights to bodily integrity as codified in international instruments will be counterproductive.

The location that religious women understand themselves to occupy may differ from others' perspectives. For instance, they may understand themselves as holders of great power because they perform genital cuttings, because they have endured such procedures, or because they have no paid employment. They may view wifehood as paid employment, a formal contractual trading of labor for other amenities. This may suggest to them that the rights to which they are entitled are essentially labor rights – fair compensation, fair productivity expectations, fair and healthy working conditions. Such an understanding of their rights may work in their favor, expanding their power and serving as a firm base from which to lobby for better overall rights enjoyment. On the other hand, understanding wifehood as paid employment may limit their choice-making related to rights. They may understand themselves to be situated in several locations at once, as paid employee, bearer of significant social power, and as a legitimately secondary member of society, all of which influences their understanding of their due rights enjoyment.

In any situation, dissatisfied actors continually assess the boundaries that they have for contesting prevailing conditions. The same is certainly true of religious women who are dissatisfied with the rights permitted to them. The boundaries that they identify may not be apparent to others. For instance, the punishments for insubordination levied by husbands, mothers-in-law, or other family and community members can be extremely heavy, and strongly influence religious women's decision-making regarding their level of accommodation. In certain contexts, women often choose not even to express their opinions or preferences unless they are absolutely sure of being proven correct, for fear of reprisal.[32] On one level, the boundaries of women's economic, social, and even physical well-being is thoroughly entwined with those of their husbands. Some women believe that their physical and economic vulnerability is so synonymous with that of their family that they dare not think of rocking the family's boat with demands for change. Two researchers of northern Indian women conclude, "[A] woman's security is far too bound up with the well-being of the household of which she is a member for major material benefits from mobilizing with other women to be apparent."[33] If young, oppressed women do not band together to change the structures that work against them, often it is because they choose to emphasize what they perceive as their short-term self-interest over against longer-term measures that may well be unsuccessful and further threaten their wellbeing. Besides, in the current system their status will only improve, to the point of one day having the power of the mother-in-law or other senior women. There is, therefore, some perceived benefit to choosing to bide one's time and wait for social power to accrue under the current system.

Some women, understanding that real resistance is not an option for them, choose to participate in and validate oppressive traditions rather than mount a hopeless or dangerous campaign. Bourdieu writes that "social categories disadvantaged by the symbolic order, such as women and the young, cannot but recognize the legitimacy of the dominant classification in the very fact that their only chance of neutralizing those of its effects most contrary to their own interests lies in submitting to them in order to make use of them (in accordance with the logic of the *éminence grise*)."[34] They choose to "go along to get along." For some women, exhibiting "good" emotions, responses, and spiritual perspectives is their only way of keeping a lid on their hostility and rage that would, should they let it out, result in severe consequences.[35] Women who are kept subordinate by religious tradition, in the end, and for a great variety of reasons, sometimes become "the most conservative force in maintaining and reinforcing that tradition,"[36] as a result of the choices they consciously make for themselves. Their choices may boil down to only two: validate the status quo or deny it and risk bodily harm. One may lament the scope of real agency in this equation, but if agency in the end is a question of whether or not individuals have choices (Giddens and others suggest this), even if the choice is accommodation or self-destruction, some women do self-consciously choose to participate in oppressive structures. A blanket equation of agency with resistance is incorrect, as is a rigid correlation between "choosing" and the perpetuation of a human rights culture.

For instance, one study has concluded that Syrian women's greatest obstacle to leaving abusive marriages or repressive family systems is the fact that to do so will certainly mean forfeiting all access to their children. Again, the menu of choices may seem terribly unjust, but women exercise their agency within their own context and often decide that their (and their children's) self-interest is better served by remaining in the marital home.[37] The choices may be terrible – even unconscionable – but given their particular circumstances, religious women enact their agency every day as they struggle to negotiate the constrictions on their lives.

A particularly vexing question regarding subordinated persons is how much agency they truly have if they do not have the power to implement their desires and broaden their choices. Agency, as Giddens has written, refers not to the intentions people have in doing things but their capability to do them.[38] The question of power and agency is a many-sided one. There are, as Jo Rowlands has noted, multiple manifestations of power.[39] There is "power over," and this is the kind of power most at issue in terms of agency. Individuals have varying levels of power over their own situation to implement their desires and "be their own boss." But there is also power *to*, power *within*, power *with*, and power *for*, and these may be the locations in which religious women are empowered to implement their agency. They may have enough power *within* their families to do some "back seat driving," influencing choices that other (more empowered) people make, without directly making such choices themselves. They may have the power *to* manipulate religious customs and practices into ones that indirectly serve their own self-interest. They may have power *for* influencing the theological perspectives of the children within their care, thus effecting gradual change in practices over the course of several generations. In short, they may not have primary decision-making power over their own lives, but they can retain other forms of power that have an impact on their wellbeing and are instances of the direct exercise of their agency.

There exists no cross-cultural rule of measure for such agency. No single standard could ever take into account all the factors that influence the innumerable situations of dominance and subordination around the world, particularly in regards to religious women. Indeed, for those women whose lives are severely circumscribed by patriarchal religious ideology, the equation of agency with significant challenge to and even overthrow of those subordinating norms is both unrealistic and unfair. As Nita Kumar has concluded,

> The degree and efficacy of agency can never be measured fully, but may be comprehended realistically only in the context of domination...it is only in comparison with larger structures that our subjects – and their weapons – come to be defined as weak, which brings us to the realization that weak subjects, weak weapons, and weak efforts cannot be expected to bear forth powerful results.[40]

Choosing to resist within discriminatory structures

Examples abound of religious women from every tradition who are able, from a position within the heart of their religious community, to navigate spiritual teachings and practices in order to gain space for themselves, to broaden their agency and their horizons, and to protest the terms of their subordination. Christian women in many countries have used their religion's teachings on charity and social uplift to make concrete improvements in the lives of other women (and also themselves).[41] Hindu widows have become shamans and ascetics and bought for themselves new spiritual and social space never before available to them.[42] Buddhist women in Sri Lanka have protested violence and government policies within the "space" of motherhood, using the rituals and curses and recourse to deities allocated to them by religious custom, banding together to form movements that withstand attack because of their unimpeachable religious integrity.[43] Muslim women who wish they could observe *purdah* but who are too poor to afford seclusion make self-affirming space for themselves in a different way, by claiming that *purdah* is actually an "internal" state. It is an attitude, a way of being that is truly accessible to them without the outer strictures.[44] With such thinking, the women increase their sense of autonomy, self-worth, and religious integrity. In myriad ways, religious women continue to reconstitute their "otherness" as space that helps them to negotiate their subordination and enhance their sense of agency and wellbeing, even if the immediate result is not to deconstruct the terms of their subordination, and even to accommodate it, or to make use of the human rights idea.

Recent contributions to women's studies in general and to subaltern studies in particular have added important nuances to the ongoing conversation on resistance and domination.[45] Scholars are now less likely to stereotype all persons of one region, sex, or religion as passive and accommodating, their voices permanently muffled by the ideologies of caste, *Shari'ah*, original sin, *karma* and *dharma*.[46] Resistance itself is now less likely to be viewed only as the public mounting of a movement or campaign. Resistance takes place in quiet ways in the home, with tactics that are rarely public, coordinated, documented, or visibly "successful." Many women whose rights are limited by religious ideology can be said neither to be passive, weak, and non-resisting nor as fully capable agents who enjoy a kind of full empowerment within whatever is allocated to them as their space or domain. As one anthropologist writes, most women "acquiesce yet protest, reproduce yet seek to transform their lives."[47] Most resistance is sometimes loyalist, sometimes subversive, and everything in between. In the end, many religious women negotiate subordinating traditions by simultaneously resisting and participating in their own subordination.

Some resistance by religious women is also non-conscious, but still legitimately understood as authentic agency. Indeed, many women will disagree with the suggestion that certain of their words or actions are a form of internal resistance.[48] These same words and actions, however, take firm if subtle aim at the domination endured by the women. Language, dance, ritual, and gossip are all ways that women counter their subordinate status, intentionally or not.[49] Non-compliance, foot-dragging, deception, and pilfering are other forms of internal resistance noted by James C. Scott during his research on subordinated peasants in Malaysia. The measures apply as well to religious women, whose resistance is relative to (and only can be understood in conjunction with) their context.[50]

Lest too rosy a glow be cast upon the situation of accommodating protest, it is important to name some remaining questions. For instance, does protest that accommodates gender subordination actually perpetuate or reinforce that subordination? Is that the by-product of the actions of women who form a mothers' group and protest, in the name of their (essentialized) role as nurturers and caregivers, the state-sponsored violence that has claimed their daughters and sons?[51] Are not these women also further entrenching biological arguments for a "woman's nature" that limits them to childrearing? They may be reconstructing motherhood as a space of protest, but are they not also reaffirming the idea that motherhood is the only space they deserve? Also, does accommodating protest in the end consume to non-practical ends the energy that could be used to really bring about change? Does internal resistance make the subject feel better, but further perpetuate her subordination by never really challenging it? What of resistance that encourages women to hate, devalue, or oppress men – is that not just an inversion of the original problem? The prevailing hierarchy is subverted in one sense, but also reproduced and strengthened in another; the fact of hierarchy itself remains in place.[52]

Some religious women intentionally participate in movements that appear to work *against* their wellbeing, all the while utilizing the rhetoric of social justice and even of human rights. Recent decades have seen a significant increase in women's participation in the public sphere in some sectors, including in traditionalist movements within politics, education, and employment. Assertive, empowered, and self-controlling women can and do use religion to accomplish what others would consider at cross-purposes with their self-interest. Because they find their traditionalist religious ideology to have integrity, they employ the human rights construct to perpetuate their own subordination or discrimination.

Some of these women find their greatest opportunity for internal resistance and the "growing" of new opportunities for themselves within the heart of fundamentalist organizations. Their participation in such movements, especially when it is self-consciously intended to increase their agency and autonomy, creates a rather bizarre situation. These women are simultaneously promoting their own personal liberation and their group subordination. The organizations may have been constructed by others with the intention of involving women in movements that, on their surface, advance pro-women agendas but that really are intended to further communal political and theological objectives, including a deeper entrenchment of patriarchal norms. In this way, women's current agency, via their desire to participate in out-in-the-open, sanctioned internal resistance, is manipulated to perpetuate their disempowerment. Some women are able, without resort to the human rights idea *per se*, and arguably by reifying the discriminatory, masculinist teachings of their religious communities, to create space for their own heightened autonomy and even rights enjoyment.

The following two examples from north India make particularly clear the advantages to religious women not only in accommodating subordinating theologies but also in becoming actual leaders in perpetuating them. The stories are not posited as ideal situations or as laudable alternatives to genuine challenges of patriarchy, but as concrete examples of how religious women exercise choice to improve their lives when they deeply believe in communal ideology (in the first example) and when the human rights rubric is essentially unavailable to them (in the second).

Kamlabehn[53] is a woman in her thirties (at the time she was interviewed by Paola Bacchetta), living in her hometown of Ahmedabad in Gujarat. She devotes much of her time to participating in a Hindu women's communal group called the Rashtra Seviki Samiti. Her main task is instructing other members in such paramilitary skills as karate, riflery, and the use of the *lathi* (a heavy stick). She is high-caste and middle class. She is an atheist. She married rather late (compared to local custom), having spent her 20s as a *pracharika*, an unmarried and celibate full-time volunteer for the Samiti. Of such a role, her interviewer Paola Bacchetta writes,

> The position has several indirect functions, one of which is to provide a legitimate space for revolt against the reproduction of the same lifestyle as their mothers, grandmothers, and so on in their feminine genealogies. Here the woman who chooses independence through celibacy, dedication to other women (the Samiti) and an ideal (the Hindu nation) in place of dedication to an individual male, and her own spacial mobility and the process of becoming a space for herself over functioning as a space for a man to come home to is respected and provided with the means to realize such choices, *albeit solely within the parameters carved out by the organization.*[54]

Indeed, Kamlabehn was able not simply to spend nights and weekends away from her family but to travel alone around the country in the second-class section of trains (often outside of the women's compartments), wear whatever clothing she chose (for her, usually blue jeans and a cotton tunic), and socialize far beyond the parameters of her extended family and neighbors. She was able to break out of decorous and demure postures when addressing men, especially those within the broader communal organization. The more similar she became to men, the more space she earned – and, in effect, the more she promoted their essentializing attitudes towards women (she herself became a prime example of some "rare" women's abilities to be goddess-avenger types). She adopted celibacy rather than striving for a traditional marriage actually based in mutuality of rights and respect, and so on.

When Kamlabehn finally did marry it was to a man very active in a brother communal group. She proposed the marriage (it had not been arranged by her parents). She then changed her dress to the more traditional *sari* with bangles, ankle bracelets and *bindi*. She vehemently denied that the clothing and accessories signaled any accommodation to standard models of normative femininity. Her interviewer agreed, concluding, "It simply reassured those in her environment by signaling that she occupies a space that in reality she does not occupy."[55]

Kamlabehn was using the dress as a kind of camouflage. It helped her to negotiate even more unorthodox opportunities for herself, such as living alone in a city different from her husband, meeting with him only when she wanted, and remaining childless. Bacchetta concludes that "she is now even less directly accountable to others for her time and spacial mobility than earlier."

Kamlabehn, proud to be atheist, makes interesting sense for herself of the difference between "Hindu culture" and "Hindu religion." In actuality, they are almost synonymous for her. But she asserts that "one can be a Hindu and not believe in any god because Hinduism is a culture and a science for living." To her, religion means the practice of god-centered rituals rooted in, as she says, "superstition." Interestingly, she pays quite a lot of attention to gods and goddesses in her own daily routine, not in worship but in study and emulation. Their warrior qualities and destruction of demons are major sources of inspiration to her in her work against the demons of her own time, which she names as "the Muslims."

Kamlabehn is vehement and vulgar in her regular verbal condemnations of "the Muslims," particularly Muslim males. But she has never met one. She bases her need for expertise in martial arts on the requirement of Hindu women to protect themselves from rape-minded Muslim men, but the only harassment she has ever received has been by Hindu men, and that has been within the larger Hindu communal organization. She explains it by saying, "among Hindus there are some who are not yet conscious. That is why we need the RSS, to teach them to respect women."[56] Bacchetta describes Kamlabehn's internalization of her anger at such harassment as follows:

> [B]y projecting such characteristics [bloodthirstiness, rape] onto Muslim men, Kamlabehn is able to discharge emotion that might otherwise accumulate into an impossible and unacceptable rebellion against the macho Hindu men in her environment. Instead, her representation of Muslim men only concretizes her solidarity with Hindu men by rendering even the most offensive of the latter as less offensive than the former. Such an attitude functions to confine Hindu nationalist women within a Hindu community whose boundaries and landscape are determined essentially by Hindu nationalist men.[57]

In the end, Kamlabehn has found a rather extraordinary way to enjoy a measure of autonomy and freedom that is unavailable to many Indian women. One senses that these things are of greatest importance to her – they are what she most wants. Without being a religious believer she has found a way to use the rhetoric of patriarchal religion to buy herself space to enjoy the freedom she desires. (One also has the sense from the transcripts of her interviews that what she does deeply believe is the rhetoric of Hindu nationalism.) She is able to use religious symbolism to further this non-spiritual agenda and even to resist the normative femininity of her religious culture. But it is also clear that Hindu men are permitting her the space she so relishes simply because Kamlabehn so ably uses it to serve their patriarchal nationalist interests. For the time being it seems to work for Kamlabehn. If she also understands – if she herself is "conscious" – that her efforts in the communal organization actually serve ultimately to negate her capacity for autonomy and freedom, she does not admit it.

A second example is Shobhag Kanvar who was, at the time of first being interviewed, in her mid-fifties, living in a joint household in rural Rajasthan.[58] She is illiterate, and has spent her life in the manner customary to the great majority of high-caste rural Hindu women – in the carefully regulated homes of her parents and husband, and identified by her status as daughter, wife, daughter-in-law, sister-in-law, mother, and grandmother. She earned for herself an additional identity that greatly expanded her sense of space, that of devotee of the Rajasthani hero-god Dev Narayan.

Shobhag Kanvar practices *purdah* in the local Hindu manner – her mobility outside her marital home is restricted as much as possible; should she leave the house she covers her face, and while in the house she veils again when in the presence of her husband's male relatives, speaking softly with her face turned away. She does not go to the village well to draw water, for to do so would be to break the rules of *purdah*. She does, however, go to the edge of the village boundary to worship Dev Narayan. There, his shrine is attended mostly by men, and all of them of lower castes. But Shobhag Kanvar has gained a reputation for particularly devout worship as well as deep religious knowledge. The male priest at the shrine, along with his associates, comes to her compound daily for tea and lively conversation. Because she also assists women pilgrims at the shrine on Saturdays, the priest gives her a percentage of their money offerings. With this income, Shobhag Kanvar has been able to build expensive stone and brick homes for herself and her adult sons.

Shobhag Kanvar continually stretches the boundaries of acceptable behavior with the license that she gains from her religious reputation.

She travels frequently to distant parts of Rajasthan for days at a time to visit other shrines to Dev Narayan. She does so in the company of the male priest and his associates. She has constructed a shrine in her own home that is considered to be spiritually legitimate. She has, in a sense, made herself into a kind of priestess. She drinks intoxicating beverages as part of religious observance during festivals (such drinking is not otherwise permissible to women). *Purdah* may require that women not leave their compounds, but Shobhag Kanvar is able to bathe in the much-valued village water tank without having her reputation impugned by others (particularly women) in the village. All the while, she is adamant that she is doing not just a respectably authentic but an exemplary job of practicing *purdah*. She is hostile to suggestions that she is not. She also clearly manifested to her interviewer a strong sense of self-worth that was only intensified by her religious practice.

It would seem, at the least, that Shobhag Kanvar wants for herself the freedom to practice her religion to the extent of her devotional interest, and that she has been able to do this. In the process she has secured for herself a measure of physical, economic, and social freedom denied to other women in her village. (It would be unsubstantiated to assume that these liberties are something that she has wanted all along, since she is very clear to limit her own comments on her agency and motives to a quest for religious integrity.) But she obviously has come to have an unusual amount of power over her personal affairs, power that she happens to retain by being so circumspect about it. Indeed, Shobhag Kanvar has found a way to both practice *purdah* and to enable it to permit her license. As her interviewer came to realize, she manipulates *purdah* so that it is not a "curtain," a veil, that prevents her from exercising autonomy or engaging the world beyond her family courtyard, but a veil that curtains off criticism of the agency she is employing. In a culture that requires women to be religious exemplars she has found a way to make such a role work for her. Other researchers have noted that once village women prove they can follow the religious rules, they are often allowed a measure of deviation.[59] Shobhag Kanvar shows just how far that deviation can go. She is, however, still required to practice *purdah*; the freedoms she has gained are considerable in the context of strong, religiously supported gender subordination, but many commonly accepted human rights are kept from her reach. Ingeniously combining accommodation and protest, she acquires as much space as her context could possibly allow without being condemned for it.

The accessibility and acceptability of human rights discourse

As noted in Chapter 1, research has shown that the very idea of human rights is problematic for some women, and so for a handful of reasons they proactively choose not to employ it. The language of human rights may be inaccessible or off-putting to some of them. In other situations it is not theoretically or practically able to address the underlying complexities of religious women's agency.

Human rights discourse inherently makes claims upon others. A study of American Christian women found the respondents socialized to be so other-oriented that they understand any claims they make as examples of selfishness.[60] Similarly, some research in Africa has also shown that the idea of making a claim against another person or institution is inimical to some women's ideas of what is appropriate. Much more accessible there are notions of corporate justice rather than individual right, even human rights.[61] Field studies in South Asia have shown that rights language in respect to women's economic development meets with broad resistance, but if the focus is shifted to women as economic producers there is general approval of the development initiatives being advocated.[62] There, a different emphasis on agency, combined with the benefits of religious women's productivity and income potential, would seem to reframe the issues in ways that are socially acceptable, while the advantage to whole families of women's income quells religious protest to women's employment.[63] In numerous contexts, then, women may choose against human rights because they perceive the concept itself to be alien, counterproductive, or inappropriate.

In addition to women's perceptions, another impediment to their use of the human rights idea is structural to the concept itself: the simultaneously individual yet corporate nature of religious life. Some critics of agency language describe it as an inappropriate emphasis on individualism within contexts and cultures that are not individualistic.[64] The idea of agency, it is said, portrays persons as complete and self-contained entities whose first commitment is to the furthering of their personal interests, rather than as beings-in-relation whose decision-making may take whole communities constantly into account. The same critique can be made of the human rights idea – that it encourages people to think individualistically about their claims for certain levels of social justice. Each religious tradition instructs adherents to understand themselves in relation to their total community and to whatever is perceived as divine. Individuals know themselves to be single entities, but also responsibility-bearing members of a greater whole. Their religious tradition may have instructed them to so thoroughly identify their wishes and needs with the larger community that any individual claims to human rights would feel incongruous.

Ultimately, assessments of what religious women "want for themselves" regarding human rights involve multiple, complicated levels. Are those who have internalized the terms of their domination the victims of false consciousness? Is it possible for women in any culture not to accept and accommodate some level or amount of patriarchal norms? What does this mean for the choices they make regarding human rights enjoyment? As Nita Kumar concludes, "[I]n all cases there is partial alignment with those very dominant structures, so that autonomy is never complete, it is often ambiguous, and is probably not always desired."[65]

Conclusion

The answer to the assertion that "what women want for themselves is what matters" is "yes, but." Yes, it always matters on principle, but it needs to be accompanied by local efforts to change subordinating, disempowering theological perspectives. Yes, women's own agency is crucial and the choices they make must be honored. But, the conversation on the matter must remain open between all who participate – women, family and religious leaders, and external critics – regarding socialization for inequality.

In the end, questions of agency in regard to compromised rights enjoyment by religious women come full circle. They point to the fact that if freedom of religion for individual women is respected, those women may choose to use their agency for ends that seem to others to be compromising of their essential agency and well-being. Especially for those commentators who are less sympathetic to religious practice, the question of agency continually returns to the issue of how much freedom a "conditioned" or negatively socialized person really has. Of course, there are many kinds of conditioning (advanced capitalist, Marxist, etc.) that have the same effect – they suggest to persons influenced by other ideologies that the subject has only limited freedom both to understand what is truly desirable for herself and to make good choices regarding her own (and others') well-being.

The focus of this study is those situations in which the human rights idea is of compromised or no assistance in securing religious women's human rights, and so these pages have necessarily dealt with women's agency as it is limited by religious ideology. Note must be made, however, of the radical resistance with which some women respond to religion-backed patriarchy. Rather than internal resistance that does not fundamentally challenge subordinating structures, some women leave subordinating institutions altogether, or remain within them to effect radical change from the inside out. Some women's response is personal – if they have the physical and economic freedom to do so they leave religious communities, be they geographically or socially constituted. They decide not to engage male dominance within religious groups but to free themselves of further concern. Others do not simply leave but also create organizations and networks to help women who choose to or who must remain. Others' radical resistance is not to religion *per se* but specifically to its patriarchal elements. These women refuse to leave their traditions to those who would subordinate women through them. They combat individual practices that have religious approbation, such as the Eyptian physician Nawal El-Saadawi in her campaign against clitoridectomy and infibulation. They challenge theologies and scriptural interpretations from a scholarly as well as a faithful perspective, such as Moroccan sociologist Fatima Mernissi. They also form their own institutions within religious institutions, such as the Women-Church movement among Roman Catholic women. If men, they say, have co-opted Christianity to support gender discrimination, we will create our own church for ourselves. They use the religion itself to challenge male domination within Christianity and without.

Meanwhile, for women in some religious communities or families, those who have internalized and accepted subordination, who have adapted their desires and choices to the self-denying religious teaching they have received, or who have found genuine short-term benefit in perpetuating rights-denying theologies and traditions, the human rights concept will be of little help, perhaps no help whatsoever, or even be detrimental. The human rights concept is not theoretically or practically able to address the underlying complexities of religious women's agency. The notion relies heavily on an individual's right to choose, yet for various reasons some women choose "against" human rights. Additionally, their right to freedom of religion solidifies their oppression and the denial of other human rights, as they choose to practice religious ideologies that perpetuate their subordination. For these women, religious ideology itself will have to change if they are to enjoy many human rights.

7 Religion, Rights and Change

> I would answer the question by a counter question: Has not the independence of man and his holding property led to the spread of immorality amongst men? If you answer "yes" then let it be so also with women. And when women have rights of ownership and the rest like men, it will be found that the enjoyment of such right is not responsible for their vices or virtues. Morality which depends upon the helplessness of a man or a woman has not much to recommend it. Morality is rooted in the purity of hearts.
>
> Mahatma Gandhi[1]

What, then, may one say of the Bangladeshi women with whose story this study began, whose morality in their community firmly depends upon their helplessness? Can the theoretical, legal, theological, and practical challenges to the implementation of rights norms be surmounted? Might the human rights idea ever be of practical assistance to them as they struggle to keep themselves and their children alive?

The human rights idea may be of practical service to them if certain criteria are met. The government of Bangladesh (which has ratified the Women's Convention) must first enforce the Convention's provisions. It must provide secular courts at every level and require their judges to render decisions without appeals to "morality" or religious sentiment. The government must provide (and/or endorse by other legitimate agencies) education for all citizens, including those who are illiterate, concerning the rights they have under the law. It must encourage acceptance of the rights idea among all citizens in order to promote compliance even in the private sphere. It must enforce those provisions of the Convention that pertain to the family and home, and it must encourage and educate every religious community to understand and accept the rights idea as an authentic articulation of common aspirations for social justice, including the particular provisions within the Women's Convention.

Enhanced legislation and compliance are always important in securing religious women's human rights. Bangladesh, however, like many countries both rich and poor, has a long way to go towards fulfilling the criteria outlined above. For example, B.R. Ambedkar, one of the framers of India's Constitution, once said, "[W]hatever else Hindu society may adopt it will never give up its social structure – the enslavement of the Shudra and the enslavement of women. It is for this reason that law must come to the rescue in order that society may move on."[2] However, the Indian experience and others have shown that religious perspectives must change or even the most progressive positive law will be stymied. For those for whom religious women's rights are of primary concern, enhanced legislation on human rights alone will not be sufficient. Familial and religious ideologies have also proven themselves stronger than both international and domestic law. The best efforts of the Government of Bangladesh will be thwarted when communities resist implementing the Women's Convention on the grounds of their human right to freedom of religion. Women's rights everywhere will continue to be subordinated to patriarchal religious ideology, and to be used as tools or leverage in the vortices of broader religious, political, social, and economic power bids. The evidence of the last 50 years of human rights lawmaking (and also of Indian statehood) reveals that such laws are not able to counteract these effects directly. At its worst, the legal imposition of human rights norms can cause a backlash that harms women.[3] The Shah Bano controversy is evidence of that in India. So, too, is the fact that a Uniform Civil Code has yet to be created there. Today, the best tactic for securing Indian women's rights is to change religious personal status laws rather than to focus on a secular, national human rights code, which some reformers think would be too contentious ever to achieve, or would essentially reflect the positions of Hindu nationalists.

The most effective response to religious arguments for self-exemption from rights norms is religious counter-arguments that support intra-familial, intra-community value change. Such theological/ideological change, rather than legislation, is the primary key to women's ability to access material resources within their families and communities, to access information and opportunities, and to ameliorate their position within the home. Without theological change, even the best positive laws and the strongest commitments to their implementation will face an uphill battle. Indigenous theological reformulation will enable women's roles at home to improve without devaluing those roles altogether, and without stripping them of the religious meaning that is cherished by and nurturing of many women. Done well, it will also avoid biological determinism and appeals to what is "natural." Both secular and religious reformers are invaluable, but especially those who work within the traditions, because they have the greater legitimacy and are less easy to dismiss.

While legal arguments can be presented to show that positive changes to divorce and inheritance laws are not incompatible with religious tenets or secular norms, the real change within communities has to be in religious rather than legal understanding about these issues. As mentioned in earlier chapters, a practice that has come to have religious meaning for people (whether or not it is an historically religious practice) must be treated as such, and challenged on religious grounds. Until religious sense has been made of the argument for change, the practice will prevail. The work must also be done in and for individual communities, first because of the diversity of theologies and religious customs within religions, and secondly because perceived efforts to homogenize or force uniformity may also be resisted.[4]

Secular legal revisions are not to be discounted, however. On the contrary, strong civil legislation on women's rights continues to be essential, even in cases of the firmest theological commitment to gender equality. Carefully, lawmakers everywhere must venture into curbs on practices that have the approval of religious communities, such as polygamy, impunity for "honor" or dowry killings, genital cutting, and so on. In some places, laws may be added that enable individual women to interpret their religion according to their own conscience. This would be a corrective to the prevailing emphasis on group religious rights that is present in the United Nations instruments and elsewhere, an emphasis (as pointed out earlier) that privileges the perspectives of religious leaders and the maintenance of intra-religious manifestations of the status quo. However, legal strengthening of enforcement for existing rights provisions is called for with the caveat that, at their heart, aspirational legislation may continue to be largely non-justiciable.

Again, the limits of legal remedies are apparent. Careful circumscription of religious practices by courts cannot be expected in non-secular governments. Furthermore, courts are not always objective in terms of religious ideology. Secular courts are often a site of contest through which religious conservatives and communalists (not to mention progressives) seek to promote their social agendas.[5] Systemic theological change can only have a positive impact on secular courts, as long as judges continue to render decisions based on their personal religious ideology. If they do continue to do so, then progressive theological change within their own communities will help them to adjudicate better.

Studies have shown that the more education a woman has, the less likely she is willing to conform to patriarchal religious practices.[6] The key to the theological change for which this book advocates is education for women and men. Formal education, however, is not available to many women (and sometimes men) and, if it is, may be at a conservative religious (or secular) school that would strongly resist progressive changes. The education called for in many instances is, therefore, at the grass-roots level, and not reliant on literacy for its effectiveness. Dialogical instruction from individual or organized women (and men), verbal text study, and the reformulation of moral norms can change women's and men's understanding of prevailing notions such as redemptive suffering. In base Christian communities in Latin America, for instance, women's Bible studies and conversation groups discuss how to preserve the notion of redemptive suffering in its positive sense for them – the ways that it confirms their central Christological beliefs and lends an affirming cosmic meaning to their own suffering – while challenging the ways that the theological tenet has been manipulated to encourage their docility or their acquiescence with unjust structures. Underneath discrete theological topics the basic education being offered is in critical analysis, applicable to many areas of life but focused especially upon naming the ways that religion is used to preserve patriarchal or class privilege and to disempower women. Inequality is based on socialization that is learned, and that can be unlearned. Discriminating theology is also learned, and may be unlearned.

The exact methods of challenging patriarchal ideology and educating for theological change will differ from community to community. Such change must be legitimate to the participants in method and content else it will not succeed. Also, those working for change must begin by helping all participants articulate what is most deeply treasured in their religious and social lives (for instance, strong families and strong communities). This is radical change in the most literal sense – it goes to the root, or radix, of what people value most. Some resistance is inevitable if people think they stand to lose something that they cherish or need in the process of reformulating religious and social norms. Women may need assurance (or proof) that physical or economic security, status, proximity to children, and other highly valued things will not be forfeited but enhanced in the reworking of religious presuppositions and the challenging of patriarchal ideology. New religious vision does not change some essential goals for happiness or self-fulfillment (such as family wellbeing), only the criteria (such as women's subordination).

Grassroots religious education has been named above as the most important mechanism for changing religious ideologies into ones that affirm women's rights. But different contexts feature different roadblocks to the integrating of rights norms and religious practices. Ignorance of theological or legal resources, homogenizing pressure from conservative religious leaders, the political and social agenda of one's government (whether religious or secular), long-held familial traditions and structures, and the legitimization of patriarchy in the wider society are just some of the impediments. In some settings an intentionally feminist critique of theologies and practices will be most helpful. Feminist thought abounds in each of the world's religious traditions (although sometimes the actors who claim the title of "feminist" within the same tradition espouse very different ideas). For instance, the major Protestant churches in Europe and North America have, since the 1960s, been significantly impacted by internal feminist critiques of theology, exegesis, liturgy, and polity. The results in particular communities include a new commitment to women's leadership on multiple levels, increased attention to domestic violence (including its public condemnation and practical support for victims), and the introduction of feminine or gender-neutral language for God.

Some women will ascertain that the best way to secure their own rights in the present moment will be to affirm that they are best found in the practice of faith. As a mechanism for positive change in women's rights enjoyment this is a problematic approach. As earlier chapters have noted, it is an argument most often put forth by religious conservatives to further entrench their power. But certain situations give women no choice but to make religious arguments if they want to improve their rights. Existing rules on inheritance and divorce, however constricted or unequal, may be preferable to alternatives, or may have no alternatives. These women may also understand the claiming of (albeit discriminatory) religious prescriptions as a way to open the conversation about their rights in general. Religious teachings serve as a stepping stone, a first crack in the door, on the way to greater rights enjoyment. These women insist on making bridges between religious and rights discourses, using the only rhetoric they have at hand.[7]

In other settings a human rights-based critique will be the best tool for change. The various challenges to that critique are the subject of this book, but if the rights idea has power and validity, if it is acceptable to people more broadly (perhaps they have used it to lobby for an item of justice outside the religious community), and if religious leaders do not adapt the concept to fit discriminating features of current religious practice, a human rights critique can be used internally to argue for gender equality. If a religious community has fought for the human right to be protected from physical assaults by neighbors or from discriminatory legislation, for example, they may also be persuaded to understand women as having a right to be protected from assault at home, no matter what the religious teaching has been on the matter.

And rights change. The current (as this book argues, limited) state of the rights idea to secure religious women's rights is, one hopes, not the ultimate evolution of the concept. Ideally, the human rights notion will evolve so as to better bridge the gap between religious practices and rights norms for women. The rights concept is, of course, always in transition, responding to broader social movements and the activism of individuals and organizations. The Women's Convention of 1979 was not the precursor to the women's liberation movement but a part of it, perhaps even a response to it. That document is only one example of many efforts to add a consciousness of women's rights to international lawmaking. During the 1970s, the particular focus was on women in the development process and the establishment of equity in that area. By the conclusion of the United Nations Decade for Women at the Nairobi conference of 1985, the areas of greatest attention were equality, development, and peace.[8] By the early 1990s the campaign of "women's rights are human rights" was in full swing, attempting to make all existing rights legislation as applicable to women as it is to men, and to combat gendered rights violations with positive law. In the opinion of Charlotte Bunch, the Fourth World Conference on Women in Beijing, 1995, became in practicality an agenda for women's rights, and proof of the successful "mainstreaming" of the "women's rights are human rights" movement.[9]

That movement had grown increasingly concerned about violence against women, insisting that it be treated as an infringement of human rights and a criminal issue, a particular instance of the violence addressed in existing international instruments that simply needed better enforcement. By the mid- to late-1990s, a further transition in rights discourse and strategizing was the introduction of brand new rights categories whose subjects were specifically women, rather than women as the fellow-humans of men. An initial action was the formulation in 1993 of the Declaration on the Elimination of Violence Against Women. The sexual, physical, or emotional violence endured particularly by women at the hands of the state, employers, husbands, boyfriends, or other relatives finally received specific attention, accompanying growing public attention to such issues.

With time, even some advocates for the "women's rights are human rights" movement have re-evaluated the viability of crow-barring a consciousness of women's issues into existing rights legislation. Like the world's religions, human rights discourse changes in response to people's personal experiences. Charlotte Bunch, for example, has more recently suggested not fitting women's justice concerns into human rights discourse but rather starting with women's experiences and from them working for the transformation of rights discourse.[10] It is a bottom-up rather than a top-down approach, and one that already is being employed in numerous societies. Questions and struggles are localized by topic and region. Women in many regions are attempting to use the rights notion to combat religiously validated violence and patriarchy, but with variations that fit their context and theological adversaries. The struggles have many commonalities (as evidenced by the Programme and Platform for Action).[11] They are specific to particular women's experiences, reflective of the ethical and religious sensibilities of their community, and permit a new kind of ownership and intentional application of the human rights idea in ways that have local integrity, authenticity, and authority.[12] Rights discourse is continually changing as different communities claim, use, and appropriate it for their own justice struggles. Having studied the use of rights discourse by lower class women in Cairo, Heba El-Kholy concludes that "conceptions of rights are socially and historically situated and are linked to both discursive elements as well as to constructions of identities."[13]

The influence of non-governmental organizations (NGO's) on rights discourse has been very significant, as attested to by a considerable body of literature, including the discourse on religious women's rights. Their impact grows with each passing year, especially as organizations focus their attention on policy-setting institutions as well as their local communities. The group Women Living Under Muslim Laws, for instance, attended the Global Tribunal on Violence Against Women at the United Nations' 1993 conference on human rights in Vienna. There they called for rights violations based in religion to be granted significantly more serious treatment at the 1995 United Nations conference in Beijing a plethora of religious organizations exerted real influence upon the resulting Programme and Platform for Action.[14] Manisha Desai reports that organizations in attendance at both meetings found that "[t]he human rights framework was both broad enough to incorporate women's issues from around the world and pliable enough to be transformed from a feminist perspective."[15] Meanwhile, organizations of religious women are transforming the rights discourse of whole governments, such as in Malaysia, where Sisters in Islam has had important domestic influence in stemming negative effects of Islamization.[16] Rights discourse on religion and women is undergoing important change because women and men are forming activist organizations in order to effect such change.

One particular change in the human rights concept that would benefit women is an expansion away from emphasis on negative liberties. Progress has already been made in this area. The Women's Convention is a fine case in point; explicit and proactive rights *to* certain issues are forthrightly articulated. Yet the historical and practical primacy of place accorded to negative liberties in rights thinking remains. Individual freedom is achieved through being unburdened of onerous external constraints in one's pursuit of happiness, justice, and fulfillment. The freedom to be left alone by those in power reifies the power of the dominant actor. The local status quo is maintained. This may be a boon to those who do not wish for state or other intrusion into their lives, but it is a great deficit to those in that local environment for whom the status quo is oppressive. If left in a situation of negative liberty, as noted in Chapter 1, women in many religious communities will find their ability to choose rights norms for themselves tremendously restricted.

Globalization is affecting structures such as economic and political systems, but it is also having an impact on the notion of human rights. The idea of human rights is being globalized; its supporters are not complaining. Feminism and other movements are experiencing similar processes (in the words of one writer, recent years have seen "a spectacular growth of a global feminist public, which has been shaped to provide a powerful political platform for making claims on the global stage about women's rights as human rights").[17] In various societies, as with El-Kholy's Egyptian example cited above, the rights idea is being shaped to fit local experiences, contexts, and identities, and thus is being transformed. But those societies are also being reshaped by globalization, presenting the possibility that lines of accountability for upholding human rights may be substantially altered.

Saskia Sassen has written of the potential for the erosion of state sovereignty, at least as it involves the reassignment of economic and political governance to international, non-governmental or partly governmental institutions. With the growth of an international public, international governance, and international norm-making, human rights may actually be more easily secured, unmoored from state authorities and shifted on to international bodies. An international legal order or a global civil society may prevail; citizenship rights will be de-emphasized and human rights will be the primary discourse for social justice.[18] Should this scenario develop, the implications for religious women could well be positive. Their human rights, regardless of their local social context, may receive significantly more attention. But the ramifications could be negative too, if international organizations (such as the United Nations) continue to give religious communities great latitude in deciding which human rights norms they will uphold. Religious communities, meanwhile, could respond to this form of globalization with even greater retrenchment than some of them do today.

As the examples throughout this study show, the issue is not whether the human rights idea is universal or adaptable to local differences; it is. The human rights idea has more than enough elasticity and breadth to lend itself to local concepts, situations, and images. As noted in the previous chapter, sometimes an argument not for human rights but for economic opportunity for women will be culturally acceptable, and therefore become a method of enhancing women's rights.[19] Rights to work and to greater autonomy are articulated and achieved by focusing on the benefit to a family from women's economic empowerment. And as noted in Chapter 6, the human rights idea is adapted in Nigeria to focus not on rights claims (which clash with local mores on appropriate selflessness) but on particular items of justice for individuals, a culturally acceptable approach.[20] Religious women's rights might be better secured in some contexts through movements whose discourse centers on a different social "good," be it citizenship benefits or maintenance of family property rather than individual human rights and women's agency per se. In every location activists are needed to articulate such indigenous concepts that promote the advancement of women's human rights.

The human rights idea may be elastic enough to apply to innumerable cultural locations, but at issue in every circumstance is whether or not those people, locally or nationally, who have the power to decide on others' rights enjoyment will choose to affirm the idea. For instance, the US government has yet to ratify the Women's Convention. A major sticking point seems to be the assertion in Article 11(d) that women have a human right to equal pay with men for equal work performed. The granting of human rights may be seen as threatening to the religious, economic (as in the case of equal pay), social, or political power of the potential grantors and therefore be denied, with religion arguably the most unimpeachable reason for doing so. In this American example, muted economic and social excuses are being made for not ratifying the Convention ("Paying women equally will be detrimental to many businesses"; "Women would thus be required to serve in equal capacity in the armed forces"). The US Senate seems to be waiting for the Women's Convention to die of neglect.

This is an important factor in the debate over the primacy of women's rights versus religious freedom, an element so large as to be omnipresent yet so evident as to go unnoticed – the role of economic, social, and political processes. Religious leaders are not incorrect to suspect that "foreign influences" and "ideological colonization" are encroaching, reorienting, and transforming traditional ways of being. The ideological bogey is not movements for gender equality, however, for which each religion has a long, indigenous tradition. Neither is the culprit the human rights idea itself. Religious leaders' sense of uneasiness and of being subject to factors beyond their control is often the result of cultural change and their communities' absorption into an economy of advanced global capitalism for which there is truly an unequal starting line. Their greatest challenge is the reification of the unjust distribution of wealth and power within and between societies, and not the empowerment of their female relatives.[21]

Meanwhile, the economic empowerment of women remains crucial. Interviews conducted for this study and others show that religious women understand a key contribution to their rights enjoyment to be improvements in their material quality of life through strengthened economies.[22] Improved status of living through food security, job availability, potable water, and other basic services helps relieve the pressure on families and communities that sometimes exacerbates patriarchal violence. National wealth is no panacea for rights infringements, yet the point is well taken that advocates for religious women's rights directly help the cause through activism for economic justice, democracy, and universal education. Those who wish to secure human rights for women in conservative religious communities would do well to work in partnership with those whose efforts are focused on the economic, political, physical, and social health of those societies.

The rights challenges to poor women are worsening with increased economic disparity, and the economic forecast for them is not promising. Of all the resources for resistance to patriarchal religious ideology, economic well-being may become less and less of an option. Now, more than ever, religious women and their allies will need to explore their multiple allegiances in order to challenge subordinating ideologies. Class, gender, regional, professional, and political identities extend beyond the boundaries of religion (much as they also establish boundaries within religion). There is globalization from above (multinational corporations, international lending institutions, and the expansion of a single, capitalistic economic order) but there is also globalization from below – transnational solidarity groups, religious organizations, feminisms, environmentalisms, and human rights activisms.[23] While the details of patriarchal religious ideologies may differ between various communities, mutual challenges such as negative stereotyping, denial of access to material resources, and intimate violence may be addressed in common. The same is true for a shared resistance to the so-called "feminization of poverty" (rather, the impoverishment of women) and the entrenchment of disparities of wealth. When she once was asked how women from the global North could be of assistance to women in poor countries, the Indian economist Bina Agarwal answered simply, "Consume less."[24] Advocacy for the elimination of patriarchal elements in religious ideologies must be partnered with advocacy for a change in the economic policies of one's own country that contribute to the same women's poverty.

And religions change, sometimes in content, sometimes in emphasis. Each of the world's religions is a philosophy and a construct in transition, in flux. None are static; they are always evolving. They are perpetually responding to stimulation from the broader society and from members' own evolving sense of what is spiritually true. The last 100 years give particular evidence of the religions' simultaneous permanency and elasticity, as traditions have responded to science and technology, information exchange and immigration, new epistemologies, ontologies, and theologies, and the ebbs and flows of their own power in various societies.

Religions change as they accommodate, on a grand or small scale, transitions in the way of thinking in the wider society. The Age of Reason, modernity, and now post-modernity, for example, each have challenged communities within every religion to strikingly new ways of thinking of deity, of the cosmos, of human value generally, and a host of other topics at the core of each religion's concern. Thinkers within each tradition have led the way; members of religious communities do not simply respond to transitional forces in society but actively help create them. Whether or not religious communities admit it, they are in constant conversation with culture and politics, giving shape to them as simultaneously they are shaped by them.

Religions change along with social attitudes, with perceptions of justice, and with ways that spiritual sense and meaning are constructed by a community. Social and theological opinions evolve, and certain practices or religious concepts are sometimes decided to be inconsistent with the ethics of a tradition. Such is the case with human chattel slavery, for instance, in most of the world's communities and the religions they practice. Capital punishment, hierarchical relations in the family, animal sacrifice, widow burning, and heterosexism are some of the practices condoned in the sacred texts and traditions of certain religions that have since been decided, by some communities, to be antithetical to the religion's essential teachings. Put another way, individuals or communities sometimes decide that what *makes* them Christian, Jain, Sikh, and so on, is not particular practices – that *purdah* is not what defines them as Hindus or Muslims – and that, in fact, the ethical imperatives of their religion require them to cease the practice in question. Identity issues are deeply at play in the conflict between women's rights and religious practices. When religious identity and subordinating practices or theologies can be unsutured from one another, when theological arguments against the practices or attitudes show its ethical inconsistency or historical untenability, revision happens, as with the case of slavery. The ability within communities to name which identities are acceptable or beyond the pale (homosexuals, independent women, persons of other faiths, etc.) is at the heart of intra-religious power conflicts. The issue is not that the religions *cannot* accommodate women's rights norms, but that some of them *do* not.

The lived experience of particular communities or of whole traditions is another reason why religious practices or beliefs change. Experience produces knowledge, yet is always mediated by theory, superstition, belief, attitude, perspective, and so on. The interpretation of experience is constructed and subjective. So are theological positions. They are manufactured formally by those persons deemed learned or orthodox, while they are also continually conjured by faithful individuals with no education at all. This "doing" of theology or framing of religious perspectives is always done in response to personal experience, even by those who claim to interpret their religion without any bias or personal influence. This fact was claimed by the first liberation theologians in the Christian tradition, and the assertion caused one of the greatest theological uproars in recent Christian history. Many in the denominations' and rites' hierarchies vigorously denied the liberationists' claims that even the opinions of figures such as Augustine and Aquinas were conditioned by their class, gender, race, and other factors. These factors, say the liberationists, shape a person's experience, and personal experience shapes the way in which each person understands the nature of God. In naming the relativity of the religious experiences and theological perspectives of classical Christian thinkers, the liberationists directly challenged the power and compromised the influence of the churches' hierarchy to define what is normative about religious thinking.

Liberation theology began in Latin America in the 1960s out of the experience of extreme economic inequity. Pastors and theologians and peasants, using their experience of grinding poverty and of marginalization, began to interpret Christian scripture, tradition, and teachings from that lens. They produced a whole new school of theological thought, a whole new tradition in biblical exegesis, both of which understood God as being radically aligned with whatever persons are oppressed in any given situation. The poor and marginalized were encouraged to follow their empowering biblical study with concrete action for social change, and to view spiritual reflection and practical response as part of the same seamless action.[25] Liberation theologies have since sprung forth from many Christian communities around the world. There are Black, African, feminist, womanist, mujerista, gay/lesbian/bisexual/transgendered, Korean, and South Asian schools of liberation theology, to name just a few. The concept of liberation theology may have gone global, but it continues to be in response to very local (and personally experienced) situations of oppression. Many of the strands of liberation theology share with Islamism and Hindutva a challenge to hegemonic neo-liberal politics, economics, and social order. Like them, liberation theology is radicalized religion in response to current events, but in a progressive rather than conservative theological key.

At a continually accelerating rate, religions are changing with the help of technology. From short-wave radios that carry religious programming into the least developed areas of the globe, to the Internet's realization of "virtual" religious communities, ideas are being exchanged faster than ever. Local belief systems are being challenged; sometimes the response is change, and sometimes it is retrenchment. Patterns of immigration are also effecting (and affecting) religious change. Some people adapt their theological perspectives as they more fully integrate the values of their new society. Some people suddenly find themselves as members of a minority rather than majority religious community, and in the struggle to articulate their beliefs in the new context find that subtly they are being altered in the retelling. Repatriation or occasional visits to one's place of origin bring the effects of religious change and challenge back to those areas as well.[26] In all, the effects of change in societies' epistemologies, of increased articulation of personal experience in the constructing of religious belief, in technology, immigration, and other facets of globalization means that the religions are changing more at the present moment than at any time in history.

There are women and men in every tradition who work to effect positive change, and to push their tradition's boundaries wider so that they include all rights for all women. Their strategies differ across traditions as well as within them, as do their opinions of where, exactly, the problem lies. Every religion has both oppressive and liberating characteristics and practices, plus reform movements with decades of experience in challenging subordinating customs.[27] Some seek change through a revisiting of the central paradigms of the faith, a return to "history" to reinterpret or rediscover the true character of founders, the original meaning of scriptures or intentions of customs and practices. These reformers accept those things that conservatives portray as normative as their own bases for theological construction, attempting to "reclaim" them.

Hindu women who wish to change gender subordination have both a harder and an easier task than women in other traditions. It is harder because it is so much more diffuse, diverse, and uncodified. Sacred texts do not have the same spiritual authority as in Islam and Christianity, for instance. Their work is easier for the very same reasons, however. In helpful ways, Hinduism is diffuse, diverse, uncodified, and its patriarchal texts lack the extreme authoritativeness of others'. In recent decades the focus of many Hindu feminist reformers has been goddesses. Proud of the fact that Hinduism is a religion with actual female deities, supporters of goddess-re-appropriation say that a female object of worship can only help to elevate the status of women. Some reformers work to refashion the image of the most popular goddesses, such as Sita and Parvati, into models of strength and autonomy. Lina Gupta, for instance, has suggested Kali as a goddess with potential for reformers of Hinduism's patriarchy. Kali has *stri shakti*, or "women's power;" she is independent, fierce, and strong. Kali transcends duality, according to Gupta, and can be a source of "social and spiritual liberation for all women and men."[28]

Other reformers, such as Kancha Ilaiah, think that even Kali is not going far enough away from the patriarchal Hindu mainstream to be an effective model for women, that she is still part and parcel of elitist Brahminical Hinduism. Rather, it is in the local, Dalit goddesses such as Pochamma (in Andhra Pradesh) who exist in a mythical world without husbands, caste or class allegiances. Pochamma is fully independent, powerful, just, and benevolent. Still other commentators, such as Rajeswari Sunder Rajan, question the ability of any goddess to aid in restructuring Hinduism along gender inclusive lines. They claim that all goddesses are figures so embedded in mythologies of subservience and *pativratya* that they are beyond all reclamation, and can only embody the religious mystique of total gender subordination. The whole project is a dicey one, as the re-appropriation of goddesses is being employed simultaneously by Hindu nationalists as well as progressive reformers. (See, for instance, the case of Kamlabehn in Chapter 6 for an example of a young woman who models herself after Kali in her efforts to support violence against Muslims and to build a "Hindu" nation.) Sunder Rajan writes that those most likely to consider Hindu goddesses as having liberating potential for women are Hindu nationalists, members of some South Asian Studies departments in the west, some radical Indian feminists, and Gandhian secularists – strange bedfellows indeed. In the end, Hindu goddesses promote women's empowerment in negative ways as well as positive ones. The conscious, intentional reinterpretation of religious history, texts, and characters is an important task, but it must always be done in the context of positive political, social, and economic changes, rather than greater ideologies (such as Hindutva) whose imagined society is thoroughly patriarchal.[29]

Christian women, likewise, are working to reform their tradition into one that affirms gender equality in every way. They understand that the Bible, classic theological formulations, history and tradition are steeped in patriarchal norms, but also believe that each of these is a matter of a particular (if popular) interpretation of the tradition that is not intrinsic to it. They work to reconstruct essential biblical exegesis, and the foundations of Christian theology and symbolism, into ones that are neither androcentric nor gynocentric. Sexism and patriarchy are named as sins, as things that separate individuals and communities from God, that encourage domination and subordination, and refute essential human equality. Some women choose to remain in the heart of congregations, seminaries, denominations, and other adjudicatories as they do their reformist work. Others think that there is little or no hope in the traditional church, and so form their own Christian communities where they feel free to explore non-androcentric scriptural study, symbolism, rituals, and ecclesiastical relationships (such as the Women-Church movement in Roman Catholicism).

Some Christian women focus their re-envisioning efforts on historical characters such as Jesus and Mary, attempting to reclaim their original, liberating intentions. Jesus is understood to have radically challenged the gender stratification of his era (and therefore he would do the same today). Biblical accounts of his interactions with women, along with the teachings attributed to him, are said to show that he viewed women and men as having radically equal human value. Mary is re-envisioned not as a meek, subservient girl who was used as an actor in a divine plan but as a strong young woman who actively and enthusiastically participated in the creation of a new social and spiritual order, defying social convention. Some women work to highlight the liberating potential of certain biblical texts and to put negative ones into historical/critical perspective, placing them in the context of the patriarchal culture in which they were written, and declaring that they are evidence not of divine will but the human writer's patriarchal bias. And women have entered the field of theology, ethics, church history, and in some denominations, church leadership. For many, the cornerstone of the Christian social message is one that defies every form of human domination, including patriarchy. The Christian faith that they genuinely experience – the very nature of God that they personally have come to know – is what informs their work, and it is antithetical to patriarchy.

Muslim women are engaged in very similar, intentional work to create theological and practical change within their religious tradition. Their efforts for change have a similar goal – more equitable gender and social relations in Islamic society[30] – but their methods, theological perspectives, and ultimate aims are different. Azza Karam identifies three kinds of feminism in her native Egypt whose focus is positive change in religious culture. The first group is the "secular feminists," those women who work for change in Islamic society without attempting to revise the discourse of Islam. Their demands for full rights for women are based in the international human rights instruments. They portray religion as a matter of individual preference and concern, and make no attempt to reconcile religious teachings and rights principles. They view religion as a completely inappropriate source for the establishment of gender rights norms.

The second group is the "Muslim feminists," whose intention is very much to harmonize religious teachings and rights norms (for instance, Fatima Mernissi, referenced in Chapter 3, who has written on the original Qur'anic context of veiling and seclusion).[31] They make full use of the Qur'an, Sunna, and other sources to support their claims for gender equality. They view the realization of human rights for women as doomed within Islamic cultures if the norms in question cannot be reconciled with texts and teachings. They are concerned that a separation of religious and feminist discourses will inevitably leave the conversation on women and religion solely in the hands of Islamists. Riffat Hassan is an example of a Muslim feminist (she is originally from Pakistan). In working to revise texts and practices that she considers misinterpreted, and to recover helpful traditions that are neglected by patriarchal interpreters, she writes of three textual/theological questions as having ultimate importance: how was woman created, was she responsible for the advent of evil and hardship in the world, and why was she created.[32]

A third group is the "Islamic feminists" (most of whom, Karam admits, would strongly object to being called feminists).[33] In their opinion, proper Islamic values are under attack from outside notions of equality, and women suffer as a consequence of trying to attain this foreign interpretation of equality. They are "forced" to go out and work, to compete with men, and be humiliated and disrespected in the process. Extra burdens are placed on women, who are expected (and expect themselves) to be "superhuman." Women are equally important as men in their fulfillment of their crucial roles both in the home and without. Their invaluable purpose and integrity will be maximized to the extent that a society lives by *Shari'a* and the idea of the "complementarity" of the sexes.[34]

Liberal Muslim scholarship accompanies these varying approaches to feminism with a similar diversity of perspectives. The first views "original" Islam as simply patriarchal; the second views the earliest forms of Islam as patriarchal in practice but not in intention, and therefore recoverable; the third permits only the Qur'an as an authoritative source, viewing all others as corrupted and therefore inauthentic; and the fourth calls for a whole new *ijtihad*, or interpretation of tradition.[35] A fifth, the Mùtazila school of rationalist Islamic theology, has challenged the traditional idea that the Qur'an is "eternal in God." Other modern epistemologies have similarly desacralized the Qur'an, emphasizing its daily applicability and contributions rather than its eternal or divine nature.[36] The debates are vigorous within various feminist and intellectual circles on the value and potential of Islam in dismantling patriarchy.

Ghazala Amwar is one intellectual who cautions against any use of fundamentalists' paradigms by fellow Muslims who wish to ground universal human rights and gender equity within an Islamic perspective. Her caveat has resonance for other traditions as well. She notes that reformers tacitly promote "the absence of a secular state"; because they do not frame a theological basis *for* a secular state, they concede ground to fundamentalists on this point. Additionally, reformers' heavy emphasis on the importance of authoritative interpretations of sacred texts, on the earliest portions of the community's history, on return to the original, guiding ethical principles of the new religious group, and on selective retrieval of traditions and texts to the exclusion of ones that challenge their agenda, only reinforce and legitimate the fundamentalists' terms of theological and doctrinal discourse. In the end, writes Amwar, "by relying on an idealized past as the authority to justify their arguments for reform, reformists tacitly consent to a patriarchal framework."[37] However, she cautions that for reformers simply to eliminate religion from the conversation altogether would subtract any legitimacy for their argument in "the hearts of the lay masses."[38] Presumably, it would confer ownership to traditionalists of all religious interpretation, and hence the power to shape moral norms. Her alternative is for reformers to begin their discussion not with the paradigms of the fundamentalists but with the idea of the secular state and, using universally acceptable tenets of faith (such as "God's justice and mercy"), construct a rationale for the secular state as *the* political arrangement that will best aid Muslims in their attempts to live as faithfully as possible.[39]

In addition, Muslim women are challenging religion-based rights infringements far from the fields of theology and scholarship. They are establishing non-governmental organizations whose purpose is religious change and rights enhancement. They are constructing new rituals and ceremonies as substitutes for ones that harm or subordinate women. One community has found that the most successful attempts to curb clitoridectomy and infibulation have come through the construction of alternative rituals for acknowledging sexual maturity. Group consensus and cultural legitimacy are the keys to successful transitions in rituals and religious attitudes. In the process, unfair maintenance and inheritance practices, among others, come to be viewed as no longer safeguarding women as they might have centuries ago.[40] In this way the claims by religious authorities that unfair practices are "justice" can be confidently, and popularly, dismantled.

The positive efforts of all religious reformers hopefully will not produce undercurrents of ethnocentrisms or contextual moralities that could be harmful to apply to human rights discourse and religious women's justice concerns. It is one thing to reformulate theologies and doctrines in positive directions regarding gender equity, but another to perpetuate an inward focus within religious discourse that produces no intersection with international rights norms. The challenge to reformers in any tradition will be to meet legitimacy requirements amongst the population, to avoid any reifying of the fundamentalists' paradigms, yet to create an authentically theological conversation that has points of access to the norms and greater discourse surrounding women's human rights.

In the end, religions change because people make them change and so, like cultures, they are constantly reshaped and reinvented. Women and men are at work in every tradition to reconcile the claims to righteousness made by those religions with women's real desire for equality. Their efforts show that the choice of "authentic religion or human rights" is a false one, and the framing of such an absolute equation inhibits movement toward social change. The subordination of or discrimination against women is not intrinsic to any religious tradition and the compatibility of religious traditions with human rights norms requires no ethical syncretism. The question is part of greater discursive struggles related to the mobilizing potential of religion in power consolidation, community cohesiveness, movements for social change, resistance to dominating societies and social/religious groups, globalization, and so on. Religious women's rights claims, so compatible with international rights norms, are in many instances presented as the surface issue, but in fact are the subtext to struggles of a much greater scale, as outlined in the preceding chapters.

While the focus of this study has been the abridgement of women's rights by religious ideology, an important note with which to conclude is that the religions have an invaluable, positive role to play in securing global gender justice. The symbolic and organizing power of religion is massive. Current government-sponsored curbs on the Falun Gong in China and on Islamists in Algeria are efforts to thwart such organizing potential. The political revolutions of Romania and the former German Democratic Republic might never have come to pass without the Lutheran (and other) churches there. The same is true regarding the role of religious institutions in the political and social revolutions of Nicaragua (its churches) and of South Africa (synagogues, mosques, temples, and churches). In each of these movements religious principles and human rights were powerful partners. The famously Islamic revolution in Iran is another example of the mobilizing power of religion for social and political change, and a reminder that religious revolutions do not always embrace a "human rights culture."

As Cornel West has noted, religions, at their worst, preserve and perpetuate "prevailing social and historical realities," while at their best present positive visions of social and historical transformation.[41] Religion is indeed a powerful tool of liberation, and religious communities currently are deeply involved in articulating alternatives to everything from the debt crisis of poor countries to militarization in rich ones. They are doing crucial work to construct alternatives to the neo-liberal economic paradigm that is so swiftly being globalized. One challenge for the religions is to separate out and eliminate gender subordination from their attempts to resist globalization's inequities and disempowerment. This is part of a greater challenge for the religions, generally, in terms of women's rights: to turn their transformative energies from external to internal matters. As noted above, religious institutions and communities have done so before, as with human chattel slavery and racial inequality. Texts and traditions certainly remain that proclaim divine approval of these institutions, but communities now view them in an historical–critical light. The same process can, must, and will happen regarding gender subordination.

Religious institutions have a tremendous cache of moral power and influence. Often, these institutions are not opposed to questions of women's rights but are tacitly in favor of them. Partnerships between human rights movements and religious groups can lure those religious institutions into the proactive support that becomes the crucial element in a movement's success. Writing of female genital cutting, Asma Abdel Haleem, a Sudanese human rights lawyer and Islamic scholar, has said, "With regards to female circumcision, it is important that there be a final religious announcement clearly stating that it is a form of mutilation and therefore forbidden. It is not sufficient for religion to shun the practice. Religion should be used as a tool for condemning and preventing its occurrence. The participation of women in the reinterpretation will be crucial."[42] Crucial indeed is women's own assertion of their interpretive insights at every level of their religion's organization. Making the equations between theological tenets and questions of social justice, women can demand that the religion's moral power be employed in the service of women's rights.

Such efforts point to another feature of the symbolic and moral power enjoyed by religions: their ability to communicate norms. Many religious institutions are currently poised to help introduce, interpret, or solidify human rights values in their societies because of their foundational assumptions regarding divine justice and the limitless value of the human being. They are natural partners for the United Nations and other organizations. Chapter 1 discussed the ways that the similar commitments and projects of both religion and the human rights idea can conflict. They can also complement one another very powerfully if the theological perspective in question affirms human equality in every category. Religious groups can provide essential help in starting cross-cultural dialogue, one intended not to enforce ethical universalism or conformity but to encourage communities to learn from one another and nurture consensus. Such a global conversation is sorely needed at a time of rapidly consolidating economic and political interests, and may keep the human rights of women, the poor, and other marginalized persons from being turned under the soil. With enough dedicated effort, the human rights idea may help to bridge the gap within religions between ethics and practice, and religion may do the same for the rights construct.

Despite, in some quarters, the post-modern rejection of normativity and universalism, the human rights idea has never been stronger, and neither (in many societies) has religion. Perhaps both are thriving because they succeed in speaking in the most elemental of ways to the nature of the human being, or to our deepest yearnings for justice. Perhaps they thrive because Auschwitz and Rwanda are so fresh and frightening in our memories, and we do not wish to lose the most potent instruments in our collective tool belt for calling a rapidly changing, globalizing world to civility. This book has critiqued the legal, theoretical, theological, and practical impediments to securing religious women's human rights. More than ever, the global human community needs for law, theory, theology, and practice to be partners. In the end, the response must be both from the top down (international and domestic lawmaking) and especially the bottom up (changes to religious familial ideology, local theologies, and local education systems). One day, then, the two efforts will meet in the middle, at a place where the human rights of women – and all – are secure.

Notes

Introduction

1. See, for example, Sultanhussein Tabandeh, *A Muslim Commentary on the Universal Declaration of Human Rights*, F.J. Goulding, trans. (Guildford: F.J. Goulding, 1970).
2. A comment made to the author in Barcelona, July 2004, by a Shiite scholar from Qum, Iran.
3. Sarah Zearfoss, "Note, The Convention for the Elimination of All Forms of Discrimination Against Women: Radical, Reasonable, or Reactionary?" *Michigan Journal of International Law* 12 (1991), p. 919.
4. Ibid., fn. 76.
5. The results of a survey of attitudes among Pakistani women have resonance in all communities. The women understood their personal problems to be rooted in whether or not their families or immediate communities were "strict" or "conservative." They did not think that these strictures were "ordained by God's word or derived from religious tenets." The researchers concluded, "Across communities, non-activist women distinguished between religion and the dictates of a male-dominated society." Patricia Jeffery and Amrita Basu, *Appropriating Gender* (New York and London: Routledge, 1998), pp. 151–152.
6. V. Spike Peterson, "Whose Rights? A Critique of 'Givens' in Human Rights Discourse," *Alternatives* XV (1990), p. 333.
7. Donna Sullivan offers a good reminder that outside observers in particular should exercise caution when deciding which religious practices are actually authentic, as opinions may necessarily be formed by majority criteria and so reflect a bias that actually works against others' freedom of religion. (The same caveat might be offered to those within a religious tradition.) See Donna Sullivan, "Advancing the Freedom of Religion or Belief Through the UN Declaration on the Elimination of Religious Intolerance and Discrimination," *American Journal of International Law* 82 (1988), p. 511.
8. A phrase coined by Tomoko Masuzawa in "Culture," in Mark Taylor, ed., *Critical Terms for Religious Studies* (Chicago: University of Chicago Press, 1998).
9. Arvind Sharma, ed., *Women in World Religions* (Albany: State University of New York Press, 1987), p. 31.

1 A conflict of rights claims

1. Paraphrased from Martha A. Chen, *A Quiet Revolution: Women in Transition in Rural Bangladesh* (Cambridge, MA: Schenkman, 1983).
2. For examples of needs-based theorists see Christian Bay, "Self-respect as a Human Right: Thoughts on the Dialectics of Wants and Needs in the Struggle for Human Community," *Human Rights Quarterly* 4 (1982), p. 67;

Abraham Maslow, *Motivation and Personality* (New York: Harper and Row, 1970), p. xiii; and Stanley I. Benn, "Rights," *The Encyclopedia of Philosophy* (New York: Macmillan, 1967).

3. See, for example, Jack Donnelly, *The Concept of Human Rights* (London: Croom, Helm, 1985), p. 2.
4. Joanna Kerr, "The Context and the Goal," in Kerr, ed., *Ours By Right: Women's Rights as Human Rights* (London and Atlantic Highlands, NJ: Zed Books, 1993), p. 5.
5. Rebecca J. Cook, "Introduction: The Way Forward," in Rebecca J. Cook, ed., *Human Rights of Women* (Philadelphia: University of Pennsylvania Press, 1994), p. 13.
6. Hilary Charlesworth, "Human Rights as Men's Rights," in Julie Peters and Andrea Wolper, eds, *Women's Rights, Human Rights* (New York and London: Routledge, 1995), p. 106.
7. Elissavet Stamatopoulou, "Women's Rights and the United Nations," in Peters and Wolper, ibid., p. 42.
8. Susan Moller Okin, "Religion, Law, and Female Identity," unpublished lecture delivered at the University of Chicago, April 4, 1997.
9. Charlotte Bunch and Samantha Frost, "Human Rights," in Cheris Kramarae and Dale Spender, gen. eds, *Routledge International Encyclopedia of Women* (New York and London: Routledge, 2000), vol. 2, p. 1079.
10. See, for instance, V. Spike Peterson, "Whose Rights? A Critique of 'Givens' in Human Rights Discourse," *Alternatives* XV (1990), pp. 303–344, and V. Spike Peterson and Laura Parisi, "Are Women Human? It's Not an Academic Question," in Tony Evans, ed., *Human Rights Fifty Years On* (Manchester and New York: Manchester University Press, 1998), p. 132.
11. Charlesworth, note 6 above, p. 103.
12. Peterson and Parisi, op. cit.
13. See Riane Eisler, "Human Rights: Toward an Integrated Theory for Action," in *Human Rights Quarterly* 9 (1987), pp. 287–308.
14. Howard Warrender, *The Political Philosophy of Hobbes* (Oxford: Clarendon Press, 1957), p. 19.
15. Joel Feinberg, *Rights, Justice and the Bounds of Liberty* (Princeton: Princeton University Press, 1980), p. 143.
16. R.C. Pandeya, "Human Rights: An Indian Perspective," in UNESCO, *Philosophical Foundations of Human Rights* (Paris: UNESCO, 1986), p. 270.
17. Carl F.H Henry, "The Judeo-Christian Heritage and Human Rights," in Carl H. Esbeck, ed., *Religious Beliefs, Human Rights, and the Moral Foundation of Western Democracy* (Columbia: University of Missouri, 1986), p. 30, quoted in Robert Traer, *Faith in Human Rights* (Washington, DC: Georgetown University Press, 1991), p. 5.
18. S. Prakash Sinha, "Human Rights: A Non-western Viewpoint," *Archiv für Rechts-und-Sozialphilosophie* 76 (1981), pp. 76–91.
19. Kate O'Donovan, *Sexual Divisions in Law* (London: Weidenfeld and Nicolson, 1985), p. 2.
20. V. Spike Peterson and Laura Parisi, note 10 above, p. 143.
21. Susan Frank Parsons, *Feminism and Christian Ethics* (Cambridge: Cambridge University Press, 1996), p. 187.

22. Ratna Kapur and Brenda Cossman, *Subversive Sites* (New Delhi: Sage Publications, 1996), p. 286.
23. Tony Evans, "Trading Human Rights," in Annie Taylor and Caroline Thomas, eds, *Global Trade and Global Social Issues* (London and New York: Routledge, 1999), p. 34.
24. See, for instance, Riane Eisler, note 13 above.
25. Fiona Robinson, "The Limits to a Rights-based Approach to International Ethics," in *Human Rights Fifty Years On*, note 10 above, p. 61.
26. Devaki Jain and Nirmala Banerjee, eds, "Introduction," in *Tyranny of the Household* (New Delhi: Shakti, 1985), p. xiii.
27. Radhika Coomaraswamy, "Reinventing International Law: Women's Rights as Human Rights in the International Community," in Peter Van Ness, ed., *Debating Human Rights* (London and New York: Routledge, 1999), p. 181.
28. Martha Nussbaum, *Women and Human Development* (Cambridge: Cambridge University Press, 2000), p. 112.
29. Fiona Robinson, "The Limits to a Rights-based Approach to International Ethics," in *Human Rights Fifty Years On*, note 10 above, pp. 61–62.
30. Parsons, note 21 above, p. 55.
31. Adetoun O. Ilumoka, "African Women's Economic, Social, and Cultural Rights," in Rebecca Cook, ed., *Human Rights of Women*, note 5 above, p. 319.
32. Natalie Hevener Kaufman and Stefanie A. Lindquist, "Critiquing Gender-Neutral Treaty Language: The Convention on the Elimination of All Forms of Discrimination Against Women," in Peters and Wolper, note 6 above, p. 118.
33. S. Bahar, "Human Rights are Women's Rights," *Hypatia* 11:1, p. 107, cited in Peterson and Parisi, note 10 above, p. 132.
34. Susan Moller Okin, note 8 above.
35. Amartya Sen, "Women's Survival as a Development Problem," *Bulletin of the American Academy of Arts and Sciences* 43; Sen, "Missing Women," *British Medical Journal* 304 (1992).
36. See Charlotte Bunch and Niamh Reilly, *Demanding Accountability* (New Brunswick, NJ: The Center for Women's Global Leadership, 1994), pp. 51–52; Susan Brooks Thistlethwaite and Rita Nakashima Brock, *Casting Stones* (Minneapolis: Fortress Press, 1996), and *Human Rights Watch World Report 2001* (New York: Human Rights Watch, 2000), p. 452.
37. Eschel M. Rhoodie, *Discrimination Against Women* (Jefferson, NC: McFarland and Co., 1989), p. 56.
38. Ibid., p. 77.
39. Ibid., pp. 347–348, for a discussion of the different international responses to race-based apartheid in South Africa and gender-based apartheid in Pakistan.
40. 54 UN ESCOR Supp. No. 5.
41. Okin, note 8 above.
42. Rhoodie, note 37 above, p. 37.
43. Ibid., pp. 346–347.
44. Ibid., p. 10.
45. *Asiaweek*, March 31, 1995, p. 14.

46. Rhoodie, note 37 above, p. 321. Interestingly, abortion is pardoned in Colombia if performed in order to "save the honor" of the husband, mother, or children.
47. *Human Rights Watch World Report 2001* (New York: Human Rights Watch, 2000).
48. Mohammed Allal Sinaceur, "Islamic tradition and human rights," in UNESCO, *Philosophical Foundations of Human Rights* (Paris: UNESCO, 1986), p. 194.
49. Ibid., p. 197.
50. Max L. Stackhouse, *Creeds, Society and Human Rights* (Grand Rapids, MI: William B. Eerdmans, 1984), p. 6.
51. Donna Sullivan, "Gender Equality and Religious Freedom: Toward a Framework for Conflict Resolution," *New York University Journal of International Law and Politics* 80 (1992), p. 803.
52. Wilfred Cantwell Smith has written, "no one has any reasonable grounds – has any 'right' – to talk about human rights who rejects metaphysics." "Philosophia, as One of the Religious Traditions of Humankind: The Greek Legacy in Western Civilization, Viewed by a Comparativist," in *Différences, Valuers, Hierarchie: Textes Offerts à Louis Dumont et Reunis par Jean-Claude Galey* (Paris: Ecole des Hautes Etudes en Sciences Sociales, 1984), p. 269.
53. Op. cit.
54. Nitin Vyas, "The Quest for Equality and Order: The Gandhian Way," in Creighton Peden and Yeager Hudson, eds, *Freedom, Dharma, and Rights* (Lewiston, NY: The Edwin Mellen Press, 1993), p. 120.
55. Warren Lee Holleman, *The Human Rights Movement* (New York: Praeger, 1987), p. 19.
56. Rhoda E. Howard, *Human Rights in Commonwealth Africa* (Totowa, NJ: Rowman and Littlefield, 1986), p. 16.
57. Op. cit.
58. See the description in James P. Piscatori, "Human Rights in Islamic Political Culture," in Kenneth Thompson, ed., *The Moral Imperatives of Human Rights: A World Survey* (Washington, DC: University Press of America, 1980), p. 143.
59. Mark Juergensmeyer, "Hindu Nationalism and Human Rights," in Irene Bloom, J. Paul Martin, and Wayne L. Proudfoot, eds, *Religious Diversity and Human Rights* (New York: Columbia University Press, 1996), p. 244.
60. Ibid.
61. Michael J. Perry, "Are Human Rights Universal? The Relativist Challenge and Related Matters," *Human Rights Quarterly* 19 (1997), p. 462.
62. Jerome Shestack, "The World Had a Dream," *Human Rights Quarterly* 15 (1988), p. 45.
63. Not all theorists of rights agree on this. See, for instance, K.R. Minogue, "Natural Rights, Ideology, and the Game of Life," in Eugene Kamenka and Alice Ehr-Soon Tay, eds, *Human Rights* (New York: St. Martin's Press, 1978), pp. 13–35.
64. Jerome Shestack, "The Philosophic Foundations of Human Rights," *Human Rights Quarterly* 20 (1998), p. 217.
65. Raimundo Panikkar, "Is the Notion of Human Rights a Western Concept?" *Diogenes* 120 (1982), pp. 80–82.

66. Perry, note 61 above, p. 478.
67. Religions such as Buddhism and Taoism, for instance, do not involve belief in a deity.
68. Wilfred Cantwell Smith, *On Understanding Islam* (The Hague: Mouton, 1981), p. 220.
69. Wilfred Cantwell Smith describes this attitude generally in *Modern Culture from a Comparative Perspective* (Albany: State University of New York Press, 1997), p. 8.
70. This dichotomy is not meant to suggest that religious persons or organizations are uninterested in issues of physical or material justice. In fact, many religious communities are extraordinary advocates for human rights on a great variety of subjects.
71. An exploration of this question is the subject of Chapter 6 of this book.
72. A multitude of teachings on specific justice-related topics exists within every religious tradition, as will be discussed later in this study.
73. The understood consequences of disobedience – in any tradition – are impossible to overestimate. For example, the important twentieth-century Iranian Sufi, Sultanhussein Tabandeh, has said "freedom of religion should not be interpreted as allowing people to reject the truth, for no one would knowingly endanger his or her salvation." Paraphrased by Robert Traer in *Faith in Human Rights* (Washington, DC: Georgetown University Press, 1991), p. 121.

2 Hierarchies of rights claims

1. See, for example, the critique of Theodor Meron, *Human Rights Law-Making in the United Nations* (Oxford: Clarendon Press, 1986), p. 64, and the discussion of his work in Chapter Five below.
2. Noreen Burrows, "The 1979 Convention on the Elimination of All Forms of Discrimination Against Women," *Netherlands International Law Review* 32 (1985), p. 424.
3. Donna Sullivan, "Gender Equality and Religious Freedom: Toward a Framework for Conflict Resolution," *New York University Journal of International Law and Politics* 24 (1992), p. 800.
4. Donna Sullivan, "Advancing the Freedom of Religion or Belief Through the UN Declaration on the Elimination of Religious Intolerance and Discrimination," *American Journal of International Law* 82 (1988), p. 490. During the drafting of the Declaration, representatives to the UN Commission on Human Rights agreed to exempt some forms of juridical relationships between the state and its religious institutions, stating that without such an exemption, "it would be difficult for a number of States to become parties to the Convention." UN ESCOR, 39th Sess., Supp. No. 8, at 35, UN Doc. E/4024 (1965).
5. Theodor Meron, "On a Hierarchy of International Human Rights," *American Journal of International Law* 80 (1986), p. 5.
6. A full treatment of theories concerning the nature and content of human rights cannot be accommodated in the scope of this study. For a survey of basic human rights theory see Morton E. Winston, ed., *The Philosophy of Human Rights* (Belmont, CA: Wadsworth, 1989).

7. Joel Feinberg, *Social Philosophy* (Englewood Cliffs, NJ: Prentice-Hall, 1973), pp. 18–19.
8. Meron, "On a Hierarchy of International Human Rights," note 5 above, p. 8.
9. Feinberg, op. cit., p. 80.
10. Maurice Cranston, *What Are Human Rights?* (New York: Basic Books, 1964).
11. Henry Shue, *Basic Rights: Subsistence, Affluence, and U.S. Foreign Policy* (Princeton: Princeton University Press, 1980).
12. Feinberg, note 7 above, p. 95.
13. Christian Bay, "Self-respect as a Human Right: Thoughts on the Dialectics of Wants and Needs in the Struggle for Human Community," *Human Rights Quarterly* 4 (1982), p. 67.
14. Abraham Maslow, *Motivation and Personality* (New York: Harper and Row, 1970), p. xiii.
15. Meron, note 1 above, p. 201.
16. Op. cit., p. 40.
17. Feinberg, note 7 above, p. 72.
18. Meron, note 5 above, p. 11.
19. Meron, note 1 above, p. 176.
20. Donna Sullivan, "Gender Equality and Religious Freedom: Toward a Framework for Conflict Resolution," *New York University Journal of International Law and Politics* 80 (1992), pp. 805–809.
21. O.A.U. Doc. CAB/LEG/67/3/Rev. 5, 21 I.L.M. 59. The African Charter may pose significant problems for religious women's rights, as the discussion makes clear in Chapter 5.
22. UN Doc. E/CN.4/AC.39/1988/L.2, at 5.
23. UN Doc. E/CN.4/Sub. 2/1987/26, at 48–49.
24. Donna Sullivan, "Advancing the Freedom of Religion or Belief Through the UN Declaration on the Elimination of Religious Intolerance and Discrimination," note 4 above, p. 488.
25. Meron, note 1 above, p. 155.
26. Op. cit., p. 498.
27. Thomas Buergenthal, "To Respect and to Ensure: State Obligations and Permissible Derogations," in Louis Henkin, ed., *The International Bill of Rights* (New York: Columbia University Press, 1981), pp. 83–84.
28. Ibid., p. 78.
29. Ibid., p. 89.
30. Alexandre Charles Kiss, "Permissible Limitations on Rights," ibid., p. 290.
31. UN Doc. A/CONF. 157/23 (12 July 1993).
32. UN General Assembly Resolution 48/104 (20 December 1993).
33. Article 29(2) of the Universal Declaration also includes morality as a ground for restricting rights.
34. 24 Eur. Ct. H. R. (ser. A) (1976).
35. Ibid., p. 22.
36. UN Doc. E/CN.4/1988/43, pp. 10–11.
37. UN Doc. E/CN.4/1987/37, p. 13.
38. Sullivan, note 4 above, p. 496.
39. Eschel M. Rhoodie, *Discrimination Against Women* (Jefferson, NC: McFarland and Co., 1989), pp. 347–348.

40. UN Doc. A/CONF. 39/27 (1969).
41. Meron, note 1 above, p. 190.
42. Anne Bayefsky, "General Approaches to Domestic Application of Women's International Human Rights Law," in Rebecca Cook, ed., *Human Rights of Women* (Philadelphia: University of Philadelphia Press, 1994), p. 361.
43. Sullivan, note 3 above, p. 817.
44. Arcot Krishnaswami, "Study of Discrimination in the Matter of Religious Rights and Practices," *New York Journal of International Law and Politics* 11 (1978), p. 229.
45. See, for example, Theodor Meron, note 1 above, p. 153.
46. See, for instance, Ian Brownlie, *Principles of International Law* (Oxford: Clarendon Press, 1990), and Anne Bayefsky, note 42 above.
47. M. McDougal, H. Lasswell and L. Chen describe the Universal Declaration "as established customary law, having the attributes of *jus cogens*...," *Human Rights and World Public Order* (New Haven: Yale University Press, 1980), p. 274.
48. Ibid., p. 185.
49. Bayefsky, note 42 above, p. 360.
50. As Hilary Charlesworth points out, these include sex-based discrimination, domestic violence, sexual degradation or violence, and other matters. Charlesworth, "Human Rights as Men's Rights," in Julie Peters and Andrea Wolper, eds, *Women's Rights, Human Rights* (New York and London: Routledge, 1995), p. 105. Christine Chinkin concurs: "[T]he choices and values incorporated into typical claims of *jus cogens* are in fact gender biased." "Remarks," in "Resolving Conflicting Human Rights Standards in International Law," *American Society of International Law Proceedings* 85 (1991), p. 350.
51. Jack Donnelly, *Universal Human Rights in Theory and Practice* (Ithaca, NY: Cornell University Press, 1989), p. 39.
52. See note 44, above.
53. Feinberg, note 7 above, p. 97.
54. See text accompanying note 64, Chapter 3.
55. 1155 UNTS 331, Art. 27.
56. Rebecca Cook, "Women's International Human Rights Law: The Way Forward," in Cook, note 42 above, p. 28.
57. Rebecca Cook, "State Accountability Under the Convention on the Elimination of All Forms of Discrimination Against Women," in Cook, note 42 above, p. 232.
58. Ibid.
59. Abdullahi Ahmed An-Na'im, "State Responsibility Under International Human Rights Law to Change Religious and Customary Laws," in Cook, note 42 above, pp. 168–169.
60. Rebecca Cook, "State Accountability Under the Convention on the Elimination of All Forms of Discrimination Against Women," in Cook, note 42 above, p. 229.
61. Ibid., pp. 236–237.
62. *Barcelona Traction, Light & Power Co., Limited (Belgium v. Spain)*, 1970 I.C.J. Rep. 4 (Judgment of February 5).
63. Ibid., p. 32.
64. [1976] 2 *Year Book of the International Law Commission* 99, UN Doc. A/CN.4/Ser.A/1976/Add. 1 (pt. 2).

65. Meron, note 5 above, p. 11.
66. Meron, note 1 above, p. 186.
67. Rebecca Cook "State Accountability Under the Convention on the Elimination of All Forms of Discrimination Against Women," note 42 above, p. 241.
68. Abdullahi Ahmed An-Na'im, "State Responsibility Under International Human Rights Law to Change Religious and Customary Laws," in Cook, note 42 above, p. 167.
69. Sullivan, note 3 above, p. 833.
70. Asma Mohammed Abdel Halim, "Challenges to Women's International Human Rights in the Sudan," in Cook, note 42 above, p. 406.
71. Meron, note 1 above, p. 157.
72. Abdullahi Ahmed An-Na'im, "State Responsibility Under International Human Rights Law to Change Religious and Customary Laws," in Cook, note 42 above, pp. 175 and 178.
73. Feinberg, note 7 above, p. 75.
74. 133 US 333 (1890).
75. AIR (1952) Bombay 1984.
76. *Reynolds v. U.S.*, 98 US 145 (1879). The Court found that religious belief and practice were distinguishable entities. See also *Cantwell v. Connecticut*, 310 US 296 (1940), in which the Court concluded that, "[The First Amendment.] embraces two concepts: freedom to believe and freedom to act. The first is absolute, but, in the nature of things, the second cannot be."
77. *Srinivasa v. Saraswati Ammal*, AIR (1952) Madras 193.
78. See, for example, *Marcx v. Belgium*, 31 Eur. Ct. H.R. (ser. A) (1979), concerning the right of unmarried mothers to custody of their children; *Abdulaziz v. United Kingdom*, 94 Eur. Ct. H.R. (ser. A.) (1985), concerning discrimination based on gender in UK immigration law; *Attorney-General v. Unity Dow*, C.A. Civil Appeal No. 4/91 Botswana (unreported), concerning the right of women to pass their nationality on to their children. Interestingly, the representative of the Attorney-General's office based his argument for the defense on the importance of perpetuating male dominance in Botswana. The important Tanzanian case of *Ephrahim v. Pastory* (PC) Civil Appeal No. 70 of 1989 (unreported), revolved around a conflict between the Tanzanian Bill of Rights and the customary law of the Haya ethnic group concerning women's ability to inherit and sell land. The court decided, quoting the Tanzanian Bill of Rights, the Women's Convention, the Political Covenant, and the African Charter on Human and People's Rights, that Haya customary law must be brought into conformity with these instruments' provisions of equal rights in the inheritance, sale and purchasing of land.
79. 112 Eur. Ct. H.R. (ser. A) (1986).
80. Communication No. 202/1986, 44 UN GAOR Supp. No. 40, at 196, UN Doc. A/44/40 (1989).
81. 1962 AIR 853, 863 (S.C.).
82. See *Badruddin v. Aisha*, ALJ 300 (1957), and *Ramprasad v. State of U.P.*, ALJ 411 (1957).
83. *Abu Bakar Siddiq v. AB Siddiq*, 38 DLR (AD) 108 (1986).
84. *Mohammed Ahmed Khan v. Shah Bano Begum*, [1985] 3 SCR 844.

85. See, for example, Donna Sullivan, note 3 above, p. 848.
86. Liesbeth Lijnzaad, *Reservations to UN-Human Rights Treaties* (Dordrecht: Martinus Nijhoff, 1995), p. 323.
87. See, for example, Cecilia Medina, "Toward a More Effective Guarantee of the Enjoyment of Human Rights by Women in the Inter-American System," in Cook, note 42 above, p. 269.

3 Theological challenges to religious women's rights

1. Cited in Riffat Hassan, "Muslim Women and Post-Patriarchal Islam," in Paula M. Cooey, William R. Eakin, and Jay B. McDaniel, eds, *After Patriarchy* (Maryknoll, NY: Orbis Books, 1991), p. 63.
2. Hassan Afchar, "The Muslim Conception of the Law," in *International Encyclopedia of Comparative Law* (Tübingen: J.C.B. Mohr, 1974), p. 98.
3. Ibid., p. 96.
4. Ibid., p. 97.
5. As one Muslim writer asserts, "[I]n Islam there are no 'human rights' or 'freedoms' admissible to man in the sense in which modern man's thought, belief, and practice understand them: in essence, the believer owes obligation or duties to God if only because he is called upon to obey the Divine Law and such Human Rights as he is made to acknowledge seem to stem from his primary duty to obey God." A.K. Brohi, "Islam and Human Rights," *PLD Lahore* 28 (1976), p. 151.
6. James P. Piscatori, "Human Rights in Islamic Political Culture," in Kenneth Thompson, ed., *The Moral Imperatives of Human Rights: A World Survey* (Washington, DC: University Press of America, 1980), p. 143.
7. Chandra Muzaffar, "Equality and the Spiritual Traditions: An Overview," in R. Siriwardena, ed., *Equality and the Religious Traditions of Asia* (New York: St. Martins Press, 1987), p. 20.
8. Chandra Muzaffar, "The Concept of Equality in Islamic Thought," in Siriwardena, ibid., p. 145.
9. Nayereh Tohidi and Jane H. Bayes, "Women Redefining Modernity and Religion in the Globalized Context," in Jane H. Bayes and Nayereh Tohidi, eds, *Globalization, Gender, and Religion* (New York: Palgrave, 2001), p. 27.
10. Op. cit., p. 148.
11. See Ann Elizabeth Mayer, *Islam and Human Rights* (Boulder: Westview Press, 1991), p. 95.
12. Ibid., p. 94.
13. For example, see the comments of Abu'l A'la Mawdudi, *Purdah and the Status of Women in Islam* (Lahore: Islamic Publications, 1981).
14. Muzaffar, "The Concept of Equality in Islamic Thought," note 8 above, p. 150.
15. CEDAW/C/5/Add.10 at 3.
16. Fouad Zakaria, "The Standpoint of Contemporary Muslim Fundamentalists," in Nahid Toubia, ed., *Women of the Arab World* (Atlantic Highlands, NJ: Zed Press, 1988), pp. 30–31.
17. Cited in Irene Bloom, J. Paul Martin, and Wayne L. Proudfoot, eds, *Religious Diversity and Human Rights* (New York: Columbia University Press, 1996), p. 320.

18. Asma Mohamed Abdel Halim, "Challenges to Women's International Human Rights in the Sudan," in Rebecca J. Cook, ed., *Human Rights of Women* (Philadelphia: University of Pennsylvania Press, 1994), p. 411.
19. Kevin Dwyer, *Arab Voices* (Berkeley: University of California Press, 1991), p. 39.
20. Muzaffar, "Equality and the Spiritual Traditions," note 7 above, p. 19.
21. Translation by Asghar Ali Engineer, "Social Dynamics and Status of Women in Islam," in Asghar Ali Engineer, ed., *Status of Women in Islam* (Delhi: Ajanta Publications, 1987), p. 84.
22. Al-Tabari, Abi Jafar Muhammad Ibn Jarir, Jamil al-Bayan Al-Tawil Ay at at-Quran (224–310AH), ed., M. Shaker, Dar al-Maaref, Cairo, vol. 8, p. 290, and quoted in Fatima Mernissi, "Democracy as Moral Disintegration," in Nahid Toubia, ed., *Women of the Arab World* (London: Zed Press, 1988), p. 38.
23. Op. cit.
24. S.T. Lokhandwala, "The Position of Women Under Islam," in Toubia, note 16 above, pp. 19–21.
25. Sultanhussein Tabandeh, *A Muslim Commentary on the Universal Declaration of Human Rights*, F.J. Goulding, trans. (Guildford: F.J. Goulding, 1970).
26. Robert Traer, *Faith in Human Rights* (Washington, DC: Georgetown University Press, 1991), p. 120.
27. Abu'l A'la Mawdudi, *Purdah and the Status of Women in Islam* (Lahore: Islamic Publications, 1981).
28. Javad Bahonar, "Islam and Women's Rights," *al-Tawhid* 1 (1984).
29. Ibid., p. 160.
30. Ibid., p. 175. This paraphrasing of Tabandeh, Mawdudi, and Bahonar follows that in Mayer, note 11 above, pp. 139–141.
31. For example, Surah 35:33: "Verily the Muslim men and the Muslim women, the believing men and the believing women, the devout men and the devout women, the men of veracity and the women of veracity, the patient men and the patient women, the humble men and the humble women, the alms-giving men and the alms-giving women, the men who fast and the women who fast, the chaste men and the chaste women, and those of men and women who remember God frequently: for them, God hath prepared forgiveness and great reward." S.T. Lokhandwala has written that this teaching was revealed to the Prophet after the women of Medina complained to him that women had rarely been referred to in the revelations up to that point. Furthermore, because this revelation came toward the end of the Prophet's life, it clearly was intended to abrogate earlier injunctions and establish equality between men and women. See note 24 above, p. 15.
32. The word *Shari'a* literally means "source of water" or "the mouth." It appears once in the Qur'an, and not in reference to legislation or law. *Shari'a* was developed in the seventh through ninth centuries. According to one Muslim scholar, "there are no consistent codified Islamic norms that can be referred to as Islamic law. What is known as Islamic law consists of interpretations of Islamic scripture." Bassam Tibi, "The European Tradition of Human Rights and the Culture of Islam," in Abdulllahi Ahmed An-Na'im and Francis M. Deng, eds, *Human Rights in Africa* (Washington, DC: The Brookings Institution, 1990), pp. 125–126.

33. Roger Garaudy, "Human Rights and Islam: Foundation, Tradition, Violation," in Hans Küng and Jürgen Moltmann, eds, *The Ethics of World Religions and Human Rights* (London: SCM Press, 1980), pp. 51–52.
34. Jane I. Smith, "Islam," in Arvind Sharma, ed., *Women in World Religions* (Albany: State University of New York Press, 1987), p. 236.
35. One Muslim modernist, Abdulaziz Sachedina, has written that this tenet simply reflects the fact that most women in early Islam were illiterate. Since testimony that is written down is more accurate than what must be remembered, those courts devised this formula to compensate for that disparity. See Miriam Cooke and Bruce B. Lawrence, "Muslim Women Between Human Rights and Islamic Norms," in *Religious Diversity and Human Rights*, note 17 above, p. 325.
36. Balraj Puri, "Personal Law and Muslim Identity," in *Status of Women in Islam*, note 21 above, p. 108.
37. Abdullahi Ahmed An-Na'im, "Qur'an, *Shari'a* and Human Rights: Foundations, Deficiencies, and Prospects," in *The Ethics of World Religions and Human Rights*, note 33 above, p. 62.
38. Nawal El-Saadawi, *The Hidden Face of Eve* (London: Zed, 1980), p. 44.
39. Fatima Mernissi, *Beyond the Veil* (New York: Schenkman Publishing, 1975), p. 15.
40. Ibid., p. 84.
41. Ibid., p. 13.
42. This dynamic is on the increase today in the United States, among families of every religion. As two incomes are increasingly necessary for the basic maintenance of the household, some men feel great shame that their wives work outside the house, seeing it as a sign of their own failure to provide. It is often the women themselves who are vilified for taking jobs, whether they want to, have to, or both.
43. Nikki Keddie, "The Rights of Women in Contemporary Islam," in Leroy S. Rouner, ed., *Human Rights and the World's Religions* (Notre Dame, IN: University of Notre Dame Press, 1988), p. 90.
44. Ibid.
45. Nahid F. Toubia, "The Social and Political Implications of Female Circumcision: The Case of the Sudan," in Elizabeth Warnock Fernea, ed., *Women and the Family in the Middle East* (Austin, TX: University of Texas Press, 1985), pp. 150–151.
46. Mernissi, note 39 above, p. 58.
47. Anant Ganesh Javadekar, "Dharma as the Foundational Principle of Cosmic Order," in C. Peden and H. Yeager, eds, *Freedom, Dharma, and Rights* (Lewiston, NY: Edwin Mellen, 1993), p. 228.
48. Bithika Mukerji, "The Foundations of Unity and Equality: A Hindu Understanding of Human Rights," in *The Ethics of World Religions and Human Rights*, note 33 above, p. 74.
49. Wendy Doniger with Brian K. Smith (trans.), *The Laws of Manu* (Harmondsworth: Penguin Books, 1991), p. lxxvi.
50. Mark Juergensmeyer, "Hindu Nationalism and Human Rights," in *Religious Diversity and Human Rights*, note 17 above, p. 245.
51. Surabhi Sheth, "Equality and Inequality in the Hindu Scriptures," in Siriwardena, note 7 above, p. 22.

52. Ralph Buultjens, "Human Rights in Indian Political Culture," in *The Moral Imperatives of Human Rights: A World Survey*, note 6 above, p. 112.
53. Surabhi Sheth, "Equality and Inequality in the Hindu Scriptures," in *Equality and the Religious Traditions of Asia*, note 7 above, p. 24.
54. Ralph Buultjens, "Human Rights in Indian Political Culture," in *The Moral Imperatives of Human Rights: A World Survey*, note 7 above, p. 113.
55. R.C. Pandeya, "Human Rights: an Indian Perspective," in UNESCO, *Philosophical Foundations of Human Rights*, (Paris: UNESCO, 1986), pp. 268–270.
56. John B. Carman, "Duties and Rights in Hindu Society," in *Human Rights and the World's Religions*, note 43 above, p. 121.
57. Bithika Mukerji, "The Foundations of Unity and Equality: A Hindu Understanding of Human Rights," note 33 above, p. 75.
58. Sheth, "Equality and Inequality in the Hindu Scriptures," in Siriwardena, note 7 above, p. 25.
59. Pandeya, note 55 above, p. 267.
60. Max L. Stackhouse, *Creeds, Society and Human Rights* (Grand Rapids, MI: William B. Eerdmans, 1984), p. 214.
61. Meera Kosambi, *At the Intersection of Gender Reform and Religious Belief* (Bombay: Research Centre for Women's Studies, 1993), p. 17.
62. Vanaja Dhruvarajan, *Hindu Women and the Power of Ideology* (Granby, MA: Bergin and Garvey Publishers, 1989), p. 29.
63. See, for example, Anant Gadesh Javadekar: "[T]he inherent biologico-psychological differences between the sexes are bound to result in differences of their rights and duties," note 47 above, p. 239.
64. Op. cit., pp. 25–26.
65. Prabhati Mukherjee, *Hindu Women, Normative Models* (Hyderabad: Orient Longman Ltd, 1978), pp. 49, 50.
66. Ralph Buultjens, "Human Rights in Indian Political Culture," in Thompson, note 6 above, p. 116.
67. Roop Rekha Verma, "Femininity, Equality, and Personhood," in Martha Nussbaum and Jonathan Glover, eds, *Women, Culture and Development* (Oxford: Clarendon Press, 1995), p. 435.
68. Mukerji, note 48 above, p. 90.
69. Kosambi, note 61 above, pp. 24, 37.
70. Katharine K. Young, "Hinduism," in *Women in World Religions*, note 34 above, p. 84.
71. Op. cit., p. 22.
72. Mukerji, note 48 above, p. 124.
73. Malladi Sabbamma, *Hinduism and Women* (Delhi: Ajanta Publications, 1992), p. 208.
74. It is understood that the Indian state is not synonymous with Hinduism. It is the majority religion, however, and the general philosophical touchstone for those drafting its rights-related documents.
75. Kirti Singh, "Obstacles to Women's Rights in India," in Rebecca Cook, ed. *Human Rights of Women* (Philadelphia: University of Pennsylvania Press, 1994), pp. 375–396.
76. Similarly, some apologists for Muslim rights schemes (e.g. Mawdudi) have claimed a special historical relationship between the idea of human rights

and the Muslim tradition, asserting that the rights concept actually originates in Islam. As with Christianity, the philosophical and metaphysical foundations of human rights theories differ widely from Islam.

77. J. Bryan Hehir, "Human Rights from a Theological and Ethical Perspective," in Thompson, note 6 above, pp. 4ff.
78. Max L. Stackhouse, "Piety, Polity and Policy," in Carl H. Esbeck, ed., *Religious Beliefs, Human Rights, and the Moral Foundation of Western Democracy* (Columbia: University of Missouri, 1986), p. 21, as summarized in Traer, note 26 above, pp. 57 and 58.
79. Edward Norman, *Christianity and the World Order* (Oxford: Oxford University Press, 1979), as summarized in Traer, note 26 above, pp. 56 and 57.
80. John Warwick Montgomery, *Human Rights and Human Dignity* (Grand Rapids: Zondervan, 1986), summarized in Traer, note 26 above, pp. 51–55.
81. Leonard Swidler, "Human Rights: A Historical Overview," in Küng and Moltmann, *The Ethics of World Religions and Human Rights*, note 33 above, p. 13.
82. Rosemary R. Reuther, "Christianity," in Sharma, note 34 above, p. 208.
83. Jerry Falwell, *Listen, America!* (New York: Bantam Books, 1981), pp. 110–111, quoted in Helen Hardacre, "The Impact of Fundamentalisms on Women, the Family, and Interpersonal Relations," in Martin E. Marty and R. Scott Appleby, eds, *Fundamentalisms and Society* (Chicago: The University of Chicago Press, 1993), p. 131.
84. Op. cit., p. 209.
85. David H. Kelsey, "Human Being," in Peter C. Hodgson and Robert H. King, eds, *Christian Theology* (2nd ed.) (Philadelphia: Fortress Press, 1985), p. 174.
86. Op. cit., p. 229.
87. Ruether "Christianity," in Yvonne Y. Haddad and John L. Esposito, eds, *Daughters of Abraham* (Gainesville: University of Florida Press, 2001), p. 77.

4 The question of relativism

1. Fernando Tesón, "International Human Rights and Cultural Relativism," *Virginia Journal of International Law* 25 (1985), pp. 869–898.
2. David Bidney, "The Philosophical Presuppositions of Cultural Relativism and Absolutism" in Leo Ward, ed., *Ethics and the Social Sciences* (Notre Dame: Notre Dame University, 1959), p. 60.
3. See, for example, Dunstan M. Wai, "Human Rights in Sub-Saharan Africa" in A. Pollis and P. Schwab, eds, *Human Rights: Cultural and Ideological Perspectives* (New York: Praeger, 1979), pp. 115–144. In fact, there are gradations of support for relativism, with some rights theorists and activists claiming to be "strong" cultural relativists fitting the description in these paragraphs. Those claiming to be "weak" relativists admit to the importance of culture in the practice of human rights, but think that some universal moral principles do exist.
4. See, for example, the arguments of Alison Dundes Renteln, *International Human Rights: Universalism Versus Relativism* (Newbury Park, CA: Sage, 1990).
5. See, for example, the work of Abu'l A'la Mawdudi, described in Ann Elizabeth Mayer, *Islam and Human Rights* (Boulder: Westview Press, 1991), pp. 117ff. Mawdudi claims and utilizes the rights notion, stating that its truest inter-

pretation is in accordance with Islamic ethics. See also Miriam Cooke and Bruce B. Lawrence, "Muslim Women Between Human Rights and Islamic Norms," in Irene Bloom, J. Paul Martin, and Wayne L. Proudfoot, eds, *Religious Diversity and Human Rights* (New York: Columbia University Press, 1996), pp. 319ff. James Piscatori notes a "resentment at liberalism's condescension" in some Muslim writers on rights, a resentment that prompts them to assert that Islamic rights schemes are better than others, and Islamic values superior to those of other cultures. James P. Piscatori, "Human Rights in Islamic Political Culture," in Kenneth Thompson, ed., *The Moral Imperatives of Human Rights: A World Survey* (Washington, DC: University Press of America, 1980), pp. 152–153.

6. See, for example, the argument presented in S. Prakash Sinha, "Human Rights: A Non-western Viewpoint," *Archiv für Rechts-und-Sozialphilosophie* 67 (1981), pp. 76–91.
7. For instance, the opinions of R.C. Pandeya, "Human Rights: An Indian Perspective," in UNESCO, *Philosophical Foundations of Human Rights* (Paris: UNESCO, 1986).
8. Ann Elizabeth Mayer, "Cultural Particularism as a Bar to Women's Rights: Reflections on the Middle Eastern Experience," in Julie Peters and Andrea Wolper, eds, *Women's Rights, Human Rights* (New York: Routledge, 1995), p. 178.
9. Id., "Universal Versus Islamic Human Rights: A Clash of Cultures or a Clash With a Construct?" *Michigan Journal of International Law* 15 (1994), p. 320.
10. Many rights theorists, such as Anant Ganesh Javadekar, root women's "special nature" in their childbearing capability. Javadekar claims that there are "inherent biologico-psychological differences" between men and women that produce "unexchangeable duties and rights arising through the sex differences." "Dharma As The Foundational Principle of Cosmic Order," in Creighton Peden and Yeager Hudson, eds, *Freedom, Dharma, and Rights* (Lewiston, NY: Edwin Mellen, 1993), pp. 339–340.
11. Abdullahi Ahmed An-Na'im, *Human Rights in Cross-Cultural Perspectives* (Philadelphia: University of Philadelphia Press, 1992), p. 345.
12. Nawal El-Saadawi, "Dissidence and Creativity in the Arab World," Amnesty International lecture at Oxford University, February 12, 1995, quoted in Miriam Cooke and Bruce B. Lawrence, "Muslim Women Between Human Rights and Islamic Norms," in Irene Bloom, J. Paul Martin, and Wayne L. Proudfoot, eds, *Religious Diversity and Human Rights* (New York: Columbia University Press, 1996), p. 315.
13. See, for example, Gustavo Esteva and Madhu Suri Prakash, *Grassroots Postmodernism: Remaking the Soil of Cultures* (New York: Zed Books, 1998). The authors reject both the national state and the human rights idea as "the Trojan horse of recolonization" and link both to the "Global Project" of western capitalism.
14. Chandra Muzaffar, *Human Rights and the New World Order* (Penang: Just World Trust, 1993), pp. 160–161, quoted in Cooke and Lawrence, op. cit.
15. Bithika Mukerji, "The Foundations of Unity and Equality: A Hindu Understanding of Human Rights," in Hans Küng and Jürgen Moltmann, eds, *The Ethics of World Religions and Human Rights* (London: SCM Press, 1990), pp. 70–71.

16. Michael J. Perry, *The Idea of Human Rights* (Oxford: Oxford University Press, 1998), p. 47. Halliday and others consider the question of universalism/particularism to be a false dichotomy. See F. Halliday, "Relativism and universalism in human rights: the case of the Islamic Middle East," *Political Studies* 43 (1995) (Special Issue), pp. 152–168.
17. Quoted in Rebecca Klatch, "Women of the New Right in the U.S.," in Valentine Moghadam, ed., *Identity Politics and Women* (Boulder, CO: Westview Press, 1994), p. 370.
18. Eschel Rhoodie, *Discrimination Against Women* (Jefferson, NC: McFarland, 1989), p. 101.
19. Christine Obbo, *African Women: Their Struggle for Economic Independence* (London: Zed Press, 1980), p. 143.
20. Zoya Hasan, *Forging Identities: Gender, Communities and the State in India* (Boulder, Colorado: Westview Press, 1994), p. xiii.
21. Asma Mohamed Abdel Halim, "Challenges to the Application of International Women's Human Rights in the Sudan," in Rebecca J. Cook, ed., *Human Rights of Women* (Philadelphia: University of Pennsylvania Press, 1994), p. 408.
22. Marie-Aimée Hélie-Lucas, "The Preferential Symbol for Islamic Identity: Women in Muslim Personal Laws," in Moghadam, note 17 above, p. 394.
23. See, for instance, official statements by representatives of the Bharatiya Janata Party regarding subjects and practices that are "antithetical to Indian social order and our cultural mooring." Kalpana Ram "The State and the Women's Movement: Instabilities in the Discourse of 'rights' in India," in Anne-Marie Hilsdon, Martha Macintyre, Vera Mackie, and Maila Stivens, eds, *Human Rights and Gender Politics* (London and New York: Routledge, 2000), p. 73.
24. Flavia Agnes, *Law and Gender Inequality* (New Delhi: Oxford University Press, 1999), p. 17.
25. See Kamala Ganesh, "Seclusion of Women and the Structure of Caste," in Maithreyi Krishnaraj and Karuna Chanana, eds, *Gender and the Household Domain* (New Delhi: Sage Publications, 1989), pp. 75–95.
26. Doranne Jacobson, *Hidden Faces: Hindu and Muslim Purdah in a Central Indian Village* (Columbia University Dissertation, copyright of the author, 1973).
27. Martha Chen and Jean Drèze, "Widows and Health in Rural North India," *Economic and Political Weekly* (October 24–31, 1992), p. WS-89.
28. Gabrielle Dietrich, *Reflections on the Women's Movement in India* (New Delhi: Horizon India Books, 1992), p. 74.
29. Wilfred Cantwell Smith, *On Understanding Islam* (The Hague: Mouton, 1981), p. 224.
30. M.C. Dinakaran, "Liberative Undercurrents in Hindu Thought – A Preliminary Inquiry," in Asghar Ali Engineer, ed., *Religion and Liberation* (Delhi: Ajanta, 1989), p. 28.
31. See, for example, Donna Sullivan, "Gender Equality and Religious Freedom: Toward a Framework for Conflict Resolution," *New York University Journal of International Law and Politics* 24 (1992), p. 825.
32. Ibid., p. 829 (fn).
33. Nawal El-Saadawi, *The Hidden Face of Eve* (London: Zed, 1980), p. 39.

34. Katherine Brennan, "The Influence of Cultural Relativism on International Human Rights Law: Female Circumcision as a Case Study," *Law and Inequality Journal* 7 (1989), p. 367.
35. Nahid Toubia, "Women and Health in Sudan," in Nahid Toubia, ed., *Women of the Arab World* (London: Zed Books, 1988), pp. 101–102.
36. Marie-Aimée Hélie-Lucas, "The Preferential Symbol for Islamic Identity: Women in Muslim Personal Laws," in Moghadam, note 17 above, p. 395.
37. Imtiaz Ahmad, *Family, Kinship and Marriage among Muslims in India* (New Delhi: Manohar, 1976).
38. Shahida Lateef, *Muslim Women in India* (London: Zed Books, 1990), p. 57. There is debate among scholars of Islam as to whether *Shari'ah* is an actual source of law or an outline of moral community guidance. There is little debate, however, as to its power to provide symbolic unity to the Muslim community, and its power as a tool of political and religious manipulation by Islamists.
39. Richard Bulliet, for example, cautions against viewing Muslim legists' presentation of *Shari'a* as canonical. "The fact is," he writes, "that despite the apparent normative force of the law, the vast preponderance of the world's Muslims have always been, at least to some degree, out of step with the letter of the *shari'a*, when they have not, indeed, marched to the beat of a different drummer altogether." Richard W. Bulliet, "The Individual in Islamic Society," in Irene Bloom, J. Paul Martin, and Wayne L. Proudfoot, eds, *Religious Diversity and Human Rights*, note 5 above, p. 176.
40. Ahmad, note 37 above, p. xxvii.
41. Ibid., pp. xxvii–xxix.
42. Ibid., p. x.
43. Zarina Bhatty, "Socio-economic Status of Muslim Women," in Zakia A. Siddiqi and Anwar Jahan Zuberi, eds, *Muslim Women, Problems and Prospects* (New Delhi: MD Publications, 1993), p. 13.
44. N. Hamsa, "Impact of Regional Tradition on Muslim Women – With Special Reference to South India," *Islam and the Modern Age* 14 (1983), p. 53.
45. Ahmad, note 37 above, p. xxii.
46. Bhatty, note 43 above, p. 16.
47. A. Aziz and Firoz Khan, "Fertility as a Function of Education and Economic Status in Muslim Women in Aligarh," in Siddiqi and Zuberi, note 43 above, pp. 77–85.
48. Zoya Hasan, *Forging Identities* (Boulder, Colorado: Westview Press, 1994), p. xi.
49. Ahmad, note 37 above, p. xxxi.
50. As noted in Chapter 2 above, an interesting challenge to this prohibition was recently filed by an Irish couple who, after 15 years of cohabitation, wished to be married but were prevented from doing so because the man previously had been married. Their challenge rested on a claim to infringement of freedom of religion, potentially a significant claim since Christianity is not uniformly opposed to divorce and remarriage. *Johnston v. Ireland*, 112 Eur. Ct. H.R. (ser. A) (1986).
51. The conservative perspective is captured in the writings of Jerry Falwell; see note 83, Chapter Three above.

52. Sultanhussein Tabandeh, for instance, has written that freedom of religion should not be understood as permitting people to reject the truth and endanger their prospects for salvation. Paraphrased in R. Traer, *Faith in Human Rights* (Washington, DC: Georgetown University Press, 1991), p. 121.
53. See, for example, Asma Mohammed Abdel Halim, "Challenges to Women's International Human Rights in the Sudan," in Cook, note 21 above, pp. 408–409.
54. Chandra Muzaffar, "Equality and the Spiritual Traditions: An Overview," in R. Siriwardena, ed., *Equality and the Religious Traditions of Asia* (New York: St. Martins Press, 1987), p. 147.
55. Valentine Moghadam, "Women and Identity Politics in Theoretical and Comparative Perspective," note 17 above, p. 11.
56. Abdullahi Ahmed An-Na'im, "State Responsibility Under International Human Rights Law to Change Religious and Customary Laws," in Cook, note 21 above, p. 188.
57. Anika Rahman, "Religious Rights Versus Women's Rights in India: A Test Case for International Human Rights Law," *Columbia Journal of Transnational Law* 28 (1990), p. 476.
58. Martha Chen, quoted in Seyla Benhabib, "Complexity, Interdependence, Community," in Martha Nussbaum and Jonathan Glover, eds, *Women, Culture, and Development* (Oxford: Clarendon Press, 1995), p. 239.
59. Some religious leaders equate westernization with promiscuity, which they claim is antithetical to their religion's core values. Consequently, some women are explicitly told that Islamization is liberating them from the evils of westernization, especially as that is manifested in international law. See Halim in Cook, note 21 above, pp. 406 and 411.
60. Walter Fernandes, "Globalisation, Liberalisation and the Victims of Colonialism," in Michael Amaladoss, S.J., ed., *Globalization and Its Victims* (Delhi: Indian Society for Promoting Christian Knowledge, 1999), p. 16.
61. Bassam Tibi, however, views majority Muslim countries as reacting against the statism they inherited in the colonization/decolonization process. Perhaps, then, practical abandonment of the nation-state is not a possibility even for those societies who wish it because of its global hegemony among political systems. See Bassam Tibi, *The Crisis of Modern Islam* (Salt Lake City: University of Utah Press, 1988), p. xiii.
62. There is a broad continuum of opinion amongst scholars from the global south and east as to what comprises "western" influence. Abdullahi Ahmed An-Na'im has written that although the human rights idea is western in origin, it remains valid for Muslim societies. ("State Responsibility Under International Human Rights Law to Change Religious and Customary Laws," in Rebecca J. Cook, ed., *Human Rights of Women* (Philadelphia: University of Pennsylvania Press, 1994), p. 171.) Valentine Moghadam, on the other hand, writes of "political discourses, movements, and institutions erroneously known as western: human rights, women's rights, equality, self-determination, social movements, parliamentarianism, socialism, democratization, privatization." Moghadam, "Introduction: Women and Identity Politics in Theoretical and Comparative Perspective," note 17 above, p. 7.

63. Ann Elizabeth Mayer, *Islam and Human Rights* (Boulder, CO: Westview Press, 1991), pp. 198–199.
64. See the discussion in Fatima Mernissi, *The Veil and the Male Elite* (Reading, MA: Addison-Wesley, 1991).
65. Mark C. Taylor, "Introduction," in Taylor, *Critical Terms for Religious Studies* (Chicago: University of Chicago Press, 1998), p. 5. Concerning religious fundamentalism/tradtitionalism, José A. Lindgren Alves writes, "Rather than an accident of history (or 'histories') or an incidental regression to archaic postmodernity, they are a 'postmodern' substitute for the vanishing metadiscourses. They constitute a resource against the cultural homogenization of the globalizing process and an ideological compensation for the cult of the free market." "The Declaration of Human Rights in Postmodernity," *Human Rights Quarterly* 22 (2000), pp. 497–498.
66. Marie-Aimée Hélie-Lucas, "The Preferential Symbol for Islamic Identity: Women in Muslim Personal Laws," in Moghadam, note 17 above, p. 393.
67. Tibi, note 61 above, p. 3.
68. Dinakaran in Engineer, note 30 above, p. 27.
69. Nikkie Keddie, "The Rights of Women in Contemporary Islam," in Leroy Rouner, ed., *Human Rights and the World's Religions* (Notre Dame, IN: University of Notre Dame Press, 1988), p. 88.
70. For example, Hasan, note 20 above, pp. 63–64. Not every instance of self-exemption from rights norms made in the name of culture or religion is a power move by elites. Thandabantu Nhlapo, for instance, writes that such appeals are sometimes authentic attempts to address issues without employing human rights concepts, and not always a defense of privilege. See "The African customary law of marriage and the human rights conundrum," in Mahmood Mamdani, ed., *Beyond Rights Talk and Culture Talk* (New York: St. Martin's Press, 2000), pp. 136–148.
71. Fouad Zakaria, "The Standpoint of Contemporary Muslim Fundamentalists," in Toubia, note 35 above, p. 27.
72. Quoted in Mayer, note 5 above, p. 397.
73. Ibid.
74. Andrea Rugh, "Reshaping Personal Relations in Egypt," in Martin E. Marty and R. Scott Appleby, eds, *Fundamentalisms and Society* (Chicago: University of Chicago Press, 1993), p. 161.
75. James Piscatori, "Accounting for Islamic Fundamentalisms," in Marty and Appleby, *Accounting for Fundamentalisms* (Chicago: University of Chicago Press, 1994), p. 361.
76. Ibid., p. 365.
77. Ibid., pp. 361–362. For example, the Muslim Brotherhood in Egypt gained strength in the 1970s based on its promises "to lessen inequality, to attack state corruption, and to bring stability and social justice." Phil Marfleet, "Globalisation and Religious Activism," in Ray Kiely and Phil Marfleet, eds, *Globalisation and the Third World* (London and New York: Routledge, 1998), p. 204.
78. Valentine Moghadam, "Economic restructuring and the gender contract: a case study of Jordan," in M.H. Marchand and A.S. Runyon, eds, *Gender and Global Restructuring* (London and New York: Routledge, 2000), pp. 102–103.
79. Piscatori, note 75 above, p. 369.

80. Philip Marfleet, "Globalization, Islam, and the Indigenization of Knowledge," in Cynthia Nelson and Shahnaz Rouse, eds, *Situating Globalization* (Bielefeld: transcript Verlag, 2000), p. 26.
81. Nancy T. Ammerman, "Accounting for Christian Fundamentalisms: Social Dynamics and Rhetorical Strategies," in Marty and Appleby, note 75 above, p. 164.
82. Robert Wuthnow and Matthew P. Lawson, "Sources of Christian Fundamentalism in the United States," in Marty and Appleby, note 75 above, pp. 27–28.
83. Peter Beyer, *Religion and Globalization* (London: Sage, 1994), p. 126.
84. Op. cit., p. 33.
85. Ibid., pp. 44–46.
86. Beyer, note 83 above, p. 114.
87. Ibid., p. 124.
88. Nancy T. Ammerman, "Accounting for Christian Fundamentalisms: Social Dynamics and Rhetorical Strategies," in Marty and Appleby, note 75 above, p. 159.
89. Martin Riesebrodt, "Fundamentalism and the Political Mobilization of Women" (Paper presented at the 85th Annual Meeting of the American Sociological Association, Washington, DC, 11–15 August, 1990), quoted in Helen Hardacre, " 'The Impact of Fundamentalisms on Women, the Family, and Interpersonal Relations,' in Marty and Appelby," note 74 above, p. 139.
90. A point made by Rhoda Howard, "Cultural Absolutism and the Nostalgia for Community," *Human Rights Quarterly* 15 (1993), pp. 315–338, and by Abdullahi Ahmed An-Na'im, unpublished lecture at the University of Chicago, April, 1996.
91. Rhoda Howard, ibid.
92. Fatima Mernissi, "Democracy as Moral Disintegration," in Toubia, note 35 above, p. 36.
93. Sadiq al-'Azm, quoted in Mayer, note 5 above, p. 382.
94. Joan Smith, "The Creation of the World We Know: The World Economy and the Re-creation of Gendered Identities," in Moghadam, note 17 above, p. 31.
95. Quoted in Maila Stivens, "Introduction," in Hilsdon et al., note 23 above, p. 3.
96. See, for example, the uses of the rights construct in Asia in Anne-Marie Hilsdon, Martha Macintyre, Vera Mackie, and Maila Stivens, eds, *Human Rights and Gender Politics: Asia-Pacific Perspectives* (London and New York: Routledge, 2000).

5 The question of privacy

1. Quoted in Leela Dube, "On the Construction of Gender: Hindu Girls in Patrilineal India," in Karuna Chanana, ed., *Socialisation, Education, and Women: Explorations in Gender Identity* (New Delhi: Orient Longman, 1988), p. 169.
2. Kate O'Donovan, *Sexual Divisions in Law* (London: Weidenfeld and Nicolson, 1985), p. 1.
3. Ibid., p. 3.

4. Linda McDowell, *Gender, Identity and Place* (Minneapolis: University of Minnesota Press, 1999), p. 175.
5. Ibid.
6. Quoted in O'Donovan, note 2 above, p. 2.
7. See, for example, Theodor Meron, notes 17ff. below.
8. Carole Pateman, *The Disorder of Women* (Oxford: Polity Press, 1989), p. 119.
9. Celina Romany, "State Responsibility Goes Private: A Feminist Critique of the Public/Private Distinction in International Human Rights Law," in Rebecca Cook, ed., *Human Rights of Women* (Philadelphia: University of Pennsylvania Press, 1994), p. 93.
10. Mary Anne Glendon, *Rights Talk* (New York: Free Press, 1991), pp. 65–66.
11. Donna Sullivan, "The Public/Private Distinction in International Human Rights Law," in Julie Peters and Andrea Wolper, eds, *Women's Rights, Human Rights* (New York: Routledge, 1995), p. 127.
12. In India, for example, this is manifested in early marriages for girls, before they can be "damaged" and therefore untradable (see P. Oldenburg, "Sex Ratio, Son Preference and Violence in India," *Economic and Political Weekly* (December 5–12, 1992), p. 2660), and in Section 497 of the Indian Penal Code's punishment of male adulterers for spoiling other men's property (see the discussion in Singh, "Obstacles to Women's Rights in India," in Cook, note 9 above, p. 395, fn. 42).
13. Pateman, note 8 above, p. 120.
14. Joan Smith "The Creation of the World We Know: The World-Economy and the Re-creation of Gendered Identities," in Valentine Moghadam, ed., *Identity Politics and Women* (Boulder: Westview Press, 1994), p. 36.
15. *Report of the Committee on the Elimination of Discrimination Against Women*, UN Doc. A/47/38 (1992), note 30, p. 8. There are, interestingly, some observers who think that the relative powerlessness of CEDAW is evidence of the acceptance by the United Nations of the public/private dichotomy, and of its tacit willingness to subordinate women's rights to male power objectives. See, for example, Hussaina Abdullah, "Religious revivalism, human rights activism, and the struggle for women's rights in Nigeria," in Mahmood Mamdani, ed., *Beyond Rights Talk and Culture Talk* (New York: St. Martin's Press, 2000), p. 118.
16. Rebecca Cook, "State Accountability Under the Women's Convention," in Cook, note 9 above, pp. 236–239.
17. Theodor Meron, *Human Rights and Law-Making at the United Nations* (Oxford: Clarendon Press, 1982), p. 62.
18. Ibid., p. 63.
19. Ibid., p. 159.
20. 104 S.Ct. 3244 (1984).
21. Meron, note 17 above, pp. 21–22.
22. Ibid., p. 22. The Convention in question is The International Convention on the Elimination of All Forms of Racial Discrimination, yet in his section concerning the Women's Convention Meron informs the reader that his opinion of the appropriate boundaries of the public and private are described earlier in his treatment of the Race Convention.
23. Liesbeth Lijnzaad, *Reservations to UN-Human Rights Treaties* (Dordrecht: Martinus Nijhoff, 1995), p. 324.

24. See text accompanying note 73, Chapter 2 above.
25. Joel Feinberg, *Social Philosophy* (Englewood Cliffs, NJ: Prentice-Hall, 1973), p. 75.
26. Feinberg uses the example of the United States' Civil Rights Act of 1964, in which the right to exclude persons from one's private property was denied to those whose property also housed a public enterprise involving the exchange of money, such as a hotel or restaurant. In all such cases, the privacy right to personal property was trumped by a law insuring nondiscrimination on the basis of race. Proprietors were required to serve all members of the public or none at all. Ibid., p. 78.
27. Another perspective on the belief/action dichotomy (religious rather than philosophical) is provided by A. Bradney who writes that the United Kingdom, while claiming to avoid religious discrimination in its legal system, actually perpetuates a pervasive if subtle kind of discrimination. British courts claim not to render judgments against individuals because they are Jain, for instance, but because of certain actions (how they treat women, for example). In actuality, one set of religious/moral/ethical principles (Christian) is being used as a rule of measure for everyone. People of any religion are entitled to hold any belief they wish, but not to act outside of accordance with reigning moral concepts. This, says Bradney, is religious discrimination, done in the name of secondary, resulting actions rather than doctrines themselves. A. Bradney, *Religions, Rights and Laws* (Leicester: Leicester University Press, 1993), p. 158.
28. Susan Moller Okin, "Inequalities Between the Sexes in Different Cultural Contexts," in Martha Nussbaum and Jonathan Glover, eds, *Women, Culture and Development* (Oxford: Oxford Clarendon Press, 1995), p. 279.
29. Onora O'Neill, "Justice, Gender, and International Boundaries," in Martha Nussbaum and Amartya Sen, eds, *The Quality of Life* (Oxford: Clarendon Press, 1993), p. 321.
30. Carole Pateman, note 8 above, p. 119.
31. Spike Peterson, "Whose Rights? A Critique of the 'Givens' in Human Rights Discourse" (1990) *Alternatives* XV, p. 319.
32. Joan Landes, quoted in Nancy Fraser, "Rethinking the Public Sphere: A Contribution to the Critique of Actually Existing Democracy," *Social Text* 25/26 (1990), p. 59.
33. Carole Pateman has written that the classic contract theorists laid the foundations within liberalism for viewing political rights as having nothing to do with "nature." They "then went on to construct the difference between men and women as the difference between natural freedom and natural subjection." Paraphrased by Celina Romany, "State Responsibility Goes Private," in Cook, note 9 above, p. 92, quoting Carole Pateman, *The Sexual Contract* (Cambridge, MA: Polity Press, 1988).
34. See text accompanying note 24 above.
35. Flavia Agnes, "Redefining the Agenda of the Women's Movement within a Secular Framework," in *Women and the Hindu Right* (New Delhi: Oxford University Press, 1999), p. 145.
36. Ibid., p. 146.
37. Ibid.

38. Nivedita Menon, "State, Community and the Debate on the Universal Civil Code in India," in Mamdani, note 15 above.
39. See text accompanying note 84 of Chapter 2.
40. *Iddat* is a period of time roughly corresponding to three months, or three menstrual cycles. Divorces do not become fully effective until this period is concluded in order to determine whether the divorced wife is pregnant.
41. M. Indu Menon, *Status of Muslim Women in India* (New Delhi: Uppal Publishing House, 1981), p. 77.
42. Werner F. Menski, "The Reform of Islamic Family Law and a Uniform Civil Code for India," in Chibli Mallat and Jane Connors, eds, *Islamic Family Law* (London: Graham and Trotman, 1990), p. 281.
43. *Talaq* is the thrice repeated phrase "I divorce you," which is considered in some Muslim communities as an authoritative method for men to divorce their wives.
44. Interestingly, the Act simultaneously requires Christians who divorce to do so in civil courts as well, stating that Christian marriages count as civil contracts. R. Monteiro, "Belief, Law and Justice for Women," *Economic and Political Weekly* (October 24–31, 1992), p. WS-75.
45. Monteiro, ibid.
46. Ibid.
47. Madhu Kishwar, "Stimulating Reform, Not Forcing It," *Manushi* No. 89 (July–August, 1995), p. 10.
48. Amrita Chhachhi, "Identity Politics, Secularism and Women: A South Asian Perspective," in Zoya Hasan, ed., *Forging Identities* (Boulder, CO: Westview Press, 1994), p. 88.
49. Donna Sullivan, "Advancing the Freedom of Religion or Belief Through the UN Declaration on the Elimination of Religious Intolerance and Discrimination," *American Journal of International Law* 82 (1988), p. 516.
50. Ratna Kapur and Brenda Cossman, *Subversive Sites* (New Delhi: Sage, 1996), p. 70.
51. For instance, the matrilineal communities of Kerala (see Chapter 4, text accompanying notes 24 and 25) perpetuate positive familial ideology in spite of institutionalized gender discrimination in inheritance, and so on.
52. Op. cit., p. 115. Interestingly, the couple has names that suggest they are Sikh, not Hindu.
53. Ibid., pp. 120–121.
54. E.M. Rhoodie, *Discrimination Against Women* (Jefferson, NC: McFarland, 1989), pp. 100–101.
55. Donna Sullivan, "Gender Equality and Religious Freedom: Toward a Framework for Conflict Resolution," *New York University Journal of International Law and Politics* 24 (1992), pp. 836–837.
56. See the discussion accompanying notes 59ff., Chapter 4.
57. Martin Marty and Scott Appleby, "Introduction: A Sacred Cosmos, Scandalous Code, Defiant Society," in *Fundamentalisms and Society* (Chicago: University of Chicago Press, 1993), pp. 1–19.
58. Max L. Stackhouse, *Creeds, Society, and Human Rights* (Grand Rapids, MI: William B. Eerdmans, 1984), pp. 242–244.
59. Marie-Aimée Hélie Lucas, "The Preferential Symbol for Islamic Identity: Women in Muslim Personal Laws," in Moghadam, note 14 above, p. 392.

60. Sullivan, note 55 above, p. 839.
61. Rebecca Cook, "Introduction," in Cook, note 9 above, p. 17.
62. Op. cit., p. 825.
63. For a discussion of India's unique understanding of secularism, see generally Brenda Cossman and Ratna Kapur, *Secularism's Last Sigh?* (New Delhi: Oxford University Press, 1999), and especially p. 56.
64. In the United States these last two items have been of particular concern to Native Americans, some of whom use peyote and other substances for religious purposes, and others of whom are denied access to holy grounds (such as the Shoshone of Nevada, some of whose most sacred sites became US military weapons ranges).
65. Fatima Mernissi, "Virginity and Patriarchy," in Aziza Al-Hibri, ed., *Women and Islam* (Oxford: Pergamon Press, 1982), p. 189.
66. See, for example, Donna Sullivan in Peters and Wolper, note 11 above, p. 130.
67. G.A. Res. 48/104 of Dec. 20, 1993.
68. Quoted in Lijnzaad, note 23 above, fn. 43 on p. 307.
69. This is a fine example of the lack of a real boundary between the private and the public.
70. As Frances Olsen writes, "Once the state undertakes to enforce some but not all rights and obligations, the state cannot avoid policy choices that will affect family life. No logical basis exists for identifying these state choices as either intervention or nonintervention." "The Myth of State Intervention in the Family," *Journal of Law Reform* 18 (1985), p. 844. Furthermore, a state is tacitly understood to be practicing "a policy of non-intervention when it bolsters family hierarchy," suggesting "that the hierarchy the state enforces is a natural hierarchy, created by God or by nature, not by law." Ibid., p. 846.
71. Donna Sullivan, "The Public/Private Distinction in International Human Rights Law," in Peters and Wolper, note 11 above, p. 127.
72. Op. cit.
73. Rebecca Cook, "Using the Convention on the Elimination of All Forms of Discrimination Against Women to Advance Women's Human Rights," in Margaret A. Schuler, ed., *Claiming Our Place* (Washington: Institute for Women, Law and Development, 1993), p. 46.

6 The question of agency

1. Quoted in Helen Hardacre, "The Impact of Fundamentalisms on Women, the Family, and Interpersonal Relations," in Martin E. Marty and R. Scott Appleby, eds, *Fundamentalisms and Society* (Chicago: University of Chicago Press, 1993), p. 142.
2. In the words of Mridula Sinha, one of the top women leaders in the (Hindu communalist) Bharatiya Janata Party in India, "For Indian women, liberation means liberation from atrocities. It doesn't mean that women should be relieved of their duties as wives and mothers. Women should stop demanding their rights all the time and think instead in terms of their responsibilities to the family." Quoted in Amrita Basu, "Appropriating Gender," in Amrita Basu and Patricia Jeffery, eds, *Appropriating Gender* (New York: Routledge, 1998), p. 179.

3. See, for example, note 1 in the Introduction, above.
4. For example, a woman in Africa who was advised, after narrowly surviving a post-partum infection, not to have intercourse with her husband for a while, told her doctor that she could not refuse her husband because it would be a "Qur'anic sin." Described in Alayne Adams and Sarah Castle, "Gender Relations and Household Dynamics," in Gita Sen, Adrienne Germain, and Lincoln Chen, eds, *Population Policies Reconsidered* (Boston: Harvard University Press, 1994), p. 168.
5. Quoted in Martha C. Nussbaum, *Women and Human Development* (Cambridge: Cambridge Universtiy Press, 200), p. 143.
6. Amartya Sen, "Well-Being, Agency, and Freedom: The Dewey Lectures 1984," *Journal of Philosophy* LXXXII(4) (April, 1985), p. 206. Emphasis in original.
7. Ibid., p. 204.
8. Amartya Sen, "Gender and Cooperative Conflicts," in Irene Tinker, ed., *Persistent Inequalities* (New York: Oxford University Press, 1990), p. 126.
9. Julia Annas, "Women and the Quality of Life: Two Norms or One?" in Martha Nussbaum and Amartya Sen, eds, *The Quality of Life* (New York: Oxford University Press, 1993), p. 282.
10. Pierre Bourdieu, *Outline of a Theory of Practice* (Cambridge: Cambridge University Press, 1977), pp. 86–87. He describes "habitus" as "systems of durable, transposable *dispositions*, structured structures predisposed to function as structuring structures, that is, as principles of the generation and structuring of practices and representations which can be objectively 'regulated' and 'regular' without in any way being the product of obedience to rules, objectively adapted to their goals without presupposing a conscious aiming at ends or an express mastery of the operations necessary to attain them and, being all this, collectively orchestrated without being the product of the orchestrating action of a conductor." (p. 72)
11. Anthony Giddens, *The Constitution of Society* (Berkeley: University of California Press, 1984), pp. 3, 25.
12. Jitka Kotalová, *Belonging to Others* (Dhaka: University Press Limited, 1993), pp. 20–21.
13. Note 10 above, p. 192.
14. Patricia Jeffery and Roger Jeffery, *Population, Gender and Politics* (Cambridge: Cambridge University Press, 1997), p. 120.
15. Patricia Jeffery and Roger Jeffery, "Killing My Heart's Desire: Education and Female Autonomy in Rural North India," in Nita Kumar, ed., *Women as Subjects* (New Delhi: Stree, 1994), p. 127. They use as their basic definition of autonomy that of Nick Dyson and Tim Moore: "the capacity to manipulate one's environment" and "the ability – technical, social, psychological – to obtain information and to use as the basis for making decisions about one's private concerns and those of one's intimates," in "On Kinship Structure, Female Autonomy, and Demographic Behaviour in India," *Population and Development Review* 9(1) (1983), p. 45.
16. Patricia Jeffery and Roger Jeffery, ibid., p. 131.
17. Patricia Jeffery and Roger Jeffery, "Gender, Community, and the Local State in Bijnor, India," in Patricia Jeffery and Amrita Basu, eds, *Appropriating Gender* (New York: Routledge, 1998), p. 137.

18. Constantina Safilios-Rothschild, "Female Power, Autonomy and Demographic Change in the Third World," in Richard Anker, Mayra Buvinic, and Nadia H. Youssef, eds, *Women's Roles and Population Trends in the Third World* (London: Croom Helm, 1982), p. 117.
19. Hanna Papanek, "To Each Less Than She Needs, From Each More Than She Can Do: Allocations, Entitlements, and Value," in Irene Tinker, ed., *Persistent Inequalities* (New York: Oxford University Press, 1990), p. 163.
20. Ibid., p. 179.
21. See the example from India below, text accompanying note 29.
22. Op. cit., p. 178.
23. Marie-Aimée Hélie-Lucas, "The Preferential Symbol for Islamic Identity: Women in Muslim Personal Laws," in Valentine Moghadam, ed., *Identity Politcs and Women* (Boulder: Westview Press, 1994), p. 394. Women who accept the valorization of their subordination in order to reconcile their anger or hurt at their subordinate status are not limited to those whose oppression is directly rooted in traditionalist religion, of course. Women in every society have made peace with the restrictions placed on their agency by accommodating and even affirming them.
24. Valentine Moghadam, "Introduction," in Moghadam, ibid., p. 20.
25. Nahid Toubia, "Women and Health in Sudan," in Nahid Toubia, ed., *Women of the Arab World* (London: Zed Books, 1988), p. 107.
26. Ibid., p. 108.
27. Grace Akello, *Self Twice-Removed: Ugandan Women* (London: Change International Reports, n.d. [1983]), p. 5. Quoted in Rhoda Howard, *Human Rights in Commonwealth Africa* (Totowa, NJ: Rowman and Littlefield, 1986), p. 19. Italics in original.
28. Grace Gredys Harris, "Individual, Self, and Person" *American Anthropologist* 91 (1989), p. 605.
29. Leela Dube, "Socialisation of Hindu Girls in Patrilineal India," in K. Chanana, ed., *Socialisation, Education, and Women: Explorations in Gender Identity* (Hyderabad: Orient Longman, 1988), p. 184.
30. Heba El-Kholy, "A Tale of Two Contracts: Towards a Situated Understanding of 'Women's Interests' in Egypt," in Cynthia Nelson and Shahnaz Rouse, eds, *Situating Globalization* (Bielefeld: Transcipt Verlag, 2000), pp. 301–335.
31. Patricia Jeffery and Roger Jeffery, "What's the Benefit of Being Educated?" in Roger Jeffery and Alaka M. Basu, eds, *Girls' Schooling, Women's Autonomy and Fertility Change in South Asia* (London: Sage, 1996), p. 154.
32. Roger Jeffery and Alaka M. Basu, "Schooling as Contraception?" in *Girls' Schooling, Women's Autonomy and Fertility Change in South Asia*, ibid., pp. 40–41.
33. Patricia Jeffery and Roger Jeffery, "A Woman Belongs to Her Husband: Female Autonomy, Women's Work and Childrearing in Bijnor," in Alice Clark, ed., *Gender and Political Economy* (Delhi: Oxford University Press, 1993), p. 110.
34. Bourdieu, note 10 above, pp. 164–165.
35. Hanna Papanek, "To Each Less Than She Needs, From Each More Than She Can Do: Allocations, Entitlements, and Value," in Irene Tinker, ed., *Persistent Inequalities* (New York: Oxford University Press, 1990), p. 180.

36. Ursula King, "The Effect of Social Change on Religious Self-Understanding: Women Ascetics in Modern Hinduism," in Kenneth Ballhatchet and David Taylor, eds, *Changing South Asia* (Hong Kong: Asian Research Service, 1984), p. 72.
37. Leila Djabari, "The Syrian Woman: Reality and Aspiration," in Haleh Afshar, ed., *Women and Empowerment* (New York: St. Martin's Press, 1998), pp. 110–111.
38. Note 11 above, p. 9.
39. Jo Rowlands, "A Word of the Times, but What Does it Mean? Empowerment in the Discourse and Practice of Development," in Afshar, note 37 above, p. 13.
40. Nita Kumar, "Introduction," in Nita Kumar, ed., *Women as Subjects* (New Delhi: Stree, 1994), p. 17.
41. For an example from the Indian Christian community, see Leslie A. Flemming, "Between Two Worlds: Self-Construction and Self-Identity in the Writings of Three Nineteenth-Century Indian Christian Women," in *Women as Subjects*, ibid., pp. 81–107.
42. See Manjusri Chaki-Sircar, *Feminism in a Traditional Society* (New Delhi: Shakti Books, 1984), pp. 215ff., and Ursula King, "The Effect of Social Change on Religious Self-Understanding: Women Ascetics in Modern Hinduism," in Kenneth Ballhatchet and David Taylor, eds, *Changing South Asia* (Hong Kong: Asian Research Service, 1984), p. 71.
43. Described in Malathi DeAlwis, "Motherhood as a Space of Protest," in *Appropriating Gender*, note 2 above.
44. Katy Gardner, "Women and Islamic Revivalism in a Bangladeshi Community," in *Appropriating Gender*, note 2 above, p. 213.
45. See, for instance, *Women as Subjects* (see note 40 above), and Douglas Haynes and Gyan Prakash, eds, *Contesting Power* (Berkeley: University of California Press, 1991), adding to the earlier *Weapons of the Weak* by James C. Scott (New Haven: Yale University Press, 1985).
46. Michael Adas, "South Asian Resistance in Comparative Perspective," in *Contesting Power*, ibid., at 292ff.
47. Jean Comaroff, *Social Bodies and Natural Ideologies* (Chicago: University of Chicago Press, 1985), p. 1, quoted in Patricia Jeffery and Roger Jeffery, "Killing My Heart's Desire: Education and Female Autonomy in Rural North India," in Nita Kumar, ed., *Women as Subjects* (New Delhi: Stree, 1994), p. 161.
48. So Katy Gardner found while researching women in rural Sylhet, Bangladesh. See *Appropriating Gender*, note 2 above, p. 219.
49. See, for example, the research of G.G. Raheja, and A.G. Gold, *Listen to the Heron's Words* (Berkeley: University of California Press, 1994).
50. *Weapons of the Weak*, note 45 above, p. xvi.
51. Malathi De Alwis, "Motherhood as a Space of Protest," in *Appropriating Gender*, note 2 above, p. 186.
52. Rosalind O'Hanlon, "Issues of Widowhood: Gender and Resistance in Colonial Western India," in *Contesting Power*, note 45 above, p. 63.
53. Not her real name. The following paragraphs summarize the research of Paola Bacchetta in her article "All Our Goddesses Are Armed: Religion, Resistance, and Revenge in the Life of a Militant Hindu Nationalist Woman," in Amrita Basu, ed., *Bulletin of Concerned South Asian Scholars* 25(4) (1993) Special Issue, pp. 38–51.

54. Ibid., pp. 43–44. Emphasis not in original.
55. Ibid., p. 47.
56. Ibid., p. 50.
57. Ibid.
58. These paragraphs summarize the research of her interviewers, Ann Grodzins Gold and Gloria Goodwin Raheja, in *Listen to the Heron's Words* (Berkeley: University of California Press, 1994), pp. 164–181, and again by Gold in Nita Kumar, ed., *Women as Subjects* (New Delhi: Stree, 1994), pp. 38–43.
59. Katy Gardner, "Women and Islamic Revivalism in a Bangladeshi Community," in Patricia Jeffery and Amrita Basu, eds, *Appropriating Gender* (New York: Routledge, 1998), pp. 213–214.
60. Research done by Carol Gilligan. See S.F. Parsons, *Feminism and Christian Ethics* (Cambridge: Cambridge University Press, 1996), p. 55.
61. Adetoun O. Ilumoka, "African Women's Economic, Social, and Cultural Rights," in Rebecca Cook, ed., *Human Rights of Women* (Philadelphia: University of Pennsylvania Press, 1994), p. 319.
62. Susan Moller Okin, "Inequalities Between the Sexes in Different Cultural Contexts," in Martha Nussbaum and Jonathan Glover, eds, *Women, Culture, and Development* (Oxford: Clarendon Press, 1995), p. 290
63. Martha Chen's research in Bangladesh found this to be the case. See Chen, *A Quiet Revolution: Women in Transition in Rural Bangladesh* (Cambridge, MA: Schenkman, 1983).
64. See, for instance, V. Spike Peterson, *Alternatives* XV (1990), p. 331, who argues that the concept of agency reifies atomization, anti-relationality, and an emphasis on the individual. Peterson also argues that "the glorification of individual agency" relegates cooperative efforts to a lesser sphere than individual ones, a process that helps support the notion that human nature is separable from social relations. In the end, more powerful people are enabled to distance themselves from others and from the consequences of their [discriminating] actions towards them, further enhancing the fallacy of "the level playing field" (p. 330).
65. Note 40 above, p. 18.

7 Religion, rights and change

1. *Harijan*, June, 1940. Quoted by S.T. Lokhandwala, "The Position of Women under Islam," in Asghar Ali Engineer, ed., *Status of Women in Islam* (Delhi: Ajanta Publications, 1987), p. 13.
2. In *Women and Human Development* (Cambridge: Cambridge University Press, 2000), p. 221, Martha Nussbaum approvingly quotes this piece from Ambedkar. I am not so sanguine about the potential of law to ensure religious women's rights.
3. For an example of such a backlash in the Indian context see Patricia Jeffery, "Agency, Activism, and Agendas," in Patricia Jeffery and Amrita Basu, eds, *Appropriating Gender* (New York: Routledge, 1998), p. 230.

4. Such is the case with the Muslim community in India, according to Balraj Puri in "Personal Law and Muslim Identity," in Engineer, note 1 above, p. 101.
5. See the examples from India in Ratna Kapur and Brenda Cossman, *Secularlism's Last Sigh?* (New Delhi: Oxford University Press, 1999).
6. See, for example, the study of women in Kerala in M. Indu Menon, *Status of Muslim Women in India* (New Delhi: Uppal Publishing House, 1991).
7. Aziza al-Hibri leaps to mind as a person who advocates for the rights of women by emphasizing the rights she believes to be codified in her religious tradition. See, for example, Aziza al-Hibri, ed., *Women and Islam* (Oxford: Pergamon Press, 1982).
8. Radhika Coomaraswamy, "Reinventing International Law: Women's Rights as Human Rights in the International Community," in Peter Van Ness, ed., *Debating Human Rights* (London and New York: Routledge, 1999), pp. 171ff.
9. The Platform for Action (PFA) adopted at the Beijing conference outlines 12 priorities for women and girls. They are violence against women, women and armed conflict, human rights, women and poverty, women and the economy, institutional mechanisms, education and training of women, women and health, women and the media, women in power and decision-making, women and the environment, and the girl child.
10. Discussed in Manisha Desai, "From Vienna to Beijing: Women's Human Rights Activism and the Human Rights Community," in Peter Van Ness, ed., *Debating Human Rights* (London and New York: Routledge, 1999), p. 189.
11. See note 9 above.
12. For references to Asian/Pacific women's activism see, for example, the chapters in Anne-Marie Hilsdon, Martha Macintyre, Vera Mackie and Maila Stivens, eds, *Human Rights and Gender Politics* (London and New York: Routledge, 2000).
13. Heba El-Kholy, "A Tale of Two Contracts: Towards a Situated Understanding of 'Women's Interests' in Egypt," in Cynthia Nelson and Shahnaz Rouse, eds, *Situating Globalization* (Bielefeld: Transcipt Verlag, 2000), p. 322.
14. See Jane H. Bayes and Nayereh Tohidi, eds, *Globalization, Gender, and Religion* (New York: Palgrave, 2001), for a description, generally, of the work of Christian and Muslim organizations at the Beijing conference.
15. Note 10 above, p. 186.
16. See Maila Stivens, "Introduction: Gender Politics and the Reimagining of Human Rights in the Asia-Pacific," in Hilsdon, et al., note 12 above, p. 21.
17. Ibid., p. 24.
18. Saskia Sassen, *Losing Control* (New York: Columbia University Press, 1996), discussed in Stivens, ibid., p. 11.
19. See text accompanying note 63, Chapter 6.
20. See text accompanying note 62, Chapter 6.
21. It might be added that conservatives' persistent attention to women's religious and social status is a brushfire, a distraction from the real forces of destabilization that ultimately and unwisely disserves the religious leaders' self-interests.
22. Interviews conducted by the present author in Chicago in April 2000, at the Indo-Pakistani Cultural Center. In the words of one respondent, a young

Muslim woman from Pakistan, "It all starts with the economy. More opportunities for girls. More independence. More education – education brings opportunities. If the economy were better, everything would change. Men know that, too. They know they couldn't use their power over a girl because she'd have more opportunities." She added, "Women wouldn't have to stay in bad marriages if there was a job they could have. They could support themselves."

23. Peter Van Ness, "Introduction," in Peter Van Ness, ed., *Debating Human Rights* (London and New York: Routledge, 1999), p. 14.
24. Bina Agarwal, "Positioning the Western Feminist Agenda: A Comment" *Indian Journal of Gender Studies* 1(2) (1994), pp. 249–255.
25. This fact was not approved of by the US government as well as those in Latin America. Worried about the political, economic and social implications of these movements, in the 1980s the US State Department's Council for Inter-American Security urged the Roman Catholic establishment to thwart it. The Council also urged the introduction of American conservative Protestant groups to the regions in order to provide "ideological counterweight." See Phil Marfleet, "Globalisation and Religious Activism," in Ray Kiely and Phil Marfleet, eds, *Globalisation and the Third World* (London and New York: Routledge, 1998), p. 187.
26. See for example, Hibba Abugideiri, "Hagar: A Historical Model for 'Gender Jihad,'" in Yvonne Y. Haddad and John L. Esposito, eds, *Daughters of Abraham* (Gainesville: University of Florida Press, 2001), p. 101.
27. Examples are too numerous to sufficiently catalogue here. For a general description of various religions' liberationist movements see Dan Cohn-Sherbok, ed., *World Religions and Human Liberation* (Maryknoll, NY: Orbis, 1992). For an example of Muslim feminists' re-exegetical work see Khawar Mumtaz and Farida Shaheed, *Women of Pakistan: Two Steps Forward and One Step Back?* (London: Zed, 1987). For feminist reform within Hinduism see, generally, the journal *Manushi*, Madhu Kishwar, ed. For Christian feminist theological ethics see Beverly Wildung Harrison *Making the Connections* (Boston: Beacon Press, 1985), and for feminist Christian exegesis, Phyllis Trible, *God and the Rhetoric of Sexuality* (Philadelphia: Fortress Press, 1978), and *Texts of Terror* (Philadelphia: Fortress Press, 1984).
28. Lina Gupta, "Kali, the Savior," in Paula M. Cooey, William R. Eakin, and Jay B. McDaniel, eds, *After Patriarchy* (Maryknoll, NY: Orbis Books, 1991), p. 15.
29. Rajeswari Sunder Rajan, "Feminism and the Hindu Goddess," in Marianne DeKoven, ed., *Feminist Locations* (New Brunswick, NJ: Rutgers University Press, 2001), pp. 212–226.
30. As defined by Azza M. Karam, "Feminisms and Islamisms in Egypt," in Marianne H. Marchand and Anne Sisson Runyon, eds, *Gender and Global Restructuring* (London and New York: Routledge, 2000), p. 200.
31. Fatima Mernissi, *The Veil and the Male Elite* (Reading, MA: Addison-Wesley Publishing Co., 1991), Chapter 7. But see Nikkie Keddie, "The Rights of Women in Contemporary Islam," in Leroy S. Rouner, ed., *Human Rights and the World's Religions* (Notre Dame, IN: University of Notre Dame Press, 1988), pp. 78–81. Keddie writes of evidence of veiling in a number of ancient cultures, and suggests that it was incorporated by Islam only after it conquered some of those regions. Keddie also takes issue with the notion

that the advent of Islam offered unqualified improvements to the quality of women's lives. She describes matriliny and high-female status in pre-Islamic Arabia, and notes that the "days of disorder" before Islam may refer to matriliny and various practices such as wife-initiated divorce. Certain practices empowering to women actually may be the things that Islam brought to "order."

32. Riffat Hassan, "Women in Post-Patriarchal Islam," in Cooey et al., note 28 above, pp. 39ff.
33. It is interesting to compare this situation with Christianity, in which some conservative Catholic women claim the title of feminist for themselves. Their critics say that they are trying to ride the coattails of the term's acknowledged power, and to wedge into feminism their conservative agenda regarding wifehood and motherhood. See Susan Marie Maloney, "United States Catholic Women: Feminist Theologies in Action," in *Globalization, Gender, and Religion*, note 14 above, p. 66.
34. See Karam, note 30 above, pp. 200–206.
35. Norani Othman, "Islam," in Cheris Kramarae and Dale Spender, gen. eds, *Routledge International Encyclopedia of Women* (New York and London: Routledge, 2000), vol. 2, p. 1161.
36. Jane Bayes and Nayereh Tohidi, "Women Redefining Modernity and Religion in the Globalized Context," in *Globalization, Gender, and Religion*, note 14 above, p. 24.
37. Ghazala Amwar, "Reclaiming the Religious Center from a Muslim Perspective," in Courtney Howland, ed., *Religious Fundamentalisms and the Human Rights of Women* (New York: St. Martin's Press, 1999), p. 305.
38. Ibid.
39. Ibid., p. 306.
40. Maila Stivens, "Introduction: Gender Politics and the Reimagining of Human Rights in the Asia-Pacific," in Anne-Marie Hilsdon, Martha Macintyre, Vera Mackie and Maila Stivens, eds, *Human Rights and Gender Politics* (London and New York: Routledge, 2000). p. 21.
41. Cornel West, "Religion and the Left: An Introduction," in Asghar Ali Engineer, ed., *Religion and Liberation* (Delhi: Ajanta, 1989), p. 14.
42. Charlotte Bunch and Niamh Reilly, *Demanding Accountability* (Rutgers and New York: The Center for Women's Global Leadership and the United Nations Development Fund for Women, 1994), p. 54.

Bibliography

Adams, E.M. *Religion and Cultural Freedom*. Philadelphia: Temple University Press, 1993.

Afchar, H. "The Muslim Conception of Law" in *International Encyclopedia of Comparative Law*. Tübingen: J.C.B. Mohr, 1974.

Afshar, H., ed. *Women and Empowerment*. London: MacMillan Press, 1998.

Agarwal, B. "Positioning the Western Feminist Agenda: A Comment" *Indian Journal of Gender Studies* 1(2) (1994), 249–255.

Agnes, F. *Law and Gender Equality*. New Delhi: Oxford University Press, 1999.

Ahmad, I., ed. *Family, Kinship and Marriage among Muslims in India*. New Delhi: Manohar, 1976.

Aleaz, K.P. *The Gospel of Indian Culture*. Calcutta: Punthi Pustak, 1994.

Al-Hibri, A., ed. *Women and Islam*. Oxford: Pergamon Press, 1982.

Allen, T. and Thomas, A., eds. *Poverty and Development in the 1990's*. Oxford: Oxford University Press, 1992.

Amaladoss, M. *Globalization and Its Victims*. Delhi: Indian Society for Promoting Christian Knowledge, 1999.

Amin, S. "The Poverty-Purdah Trap in Rural Bangladesh: Implications for Women's Roles in the Family" *Development and Change* 28 (April 1997), 213–233.

Anker, R., Buvinic, M., and Youssef, N., eds. *Women's Roles and Population Trends in the Third World*. London: Croom Helm, 1982.

An-Na'im, A.A. *Human Rights in Cross-Cultural Perspectives*. Philadelphia: University of Pennsylvania Press, 1992.

—— and Deng, F.M., eds. *Human Rights in Africa*. Washington, DC: The Brookings Institution, 1990.

Antony, M.J. *Women's Rights*. New Delhi: Dialogue, 1985.

Aravamudan, G. *Voices in My Blood*. New Delhi: Sterling Publishers, 1990.

Arslan, M. and Janaki, R., eds. *Communalism in India*. New Delhi: Manohar, 1994.

Baird, R.D., ed. *Religion and Law in Independent India*. New Delhi: Manohar, 1993.

Ballhatchet, K. and Taylor, D., eds. *Changing South Asia*. Hong Kong: Asian Research Service, 1984.

Basu, A., ed. *Women and Religious Nationalism in India*. Special Issue, *Bulletin of Concerned Asian Scholars* 25(4) (1993).

Basu, S. *She Comes to Take Her Rights*. Albany: State University of New York Press, 1999.

Bay, C. "Self-respect as a Human Right: Thoughts on the Dialectics of Wants and Needs in the Struggle for Human Community" *Human Rights Quarterly* 4 (1982), p. 67.

Bayes, J.H. and Tohidi, N., eds. *Globalization, Gender, and Religion*. New York: Palgrave, 2001.

Benhabib, S. *Situating the Self: Gender, Community, and Post-modernism in Contemporary Ethics*. London: Routledge, 1992.

Benn, S.I. "Rights" *The Encyclopedia of Philosophy*. New York: Macmillan, 1967.

Beyer, P. *Religion and Globalization*. London: Sage, 1994.

Blakely, T.D., van Beek, W.E.A., and Thomson, D.L., eds. *Religion in Africa*. London: James Curry, 1994.

Bloom, I., Martin, J.P., and Proudfoot, W.L., eds. *Religious Diversity and Human Rights*. New York: Columbia University Press, 1996.

Bourdieu, P. *Outline of a Theory of Practice*. Cambridge: Cambridge University Press, 1977.

Bradney, A. *Religions, Rights and Laws*. Leicester: Leicester University Press, 1993.

Brennan, K. "The Influence of Cultural Relativism on International Human Rights Law: Female Circumcision as a Case Study" *Law and Inequality* 7 (1989), 367–398.

Brownlie, I. *Principles of International Law*. Oxford: Clarendon Press, 1990.

Bryant, C.G.A. and Jary, D., eds. *Giddens' Theory of Structuration: A Critical Appreciation*. London: Routledge, 1991.

Bunch, C. and Reilly, N. *Demanding Accountability*. New York: The Center for Women's Global Leadership and the United Nations Development Fund for Women, 1994.

Burrows, N. "The 1979 Convention on the Elimination of All Forms of Discrimination Against Women" *Netherlands International Law Review* 32 (1985), 419–460.

Byrnes, A.C. "The 'Other' Human Rights Treaty Body: The Work of the Committee on the Elimination of Discrimination Against Women" *The Yale Journal of International Law* 14 (1989), 1–67.

Capps, W.H. *Religious Studies*. Minneapolis: Fortress Press, 1995.

Chaki-Sircar, M. *Feminism in a Traditional Society*. New Delhi: Shakti, 1984.

Chanana, K., ed. *Socialisation, Education, and Women: Explorations in Gender Identity*. Hyderabad: Orient Longman, 1988.

Charlesworth, H., Bayefsky, A., Cook, H.M., Sullivan, D.J., Chinkin, C.M., and Farer, T. "Resolving Conflicting Human Rights Standards in International Law" *American Society of International Law Proceedings* 85 (1991), 336–358.

Charrad, M. "State and Gender in the Mahgrib" *Middle East Report* No. 163, 20(2) (1990), 19–24.

Chaturvedi, D.C. *Indian Fundamental Rights*. Meerut, UP: Saru Publishing House, 1992.

Chen, M.A. *A Quiet Revolution*. Cambridge, MA: Schenkman, 1983.

—— and Drèze, J. "Widows and Health in Rural North India" *Economic and Political Weekly* (October 24–31, 1992), WS81–WS92.

Clark, A.W., ed. *Gender and Political Economy*. Delhi: Oxford University Press, 1993.

Clark, R.S. "The United Nations and Religious Freedom" *New York University Journal of International Law and Politics* 11 (1979), 197–225.

Cohn-Sherbok, D., ed. *World Religions and Human Liberation*. Maryknoll, NY: Orbis Books, 1992.

Cooey, P.M., Eakin, W.R., and McDaniel, J.B., eds. *After Patriarchy*. Maryknoll, NY: Orbis Books, 1991.

Cook, R.J., ed. *Human Rights of Women*. Philadelphia: University of Pennsylvania Press, 1994.

——. "International Human Rights Law Concerning Women: Case Notes and Comments" *Vanderbilt Journal of Transnational Law* 23 (1990), 779–818.

——. "Reservations to the Convention on the Elimination of All Forms of Discrimination Against Women" *Virginia Journal of International Law* 23 (1990), 643–716.

Cranston, M. *What Are Human Rights?* New York: Basic Books, 1964

Davies, M. *Third World – Second Sex* (vol. 1). London: Zed Books, 1983.

——. *Third World – Second Sex* (vol. 2). London: Zed Books, 1987.

Dekoven, M., ed. *Feminist Locations.* New Brunswick, NJ: Rutgers University Press, 2001.

Devasia, V.V. and Devasia, L., eds. *Women, Social Justice, and Human Rights.* New Delhi: APH Publishing Corporation, 1998.

Devendra, K. *Changing Status of Women in India.* 3rd ed. New Delhi: Vikas Publishing House, 1994.

Dhagamwar, V. *Law, Power and Justice.* New Delhi: Sage, 1992.

Dharmalingam, A. "Economics of Marriage Change in a South India Village" *Development and Change* 25 (July 1994), 569–590.

Dhruvarajan, V. *Hindu Women and the Power of Ideology.* Granby, MA: Bergin and Garvey, 1989.

Diemer, A., Hersch, P.J., Hountondji, J., Humphrey, R., Inagaki, E. Kamenka, P., Kirpal, V.N., Kudravtsev, M., Markovic', V., Matthieu, A.A., Mazrui, F.M., Quesada, R.C., Pandeya, P. Ricoeur, M., Allal Sineceur, A., Ehr-Soon Tay, C., Taylor, R., Tuck, F., and Zakaria, F. eds. *Philosophical Foundations of Human Rights.* Paris: UNESCO, 1986.

Dietrich, G. *Reflections on the Women's Movement in India.* New Delhi: Horizon India Books, 1992.

Doniger, W. with Smith, B.K. (trans.) *The Laws of Manu.* Harmondsworth: Penguin Books, 1991.

Donnelly, J. and Howard, R.E., eds. *International Handbook of Human Rights.* Westport, CT: Greenwood Press, 1987.

Donnelly, J. *Universal Human Rights in Theory and Practice.* Ithaca, NY: Cornell University Press, 1989.

Dyson, T. and Moore, M. "On Kinship Structure, Female Autonomy, and Demographic Behavior in India" *Population and Development Review* 9(1) (1983), 35–60.

Dwyer, K. *Arab Voices.* Berkeley: University of California Press, 1991.

Eide, A.E. and Hagtvet, B., eds. *Human Rights in Perspective.* Oxford: Basil Blackwell, 1992.

Eisenstein, Z.P., ed. *Capitalist Patriarchy and the Case for Socialist Feminism.* New York: Monthly Review, 1979.

Eisler, R. "Human Rights: Toward an Integrated Theory for Action" *Human Rights Quarterly* 9 (1987), 287–308.

Elshtain, J.B. *Public Man, Private Woman.* Princeton: Princeton University Press, 1981.

Engineer, A.A. *Religion and Liberation.* Delhi: Ajanta, 1989.

——, ed. *Status of Women in Islam.* Delhi: Ajanta Publications, 1987.

——. *Islam and Liberation Theology.* New Delhi: Sterling Publishers Private Ltd., 1990.

Engle, K. "International Human Rights and Feminism" *Michigan Journal of International Law* 13 (1992), 517–610.

Erricker, C., ed. *Teaching World Religions.* Oxford: Heinemann Educational, 1993.

Esbeck, C.H., ed. *Religious Beliefs, Human Rights, and the Moral Foundation of Western Democracy.* Columbia: University of Missouri, 1986.

Esteva, G. and Prakash, M.S. *Grassroots Postmodernism: Remaking the Soil of Cultures*. New York: Zed Books, 1998.
Evans, T., ed. *Human Rights Fifty Years On*. Manchester and New York: Manchester University Press, 1998.
Falk, N.A. *Women and Religion in India*. Kalamazoo: Western Michigan University, 1994.
Falk, R. *Predatory Globalization*. Cambridge: Polity Press, 1999.
Feinberg, J. *Social Philosophy*. Englewood Cliffs, NJ: Prentice-Hall, 1973.
——. *Rights, Justice and the Bounds of Liberty*. Princeton: Princeton University Press, 1980.
Fernea, E.W., ed. *Women and the Family in the Middle East*. Austin: University of Texas Press, 1985.
Fowler, B. *Pierre Bourdieu and Cultural Theory*. London: Sage, 1997.
Franke, W.F. and Chasin, B.H. "Women and Kerala Model" *Economic and Political Weekly* (March 9, 1996), 625–630.
Fraser, N. "Rethinking the Public Sphere: A Contribution to the Critique of Actually Existing Democracy" *Social Text* 25/6 (1990), 56–79.
Fudge, J. "The Public/Private Distinction: The Possibilities of and the Limits to the Use of Charter Litigation to Further Feminist Struggles" *Osgoode Hall Law Journal* 25 (1988), 485–554.
Gaus, G.F. *Political Concepts and Political Theories*. Boulder: Westview Press, 2000.
Giddens, A. *Studies in Social and Political Theory*. New York: Basic Books, 1977.
——. *The Constitution of Society*. Berkeley: University of California Press, 1984.
Gills, B., Rocamora, J., and Wilson, R., eds. *Low Intensity Democracy*. London and Boulder: Pluto Press, 1993.
Glendon, M.A. *Rights Talk*. New York: The Free Press, 1991.
Goddard, V.A., ed. *Gender, Agency and Change*. London and New York: Routledge, 2000.
Government of Kerala. *Women in Kerala*. Trivandrum: Department of Economics and Statistics, 1989.
Gremillion, J., ed., *The Gospel of Peace and Justice: Catholic Social Teaching Since Pope John*. Maryknoll, NY: Orbis Books, 1976.
Gulati, L. "Dimensions of Female Aging and Widowhood; Insights from Kerala Experience" *Economic and Political Weekly* (October 24–31, 1992), WS93–WS99.
Gustafson, C. and Juviler, P., eds. *Religion and Human Rights: Competing Claims?* Armonk, NY: M.E. Sharpe, 1999.
Haddad, Y.H. and Esposito, J.L., eds. *Daughters of Abraham*. Gainesville: University Press of Florida, 2001.
Halliday, F. "Relativism and Universalism in Human Rights: The Case of the Islamic Middle East" *Political Studies* 43 (Special Issue) (1995), 152–168.
Hamsa, N. "Impact of Regional Tradition on Muslim Women – With Special Reference to South India" *Islam and the Modern Age* 14 (1983), 49–58.
Haragopal, G. *Political Economy of Human Rights*. Mumbai: Himalaya Publishing House, 1997.
Harker, R., Mahar, C., and Wilkes, C., eds. *An Introduction to the Work of Pierre Bourdieu*. New York: St. Martin's Press, 1990.
Harlan, L. *Religion and Rajput Women*. Berkeley: University of California Press, 1992.
—— and Courtright, P.B., eds. *From the Margins of Hindu Marriage*. New York: Oxford University Press, 1995.

Harris, G.G. "Concepts of Individual, Self, and Person in Description and Analysis" *American Anthropologist* 91 (1989), 599–612.
Harrison, B.W. *Making the Connections*. Boston: Beacon Press, 1985.
Hasan, Z., ed. *Forging Identities: Gender, Communities and the State in India*. Boulder, Colorado: Westview Press, 1994.
Haynes, D. and Prakash, G., eds. *Contesting Power*. Berkeley: University of California Press, 1991.
Henkin, L., ed. *The International Bill of Rights*. New York: Columbia University Press, 1981.
Hijab, N. *Womanpower*. Cambridge: Cambridge University Press, 1988.
Hilsdon, A., Macintyre, M., Mackie, V., and Stivens, M., eds. *Human Rights and Gender Politics*. London and New York: Routledge, 2000.
Hodgson, P.C. and King, R.H., eds, *Christian Theology*. 2nd ed. Philadelphia: Fortress Press, 1985.
Holleman, W.L. *The Human Rights Movement*. New York: Praeger, 1987.
Howard, R.E. *Human Rights in Commonwealth Africa*. Totowa, NJ: Rowman and Littlefield, 1986.
——. "Cultural Absolutism and the Nostalgia for Community" *Human Rights Quarterly* 5 (1993), 315–338.
Howland, C.W., ed. *Religious Fundamentalisms and the Human Rights of Women*. New York: St. Martin's Press, 1999.
Human Development Report 1995. New York: United Nations Development Programme, 1995.
Human Development Report 2000. New York: Oxford University Press, 2000.
Human Rights Watch World Report 2001. New York: Human Rights Watch, 2000.
Jackson, C. and Pearson, R., eds. *Feminist Visions of Development*. London: Routledge, 1998.
Jacobson, D.A. *Hidden Faces: Hindu and Muslim Purdah in a Central Indian Village*. (Columbia University Dissertation, copyright of the author, 1973).
—— and Wadley, S.S. *Women in India: Two Perspectives*. New Delhi: Manohar, 1992.
Jain, D. and Banerjee, N., eds. *Tyranny of the Household*. New Delhi: Shakti, 1985.
Jain, R. *Family Violence in India*. New Delhi: Radiant, 1992.
Jeffery, P. *Frogs in a Well*. London: Zed, 1979.
Jeffery, R. and Basu, A., eds. *Girls' Schooling, Women's Autonomy and Fertility Change in South Asia*. New Delhi: Sage, 1996.
Jeffery, P. and Jeffery, R. *Don't Marry Me to a Plowman*! Boulder: Westview, 1996.
——. *Population, Gender and Politics*. Cambridge: Cambridge University Press, 1997.
Jeffery, P. and Basu, A. *Appropriating Gender*. New York and London: Routledge, 1998.
Joseph, M. *Marriage Among Indian Christians*. New Delhi: Rawat, 1994.
Juviler, P. and Gross, B., eds. *Human Rights for the 21st Century*. Armonk, NY: M.E. Sharpe, 1993.
Kamenka, E. and Tay, A.E.-S., eds. *Human Rights*. New York: St. Martin's Press, 1978.
Kandiyoti, D. *Women, Islam, and the State*. Philadelphia: Temple University Press, 1991.
Kapur, R. and Cossman, B. *Subversive Sites*. New Delhi: Sage, 1996.
——. *Secularism's Last Sigh*? New Delhi: Oxford University Press, 1999.
Kaur, I. *Status of Hindu Women in India*. Allahabad: Chugh Publications, 1983.

Keller, N. *Women Under the Cross*. New Delhi: Cosmo, 1997.
Kerr, J., ed. *Ours By Right: Women's Rights as Human Rights*. London and Atlantic Highlands, NJ: Zed Books, 1993.
Kiely, R. and Marfleet, P., eds. *Globalisation and the Third World*. London and New York: Routledge, 1998.
King, U. "The Effect of Social Change on Religious Self-Understanding: Women Ascetics in Modern Hinduism" in K. Ballhatchet and D. Taylor, eds. *Changing Asia*. Hong Kong: Asian Research Service, 1984.
Kishwar, M. *In Search of Answers*. London: Zed Books, 1984.
——. "Stimulating Reform, Not Forcing It" *Manushi* (July–August, 1995), 5–14.
——. "When Daughters Are Unwanted" *Manushi* (January–February, 1995), 15–22.
Kosambi, M. *At the Intersection of Gender Reform and Religious Belief*. Bombay: Research Centre for Women's Studies, 1993.
Kotalová, J. *Belonging to Others*. Dhaka: University Press, 1996.
Krausz, M. *Relativism*. Notre Dame, IN: University of Notre Dame Press, 1989.
Kramarae, C. and Spender, D., general eds. *Routledge International Encyclopedia of Women*. New York and London: Routledge, 2000.
Krishnaraj, M. and Chanana, K., eds. *Gender and the Household Domain*. New Delhi: Sage, 1989.
Krishnaswami, A. "Study of Discrimination in the Matter of Religious Rights and Practices" *New York Journal of International Law and Politics* 11 (1978), 227–296.
Kritzman, L.D., ed. *Michel Foucault: Politics, Philosophy, Culture*. New York: Routledge, 1998.
Kumar, N., ed. *Women as Subjects*. New Delhi: Stree, 1994.
Kumar, R. "From Chipko to Sati: The Contemporary Indian Women's Movement" in Basu, A., ed. *The Challenge of Local Feminisms*. Boulder: Westview Press, 1995, 58–86.
Küng, H. and Moltmann, J., eds. *The Ethics of World Religions and Human Rights*. London: SCM Press, 1990.
Kynch, J. and Sen, A. "Indian Women: Well-Being and Survival" *Cambridge Journal of Economics* 7 (1983), 363–380.
Kymlicka, W., ed. *The Rights of Minority Cultures*. Oxford: Oxford University Press, 1995.
Laqueur, W. and Rubin, B., eds. *The Human Rights Reader*. New York: Penguin, 1989.
Lateef, S. *Muslim Women in India*. London: Zed Books, 1990.
Leslie, J., ed. *Roles and Rituals for Hindu Women*. London: Pinter Publishers, 1991.
——. *The Perfect Wife*. Oxford: Oxford University Press, 1989.
Lijnzaad, L. *Reservations to UN-Human Rights Treaties*. Dordrecht: Martinus Nijhoff, 1995.
Lindgren Alves, J.A. "The Declaration of Human Rights in Postmodernity" *Human Rights Quarterly* 22 (2000), 478–500.
Little, D., Kelsay, J., and Sachedina, A.A. *Human Rights and the Conflict of Cultures*. Columbia, SC: University of South Carolina Press, 1988.
MacLoed, A.E. "Hegemonic Relations and Gender Resistance: The New Veiling as Accommodating Protest in Cairo" *Signs: Journal of Women in Culture and Society* 17(3) (1992).
Mahoney, K.E. and Mahoney, P., eds. *Human Rights in the Twenty-First Century: A Global Challenge*. Dordrecht: Martinus Nijhoff, 1993.

Mallat, C. and Connors, J., eds. *Islamic Family Law*. London: Graham and Trotman, 1990.
Mamdani, M., ed. *Beyond Rights Talk and Culture Talk*. New York: St. Martin's Press, 2000.
Mandaville, P. *Transnational Muslim Politics*. London: Routledge, 2001.
Marchand, M.H. and Runyon, A.S., eds. *Gender and Global Restructuring*. London and New York: Routledge, 2000.
Marty, M.E. and Appleby, R.S., eds. *Accounting for Fundamentalisms*. Chicago: University of Chicago Press, 1994.
——, eds. *Fundamentalisms and the State*. Chicago: University of Chicago Press, 1993.
——, eds. *Fundamentalisms Observed*. Chicago: University of Chicago Press, 1991.
——, eds. *Fundamentalisms and Society*. Chicago: University of Chicago Press, 1993.
Maslow, A. *Motivation and Personality*. New York: Harper and Row, 1970.
Mawdudi, A.A. *Purdah and the Status of Women in Islam*. Lahore: Islamic Publications, 1981.
Mayer, A.E. *Islam and Human Rights*. Boulder, CO: Westview Press, 1991.
——. "Universal Versus Islamic Human Rights: A Clash of Cultures or a Clash With a Construct?" *Michigan Journal of International Law* 15 (1994), 307–404.
McDowell, L. *Gender, Identity and Place*. Minneapolis: University of Minnesota Press, 1999.
McDougall, M.S., Lasswell, H.D., and Chen, L. *Human Rights and World Public Order*. New Haven: Yale University Press, 1980.
McKean, W. *Equality and Discrimination Under International Law*. Oxford: Clarendon Press, 1984.
Menon, M.I. *Status of Muslim Women in India*. New Delhi: Uppal Publishing House, 1981.
Menon-Sen, K. and Shiva Kumar, A.K. *Women in India: How Free? How Equal*? New Delhi: Office of the [UN] Resident Coordinator in India, 2001.
Mernissi, F. *Beyond the Veil*. New York: Schenkman Publishing, 1975.
——. *The Veil and the Male Elite*. Reading, MA: Addison-Wesley, 1991.
Meron, T. "Enhancing the Effectiveness of the Prohibition of Discrimination Against Women" *American Journal of International Law* 84 (1990), 213–217.
——. *Human Rights and Humanitarian Norms as Customary Law*. Oxford: Clarendon Press, 1989.
——. *Human Rights in International Law, Vols. I and II*. Oxford: Clarendon Press, 1984.
——. *Human Rights Law-Making in the United Nations*. Oxford: Clarendon Press, 1986.
——. "Norm Making and Supervision in International Human Rights: Reflections on Institutional Order" *American Journal of International Law* 76 (1982), 754–778.
——. "On a Hierarchy of Human Rights" *American Journal of International Law* 80 (1996), 1–23.
Moghadam, V.M. *Modernizing Women*. Boulder, CO: Lynne Rienner, 1993.
——, ed. *Identity Politics and Women*. Boulder, CO: Westview Press, 1994.
Mohanty, C.T., Russo, A., and Torres, L., eds. *Third World Women and the Politics of Feminism*. Bloomington: Indiana University Press, 1991.
Moltmann, J. *On Human Dignity*. Philadelphia: Fortress Press, 1984.

Monteiro, R. "Belief, Law and Justice for Women" *Economic and Political Weekly* (October 24–31, 1992), WS74–WS80.
Mumtaz, K. and Shaheed, F. *Women of Pakistan: Two Steps Forward and One Step Back*? London: Zed Books, 1987.
Nelson, C. and Rouse, S., eds. *Situating Globalization*. Bielefeld: transcript Verlag, 2000.
Nhlapo, T. "Cultural Diversity, Human Rights and the Family in Contemporary Africa: Lessons from the South African Constitutional Debate" *International Journal of Law and the Family* 9 (1995), 208–225.
Nirmal, C.J., ed. *Human Rights in India*. Oxford: Oxford University Press, 1999.
Nussbaum, M. and Sen, A., eds. *The Quality of Life*. Oxford: Clarendon Press, 1993.
Nussbaum, M. and Glover, J., eds. *Women, Culture and Development*. Oxford: Clarendon Press, 1995.
Nussbaum, M. *Women and Human Development*. Cambridge: Cambridge University Press, 2000.
Obbo, C. *African Women: Their Struggle for Economic Independence*. London: Zed Press, 1980.
O'Donovan, K. *Sexual Divisions in Law*. London: Weidenfeld and Nicolson, 1985.
Oldenburg, P. "Sex Ratio, Son Preference and Violence in India" *Economic and Political Weekly* (December 5–12, 1992), 2657–2662.
Olsen, F.E. "The Myth of State Intervention in the Family" *Journal of Law Reform* 18(4) (1985), 835–864.
Papanek, H. and Minault, G., eds. *Separate Worlds: Studies of Purdah in South Asia*. Delhi: Chanakya Publications, 1982.
Parsons, S.F. *Feminism and Christian Ethics*. Cambridge: Cambridge University Press, 1996.
Pateman, C. *The Disorder of Women*. Oxford: Polity Press, 1989.
Parrinder, G. *Sexual Morality in the World's Religions*. Oxford: Oneworld, 1980.
Peden, C. and Yeager, H., eds. *Freedom, Dharma, and Rights*. Lewiston, NY: Edwin Mellen, 1993.
Perry, M.J. "Are Human Rights Universal? The Relativist Challenge and Related Matters" *Human Rights Quarterly* 19 (1997), 461–509.
——. *The Idea of Human Rights*. Oxford: Oxford University Press, 1998.
Peters, J. and Wolper, A., eds. *Women's Rights, Human Rights*. New York and London: Routledge, 1995.
Peterson, V.S. "Whose Rights? A Critique of 'Givens' in Human Rights Discourse" *Alternatives* XV (1990), 303–344.
Piper, C.L. "Reservations to Multilateral Treaties: The Goal of Universality" *Iowa Law Review* 71 (1985), 295–322.
Pollis, A. and Schwab, P., eds. *Human Rights: Cultural and Ideological Perspectives*. New York: Praeger, 1979.
Raheja, G.G. and Gold, A.G. *Listen to the Heron's Words*. Berkeley: University of California Press, 1994.
Rahman, A. "Religious Rights Versus Women's Rights in India: A Test Case for International Human Rights Law"*Columbia Journal of Transnational Law* 28 (1990), 473–498.
Randell, V. and Waylen, G., eds. *Gender, Politics and the State*. London: Routledge, 1998.
Ray, B. and Basu, A., eds. *From Independence Towards Freedom*. New Delhi: Oxford University Press, 1999.

Reanda, L. "Human Rights and Women's Rights: The United Nations Approach" *Human Rights Quarterly* 3 (1981), 11–31.

Rehof, L.A. *Guide to the Travaux Preparatoires of the United Nations Convention on the Elimination of All Forms of Discrimination Against Women*. Dordrecht: Martinus Nijhoff, 1993.

Renteln, A.D. *International Human Rights: Universalism Versus Relativism*. Newbury Park, CA: Sage, 1990.

Rhoodie, E.M. *Discrimination Against Women*. Jefferson, NC: McFarland, 1989.

Rosaldo, S.Z. and Lamphere, L., eds. *Woman, Culture, and Society*. Stanford: Stanford University Press, 1974.

Rosas, A. and Helgesen, J., eds. *The Strength of Diversity*. Dordrecht: Martinus Nijhoff, 1992.

Rose, N. "Beyond the Public/Private Division: Law, Power and the Family" *Journal of Law and Society* 14 (1987), 61–76.

Rosenbaum, A.S., ed. *The Philosophy of Human Rights*. Westport, CT: Greenwood Press, 1980.

Rouner, L.S., ed. *Human Rights and the World's Religions*. Notre Dame, IN: University of Notre Dame Press, 1988.

Rozario, S. *Purity and Communal Boundaries*. London: Zed, 1992.

Rupert, M. *Ideologies of Globalization*. London and New York: Routledge, 2000.

el Saadawi, N. *The Hidden Face of Eve*. London: Zed, 1980.

Sabbamma, M. *Women: Tradition and Culture*. New Delhi: Sterling, 1985.

Sahai, S. *Social Legislation and the Status of Hindu Women*. Jaipur: Rawat Publications, 1996.

Said, E. *Culture and Imperialism*. New York: Knopf, 1983.

Saksena, K.P., ed. *Human Rights Perspective and Challenges*. New Delhi: Lancers Books, 1994.

Sarkar, T. and Butalia, U., eds. *Women and the Hindu Right*. New Delhi: Kali for Women, 1995.

Schuler, M.A., ed. *Claiming Our Place*. Washington: Institute for Women, Law and Development, 1993.

Scott, J.C. *Weapons of the Weak*. New Haven: Yale University Press, 1985.

Sen, A. "Well-Being, Agency, and Freedom: The Dewey Lectures 1984" *Journal of Philosophy* LXXXII(4) (April 1985).

——. *Development as Freedom*. New York: Anchor Books, 1999.

—— and S. Gupta, "Malnutrition of Rural Children and the Sex Bias," *Economic and Political Weekly* XVIII (May 1983), 855–864.

Sen, G., Germain, A., and Chen, L., eds. *Population Policies Reconsidered*. Boston: Harvard University Press, 1994.

Sharistanian, J., ed. *Beyond the Public/Domestic Dichotomy*. Westport, CT: Greenwood Press, 1987.

Sharma, A., ed. *Women in World Religions*. Albany: State University of New York Press, 1987.

——, ed. *Today's Woman in World Religions*. Albany: State University of New York Press, 1994.

Sherman, J.A. and Beck, E.T., eds. *The Prism of Sex*. Madison: University of Wisconsin Press, 1979.

Shestack, J.J. "The Philosophical Foundations of Human Rights" *Human Rights Quarterly* 20 (1998), 201–234.

Shiva, V., Jafri, A.H., Emani, A., Bhutani, S., Antony, A., and Prasad, U., eds. *Licence to Kill*. New Delhi: Research Foundation for Science, Technology and Ecology, 2000.

Shue, H. *Basic Rights: Subsistence, Affluence, and U.S. Foreign Policy*. Princeton: Princeton University Press, 1980.

Siddiqi, Z.A. and Zuberi, A.J., eds. *Muslim Women: Problems and Prospects*. New Delhi: M D Publications, 1993.

Sinha, K. and Dutta, P., eds. *Globalisation and Developing Countries*. New Delhi: New Age International Publishers, 1999.

Sinha, R. *Dynamics of Change in the Modern Hindu Family*. New Delhi: Concept Publishing Company, 1993.

Sinha, S.P. "Human Rights: A Non-western Viewpoint," *Archiv für Rechts- und-Sozialphilosophie* 67 (1981), 76–91.

Siriwardena, R. *Equality and the Religious Traditions of Asia*. New York: St. Martins, 1987.

Smith, W.C. *On Understanding Islam*. The Hague: Mouton, 1981.

——. *Modern Culture from a Comparative Perspective*. Albany: State University of New York Press, 1997.

——. *The Meaning and End of Religion*. Minneapolis: Fortress Press, 1991.

——. "Philosophia, as One of the Religious Traditions of Humankind: The Greek Legacy in Western Civilization, Viewed by a Comparativist" in *Différences, Valuers, Hierarchie: Textes Offerts à Louis Dumont et Reunis par Jean-Claude Galey*. Paris: Ecole des Hautes Etudes en Sciences Sociales, 1984.

Stackhouse, M.L. *Creeds, Society, and Human Rights*. Grand Rapids, MI: William B. Eerdmans, 1984.

Stahnke, T. and Martin, J.P., eds. *Religion and Human Rights: The Basic Documents*. New York: Center for the Study of Human Rights, Columbia University, 1998.

Standing, H. *Dependence and Autonomy*. London: Routledge, 1991.

Stromquist, N. and Monkman, K., eds. *Globalization and Education*. Lanham, MD: Rowman and Littlefield, 2000.

Suguna, B. *Working Women and Religion*. New Delhi: Discovery Publishing House, 1994.

Sullivan, D.J. "Advancing the Freedom of Religion or Belief Through the UN Declaration on the Elimination of Religious Intolerance and Discrimination" *American Journal of International Law* 82 (1988), 487–520.

——. "Gender Equality and Religious Freedom: Toward a Framework for Conflict Resolution" *New York University Journal of International Law and Politics* 24 (1992), 795–856.

Swidler, L., ed. *Religious Liberty and Human Rights in Nations and Religions*. Philadelphia: Ecumenical Press; New York: Hippocrene Books, 1986.

Tabandeh, S. *A Muslim Commentary on the Universal Declaration of Human Rights*. F.J. Goulding (trans.). Guildford: F.J. Goulding, 1970.

Tanner, K. *Theories of Culture*. Minneapolis: Fortress Press, 1997.

Taubenfeld, R.F. and Taubenfeld, H.J. "Achieving the Human Rights of Women: The Base Line, the Challenge, the Search for a Strategy" *Human Rights* 4 (1975), 125–169.

Taylor, A. and Thomas, C., eds. *Global Trade and Global Social Issues*. London and New York: Routledge, 1999.

Taylor, M.C., ed. *Critical Terms for Religious Studies*. Chicago: University of Chicago Press, 1998.

Tesón, F. "International Human Rights and Cultural Relativism" *Virginia Journal of International Law* 25 (1985), 869–898.

Thompson, K., ed. *The Moral Imperatives of Human Rights: A World Survey*. Washington, DC: Council on Religion and International Affairs, 1980.

Tibi, B. *The Crisis of Modern Islam*. Salt Lake City: University of Utah Press, 1988.

Tilley, J.J. "Cultural Relativism" *Human Rights Quarterly* 22 (2002), 501–547.

Tinker, I., ed. *Persistent Inequalities*. New York: Oxford University Press, 1990.

Toubia, N., ed. *Women of the Arab World*. London: Zed, 1988.

Traer, R. *Faith in Human Rights*. Washington, DC: Georgetown University Press. 1991.

Trible, P. *God and the Rhetoric of Sexuality*. Philadelphia: Fortress Press, 1978.

——. *Texts of Terror*. Philadelphia: Fortress Press, 1984.

UNESCO. *Philosophical Foundations of Human Rights*. Paris: UNESCO, 1986.

Van Ness, P., ed. *Debating Human Rights*. London and New York: Routledge, 1999.

Walby, S. *Theorizing Patriarchy*. Oxford: Basil Blackwell, 1990.

Waldman, M.R. "Tradition as a Modality of Change: Islamic Examples" *History of Religions* 25(4) (1986), 318–340.

Ward, L., ed. *Ethics and the Social Sciences*. Notre Dame: Notre Dame University, 1959.

Warrender, H. *The Political Philosophy of Hobbes*. Oxford: Clarendon Press, 1957.

Waters, M. *Globalization*. London: Routledge, 1995.

Weithman, C., ed. *Religion and Contemporary Liberation*. South Bend, IN: University of Notre Dame Press, 1997.

Welch, C.E., Jr. and Leary, V.A., eds. *Asian Perspectives on Human Rights*. Boulder, CO: Westview, 1990.

Zaehner, R.C. *Hinduism*. Oxford: Oxford University Press, 1966.

Zearfoss, S. "Note, The Convention for the Elimination of All Forms of Discrimination Against Women: Radical, Reasonable, or Reactionary?" *Michigan Journal of International Law* 12 (1991), 903–942.

Zoelle, D.G. *Globalizing Concern for Women's Human Rights*. New York: St. Martin's Press, 2000.

Index